EDDIE
HAPGOOD
FOOTBALLER

LYNNE HAPGOOD

EDDIE HAPGOOD

FOOTBALLER

From Beyond the Touchline

First published by Pitch Publishing, 2022

Pitch Publishing
A2 Yeoman Gate
Yeoman Way
Worthing
Sussex
BN13 3QZ
www.pitchpublishing.co.uk
info@pitchpublishing.co.uk

ISBN 978 1 80150 049 4

Typesetting and origination by Pitch Publishing
Printed and bound in Great Britain by TJ Books, Padstow

Contents

In memory of our parents
Eddie and Maggie Hapgood
who gave all their children the
great gift of loving security

'What does it feel like seeing your dad up there?' Samir Singh, the Arsenal community officer, asked me, gesturing upwards to the vast mural of Arsenal legends embracing the Emirates Stadium. I hesitated. 'I'm not sure; it's very hard to understand.'

Introduction

Perhaps because I was born after he had finished playing, I could never quite grasp the simple fact that Eddie Hapgood, captain of Arsenal and England in the 1930s and whose name is indelibly recorded in football history, was my father. I always knew he was special but I also knew that I shared him with many unknown people who also thought he was special. As I grew up, the stories he told, the discussions I half heard and intriguing family conversations filtered through to me. Even so, for a long time the life of my parents remained a multi-piece jigsaw puzzle without a picture. As an adult, when I decided to try and make sense of it, I had to start at the beginning. I collected together the fragments I knew, I researched history books and club records, I read tales and recollections of fans from the past, autobiographies and comments of team-mates. I trawled through journalists' accounts and opinions, football programmes, contemporary football biographies and the almost infinite resource of the press past and present. I hunted for anything and everything that would bring what was special about my father into the present.

I was anxious that such piecemeal information should not end up simply as a collection of random anecdotes. What happened was quite the opposite. From the heap of loosely connected bits and pieces emerged a personality whose consistency and integrity were remarkably sustained through a period of profound personal and social change and whose values are just as relevant to sport today. As I read and listened to what everyone else had to say and what had happened during the tumultuous years of the 1930s and 40s, the famous footballer began to connect with the father I remembered. The defender so often applauded for his passion and commitment on the pitch brought into focus the equally passionate and committed defender of his personal and family values. For him, the two worlds were one and the same.

It can seem that his public story stopped when the football stopped. That isn't true. When Arsenal moved into their new stadium in 2006, it was to the images and words of my father and to those of the great players of the past that the club turned to revitalise its identity. In a very different present, the whole story is now held only in my younger brother's memory and mine. My older brother Tony and my older sister Margot died before they could share this project with us. I have done my best to keep faith with them. As I wrote, they were always in my mind jostling to insert what we talked about, the memories we shared, what I imagined or sensed were their points of view.

Too often the story of great sportsmen and women of the past is reduced to their sporting record while the identity of those who embodied it is forgotten. I want to share Eddie Hapgood's whole story with you: footballer, father – and defender.

Lynne Hapgood

Preface

One morning my father woke to find the world bathed in a yellowish glow. He also found he couldn't speak, or rather what he tried to say emerged as incoherent, unformed sounds. I don't know what other difficulties he may have encountered; he told me only fragments of that morning encased in amber. Somehow he got dressed and went downstairs. He said nothing to my mother but, knowing that something was wrong, he took himself off to the nearest doctor. Did he walk, did he drive? I don't know how he managed it, but he somehow found himself in the consulting room of a doctor he had never met before.

Whatever the doctor's initial question was, the answer was only stumbling noises and ugly guttural sounds.

The next question was, 'Are you drunk?' At which point he was able to form a word that encapsulated a life, a belief and a way of being, and was pronounced – completely and audibly.

'Footballer.'

Maybe for the doctor the word was enough. Maybe he would have been surprised to find that his patient, who couldn't speak, had indeed spoken, but he wouldn't have understood the significance of the word as a word. He would merely have heard three surprisingly clear syllables, that should not have been possible to pronounce, but were. 'Foot-ball-er,' a word brought up from some deeply internalised realm of identity and spoken.

'Footballer.' Colours returned to normal, speech returned, and indeed, for a time, it seemed as if life reverted to normal, nearly normal. It was 1968. He was 60 years old.

On the stone that marks his grave, and which is now also our mother's, is inscribed one word: Footballer.

1

A Suitcase of Stories

The whole of our father's history, it seemed to us children, was held in two large leather suitcases, his informal archive. It never occurred to us to ask how a life lived for many years in the public eye could settle so easily into just two suitcases because then, in the 1950s, we had no idea our father was famous, let alone how famous or for how long. To us, the suitcases simply contained his props and, like a magician, he spun stories, fables, and dreams out of them.

The suitcases were extraordinary in themselves. Heavy brown leather with brass clip-snap closings, their corners damaged, their handles loose, the stitching unravelling. Faded travel labels hinting at exotic destinations had been scraped and torn leaving blue fragments which we tried to decipher, following the lines with curious fingers. Only Dad was strong enough to carry them.

Occasionally, on a winter evening, one or other of the suitcases would be retrieved from our mysterious spare room and opened on to the sitting room floor, spilling out photographs, scrapbooks, papers, and a glorious muddle of souvenirs, letters and newspapers.

This usually happened in response to a request from somebody – a journalist, a fan or football historian as we later realised – for information or a particular photograph but it was also our opportunity to explore among the papers and to ask questions which we knew would trigger Dad's reminiscences. We children would settle down to listen expectantly to stories we had heard many times before, always familiar but always different. Dad was a sparkling raconteur. We were smiling before he even began to reminisce and we were helpless with laughter by the time the performance was under way. The more we laughed, the more he added to his stories so that we were always surprised by new details, a change of tone, the introduction of a new character energetically imitated, spellbound as our familiar room was transformed into a circus of wonderful events. Over the years, the stories seemed to expand – one story into another – until we believed we must surely have the whole story.

The time I am describing began when we moved to Bath in 1950. It seemed that in our confusing family history there were four of everything; four towns, four houses, four football clubs, four children. In fact, by the time we moved to Bath from Blackburn via Kettering and Watford there were only three. The fourth one was the oldest, our brother Tony, already 20 and out in the world, building his life and career in Burnley. Only Margot who was ten, my brother Mike who was three and me at seven moved into the house which was the nearest we ever got to a home. For us younger children it seemed that our life started right there in that house, there in Bath. We were too young to have a remembered past, just a few fragments that barely added up to memories. We didn't anticipate a future either, or at least nothing had been mentioned. Whatever the future held, it was somehow anchored here in this house, in Bath. Our parents moved in and organised their possessions, and we spilled out behind the removal men, happily flowing like water into every room, through doors and into the large garden with fields beyond. We flourished in the deep breath of relief our parents took. We felt them gather us close and for the first time in 11 years allow themselves to feel safe. They fostered that feeling and we enjoyed it for the five short years we were able to. We seemed to understand that, for the time being and for some unknown reason, the now was more important than any past or any future and that we were safe.

One reason, I was to learn later, was that their past simply refused to make sense. It had been too quick in passing, too dramatic. They had lost track of whatever logic it might have had in the shock of change. There had been the rapid turnover of houses and towns, a growing family, the struggle for familiar securities after six long years of war. And there had been the loss of youth, behind which was a story of fame and glory.

Like many other young men and women who were barely 31 when war was declared and 37 when demobilisation began, there was stolen time to be retrieved or grieved for. My father carried his own particular sense of loss and his own particular grief. Age and injury had stalked his body during the war years and brought his footballing career to a virtual end in 1943. When the war ended, he was completely unprepared for a future he could not imagine and set adrift from himself by what he considered a betrayal. My mother, struggling in the slipstream of his career, alone for long periods during the war with two and then three children, had not been well since the birth of my younger brother in 1947. Even as they both embraced the apparent respite of Bath I think they must have feared that security was as far away as before. And so it turned out that Dad, drawing on his characteristic energy and optimism, had little option but to embrace the present. Perhaps this is why he shared little of his past with us. Although he was only 42 by the time we arrived in Bath, whatever had gone before seemed a very long time ago and he had lost touch with the reality of much of it himself.

Of his Bristol past, of the city where we later learned he was born and grew up, of his childhood we had only the briefest glimpses. In 1950, when I was seven, I didn't know Bristol was just around the corner from us in Bath. There were a few occasions when clues rather than stories from his Bristol childhood slipped out on the flow of memory. There was so much he couldn't or wouldn't tell his young family about a poverty-stricken and struggling childhood. And the scale of what he couldn't tell us, of crowded houses, of unemployment, of street gangs, of ugly streets and hungry faces meant that only the tiniest anecdotal glimpses found their way into our lives. It would be many years before, shocked by my mother's illness and with his dinner uneaten in front of him, he began talking without prompting and without restraint about his early years, as if her temporary absence had stripped him of his adult life and returned him to his youthful experiences in Bristol.

I would like to write that the first Bristol story began at the beginning. It would be comfortably reassuring to state, 'Eddie

Hapgood was born...' but we could never be sure when the beginning began. 'You can pick any date you want for the date of Eddie Hapgood's birth,' or so he would say with a laugh. The vagueness became a family joke and quite irrelevant beside the fact that he was definitely born, the ninth of Emily and Harry Hapgood's ten children, in Bristol on 14, 24 or 27 September in 1908 or 1909. We celebrated his birthday on 27 September which, he said, had become the accepted date although, he would continue, he was really born on 14 September. The vagueness was no affectation. At that time we thought it rather fairytale-like, distinctive and eccentric, but in fact I think it was simply a reflection of the difficult social and family times into which he arrived. His brother Percy had been born in 1906, and the last of the family, Iris, was to come in 1911. There was also a house move in 1908. It would have been easy for those September dates when Dad arrived to slip and slide.

The first story (as we saw it), and certainly the earliest memory he shared with us, was about his mother and was told many times. Emily Hapgood was always a shadowy figure to us. She had died as World War II came to an end and we youngest children were just beginning our lives or had yet to be born. Sometime between the end of a war and the confusion of peacetime, it seems her presence was lost to us. Yet memories of her bracket the story of Dad's early life in Bristol and gave us momentary but abiding glimpses of her and of his childhood. As a boy, or so he said, he would sit on the steps leading from the kitchen to the street and watch her doing the weekly wash. He enjoyed looking outwards watching people moving up and down the street, anticipating the time when he was old enough to run free with his older brothers, Tom and Percy. Meanwhile, he shared the kitchen with toddler Iris, no doubt keeping an eye on her while his mother worked her way through the relentless demands of an early-20th-century washday. She used her arms as mangles, he told us, and he would twist imaginary sheets around and around his own arms as if they were massive snakes in imitation of her much-practised actions. He was fascinated, he said, by the way they coiled in muscular folds across her body, in and out of her arms and over her shoulder, as the water ran into the sink. 'When the last drops fell, the sheet was shaken out, folded and stacked on top of the others waiting to be run through the metal and wood mangle standing in the corner,' he continued, acting out the stages one by one. The intensity of his description conjured up the force of a specific moment and yet washday and its ritual activities must have seeped through the days, weeks and years of his memory.

This story was extraordinary, almost disturbing in its vividness. What he didn't tell us – and was not part of the story; he barely knew it himself – is that, before he was born, Emily Hapgood, with eight children of her own to wash for, had taken in washing from others. In 1906 she became the chief supporter of the family; 'Washerwoman' was the contemporary label. Perhaps she still needed to do washing even when pregnant with Eddie and after he was born. Perhaps, too, that is why the picture remained so vivid for him, witnessing if not understanding his mother's labour and surely her exhaustion.

Another part of the story we were never told was why Emily had been so poor. We knew all about being poor; it was a frequent and powerful element of any number of fairy stories and folk tales so we had no need to ask questions. Dad would have no desire to tell. The truth was that in 1905 Emily had chosen poverty over an unhappy marriage. She and Dad's father Harry had been separated for nearly two years before Dad was born. In fact, he almost missed being born in Bristol, or indeed, being born at all.

Shortly after getting married in 1892, Emily and Harry had moved from Bristol's shrinking industrial base to find work in the coal mines of South Wales with their two children. No doubt they were also trying to leave behind the dirt and pollution of industrial Bristol and the dangers of an area which, in 1889, was increasingly squalid, lawless and violent. They stayed in South Wales for 15 years, moving house on several occasions. Then, in 1907, Emily, with six more children, decided to take herself and all the children back on her own to Bristol. If Dad ever knew what triggered such a drastic action then he never told us, but Emily must have been desperate to risk possible social ignominy and subsistence living over a working husband. She returned to the district she grew up in where industrial decline was now chronic, unemployment steadily rising and workers' houses sinking into slums.

Tucked behind the magnificent facade of Bristol Temple Meads Station, just a few minutes' walk to the north-east was the Dings, a tiny, tightly packed community of about 130 houses on interlinked streets. In this unhappy year Emily found a home for herself and her children in Anvil Street, in the shadow of the railway arches, in the Dings area, a stone's throw from where she had first met Harry. They had moved into empty rooms and Emily set about rebuilding her family's life. 'A hovel with sacks for carpets, boxes for furniture and frequent infestations of bugs,' her daughter Stella, aged eight at this time, recalled much later in life. It was here that Emily first took in washing. Her elder sister, Kate, and her daughters Kate and Edith, who were now working, helped out. It was not long before Harry made his own way back to Bristol and persuaded Emily to start again. They moved into better accommodation and it was at 4 Clarks Building, Union Road, in the heart of the Dings, that Dad was born. Whichever way you look at it, Union Road symbolically announced Dad's conception and birth, the reuniting of the Hapgood family and Harry's return to Bristol.

As times improved for the Hapgood family, they moved again. Only Iris, Percy and Dad still lived with their parents. The front door of 23 Ranelagh Street, Barton Hill, frames Dad's last memory of Bristol and of home before he left to begin his professional footballing career in Kettering. Emily had packed a bag for him. She leaned against the door jamb accepting his departure, perhaps proud, but surely saddened by the loss of her youngest son. As he walked away he looked back to wave. That was how he saw her then and it was an image he never forgot.

This story was not one of those we heard so often. It was prompted many years later by reading Laurie Lee's autobiography, *As I Walked out One Midsummer Morning*. Lee was a few years younger than my father and grew up in rural Gloucestershire not urban Bristol, but the book opens with an account of a common experience – that of a young man leaving his mother and his childhood home to take on the world. 'She stood old and bent at the top of the bank,' Dad read out loud, 'silently watching me go … not questioning why I went. At the bend of the road I looked back again and saw the golden light die behind her; then I turned the corner … and closed that part of my life forever.'

The book was a Christmas present and when he looked up there were tears in his eyes as he shared with us all how he had said goodbye to his mother, to Bristol and to his childhood. He had walked away, he said, with anticipation and perhaps something of a swagger. Just in time, his nephew Jack raced after him to say goodbye and at the end of the street was rewarded with a silver threepenny piece. That was the gesture of a young man convinced that, at last, his adult life was beginning. Surprised by his emotion, we understood or guessed perhaps, how much he had loved her. But if that was the case, I find it even harder to explain how little we learned. If Tony had not been divided from us by age and experience we would certainly have heard his stories. We all had our own stories but when do families ever sit around a table and sort out who heard what, knew what?

Another familiar anecdote was about his time at Hannah More School in St Philips Marsh. It was not a pleasant experience. Twisting his hands into rigid arthritic shapes, he would demonstrate to us how the teacher held his hand, squeezing his fingers so painfully against his pen that he could barely concentrate on the task of improving his handwriting. He told the story as a joke with extravagant, pantomime gestures, but we knew it had a bitter edge. Perhaps he didn't sit easily under the unyielding and conformist discipline of the time. Perhaps he felt picked on as most children do at some point of their school lives. Fairness is a value that children weigh precisely. It seemed trivial, not so very different from our own groans and moans about our day at school, but we felt his emotions flowed far more deeply than we understood from this simple story. Is this why I remember my mother's often expressed embarrassment with her own immaculately neat handwriting which, she said, was more printing than writing? Mum did the letter-writing to us all in those pre-digital days, but I remember too my father's handwriting, confident, and 'joined-up' and usually indicating important messages. 'Dear Michael,' he wrote to my brother on 2 February 1972, 'Lynne had a baby boy on Feb 1st @ 8.15 p.m. Dad.' I can't remember why this note got back to me but as I slipped it from the envelope, I recognised his flowing writing instantly.

Mike had discovered his father's Bristol when he worked there in the 1990s and he had located Hannah More School some time previously. Over the years, we had fallen into an informal routine of occasional days out together, using the excuse of some event or other to walk and talk and catch up. As we explored Bristol's hinterland where our father grew up, we arrived at the school gates when afternoon playtime was ending and the children were trailing back into the school building. The supervising teacher, startled and slightly defensive, finally agreed to show us the school. Built on the Victorian model with classrooms leading from the main assembly area and a mezzanine floor raised on painted steel columns leading to further classrooms and offices, it must have looked exactly the same a century ago. We stood in the assembly area on a gleaming parquet floor that must surely have been the original one where my father and his brothers had gathered each term-time morning, and where morning prayers would have been recited. It was a strange experience, the nearest I had yet come to something concrete connecting the story-telling of the father I knew with the little boy he was. I didn't want to leave. I wanted to stand, to allow my father's story of pain and humiliation to find its place among the run-of-the-mill experiences of generations of children. I wanted to take the time to imagine him, and perhaps Percy and Tom, lining up with their peers, sitting cross-legged to listen to the headmistress, where I was now standing. I wanted, at least, to take some photographs. Schools do not, of course, have time for dreaming, and casual photographs are now banned for security reasons so, with many thanks, we walked away.

Dad's other favourite Bristol story and the most dramatic was an example of derring-do in which he emerged in a more heroic guise than an anguished schoolboy. He would dive, he told us, into the harbour where the ships were moored and on one never-to-be-forgotten day brought home a haul of peanuts. The piratical glory of this deed fitted perfectly the drama of his narration and stoked our admiration of an adolescent life lived with such gusto. How could a boy, even my startlingly capable father, board a huge cargo ship from harbour waters? How possible was it to dive between concrete harbour walls and the walls of a cargo steamer and come out alive? Was making off with a haul of peanuts the same as us scrumping forbidden pears from a low-hanging branch on the way to school? It sounded much, much more dangerous and altogether more awe-inspiring.

Of course, I had never seen a harbour so it was all guesswork and he left out most of the story; perhaps he didn't know it. In

1924, when Dad was 16, the SS *Ettrick* grounded at Horseshoe Bend in the River Avon, a common event in a tidal river which flowed over a narrowing, silted-up quagmire of deep, silky mud. The routine was familiar and most were able to be re-floated on the incoming tide. On this occasion her crew failed to re-float her. During the night the *Ettrick* capsized, emptying her gifts of tobacco, cigarettes, sweets and, no doubt, peanuts on to the sloping, slippery banks. News must have spread quickly, drawing youths from the city and surrounding villages to see what they could scavenge for themselves and their families. An eyewitness account claimed that his whole village had boots for the winter. This was fair gain; few children would have hesitated to help themselves to heaven-sent booty. Whether or not the *Ettrick* was the source of Dad's story I'll never know, but I can guess that, even if it wasn't, local legend can rapidly be appropriated and embroidered into personal history by an adventurous teenager.

These briefest hints of a past time were intermingled and obscured with many other equally familiar and often repeated stories. These stories were of football, of Arsenal Football Club, of travel, of adventures in Europe, of players he had played with and players he had played against, reminiscences as photos were brought out and put back, demonstrations of this footballer's style, or that footballer's tackles. Stories about men whose names and personalities peopled our sitting room. Stories about Mum and stories about Tony's childhood. Stories about kings, film stars and dictators. Such evenings were a phantasmagoria of events, memories, characters without context or chronology. But those three stories were all we were told and all we knew about Dad's

Bristol childhood. Then everything was tipped back into the suitcases; the lids were closed; it was time for baths and bed. Mike was swept off and ordinary squabbles and complaints took over. Margot announced firmly as she did every night that she should go to bed later than me because she was older. I lurked behind the sofa, sure that if I stayed quiet I would be forgotten. Soon we were all in bed. We had heard the very best of bedtime stories. For many years that is just what they remained – stories.

2

Beginning with Bristol

Yes. Incredibly, that was all we were told, and all we knew until, as adults, questions about 'Eddie Hapgood' began to float to the front of our minds. We looked for some kind of order, swapped what information we had, shared what we knew. We were astonished at the number of missing pieces in the jigsaw of our memories, of what had never been shared with us, about a past so absent we had never considered what might have been lost. We were equally astonished at what seemed like our lack of curiosity over the years. It wasn't that we were lacking facts. Journalists and historians of football and of Arsenal Football Club had already done that for us in numerous articles and books from the very start of his career. Perhaps that was a factor contributing to our ignorance because, in that sense, it seemed there was nothing we didn't know about him.

By the time we had grown up, 'Eddie Hapgood' had long become a parallel persona, a hologram of the father we knew and loved. Now we wondered about 'Eddie Hapgood' and began to bring the two identities, footballer and father, together. We wanted to understand what had shaped this double identity or whether it was a double identity at all. We wanted to understand what we were beginning to feel we instinctively knew. How did football evolve into the language of the deepest feelings of the boy from Bristol? How did playing a game become living a philosophy? What made a 60-year-old man suffering from a stroke and unable to frame his words, think that saying 'footballer' explained all that it was necessary for a doctor to know? And so we began to look for the threads that might knit his story together.

Now I *can* begin at the beginning. Dad was born on the edge of the Dings at 2 Union Road in the Barton Hill district of Bristol in 1908. Emily Clarke had been beguiled and dazzled by Harry Hapgood for as long as she could remember. She grew up in Bread Street, just across the road from Harry and his sister, Ellen, a close friend from early childhood. They lived in a dense area of terraced housing already overcrowded in 1881 facing each other across narrow streets. Number 25, where Harry grew up, housed 14 people. Opposite, where the Clarkes lived, number 28 was comparatively luxurious with only eight occupants, other members of the family returning from various jobs away to swell the numbers from time to time.

Living at such close quarters, it is not surprising that, at some point, Emily's admiration of Ellen's dashing brother, two years older than she was, matured into a more dangerous fascination. At 19 she became pregnant. Her first daughter and Dad's oldest sister, Hilda, was born in the Stapleton Road workhouse. It is very easy today to condemn what seems to be a naked callousness that not only stigmatised a young woman but consigned her to possible destitution. And, of course, those were the stark facts facing Emily carrying an illegitimate child in 1889. More likely they accepted that, however undesirable, the workhouse offered free temporary shelter and care for mother and baby, and, more important, was not necessarily a lifelong sentence. Whatever Emily endured during that difficult time, for her it was temporary and did not stop her loving Harry. Their second daughter, Edith, was born before she and Harry finally married in 1892. Ellen Hapgood had proved to be a loyal friend and a persevering sister; she is said to have finally persuaded Harry to formalise his relationship with Emily.

By all accounts Dad's father, the man who entranced Emily Clarke, was a charming, energetic man, with a zest for life, for company, and for drinking. He was sociable and attractive, a gifted raconteur who charmed a roomful of people by singing as he accompanied himself on the penny whistle or squeeze-box. Apparently he never lost his charm or his gift of energising those around him although in his later years he drank heavily. It was Mum who told me that Dad would never touch alcohol because of what he had witnessed in his father's condition. During the 1930s, when Dad was at the height of his fame and it seemed that youth would last forever, he, Mum and Tony would holiday in Cornwall. Footballers didn't earn much in those days but with bonuses and long summer holidays on pay, life must have seemed luxurious. On their way back, they would stop off in Bristol, the family would gather round and Gran'fer Harry would play and sing. My mother remembered him from their visits with a mixture of resentment and awe. 'I didn't meet him until after he had a stroke,' she told me, 'but although he was fragile, he drew people to him with his singing and playing. Gran'fer Harry was always the life and soul of the party and it was impossible not to like him.' My brother Tony, only a little boy on those visits, said the same. 'Gran'fer made me laugh. He was always singing.' He had an energy, a gaiety, a sense of his own superiority that, in his own eyes, gave him freedom to bend the rules. He passed that attitude on to his family. The Hapgoods were special, brought low by circumstances perhaps, but always different, aspiring. If Iris, the youngest of his children, wanted piano lessons, then she should have them even if tuition fees had to be funded by the illicit selling of a questionably calculated 'angels' share' siphoned off at the local whisky distillery where he had found a job.

Dad's vigorous enjoyment of life, his powerful presence and the infectious charm for which he was noted were, I imagine, inherited from his father but there, it seems, the connection ends. Gran'fer Harry never entered any of Dad's stories. As a child I never heard him mentioned and we younger children knew nothing about him. Mum's brief comments and Tony's reminiscences occurred long after Dad had died. Harry Hapgood died in 1939 just as war was declared so it is possible that the storm of destruction that followed possibly took memories of him, along with my father's career, as collateral damage. For Harry's older children, even for Dad whose knowledge of his parents' history can only have been gleaned in bits and pieces over the years from his older siblings, his undoubted charm and conviviality appears to have been obscured by his thoughtless and cavalier treatment of his wife. It is very tempting to imagine a genetic tree. Emily seems to have offered love and the very best of herself, her strength, determination and self-respect, to her husband and children but at considerable personal cost. With a song and a laugh and a swig of whisky, Harry, with class, style and charisma, seems simply to have claimed to be the 'best'. Which values were really important, what being the 'best' really meant, was something Dad had to work out for himself.

Paradoxically, the heart of this teeming industrial hub where the Hapgood family lived seemed isolated and fragmented. Railway arches spanned the district, darkening the streets and houses. They cut off the skies and neighbouring streets from one another as they carried the noise and smoke of trains thundering over the residents' heads across the city. Throughout Dad's childhood, crude tar was still being poured directly from the tanks on the railway wagons into the boilers in the depots that backed on to Barton Hill district, thickening the toxic fumes over the bridges. The pig farm on Barton Hill itself and the accompanying slaughterhouse were still open in the early 1920s.

Although only a short walk from the magnificence of St Mary Redcliffe Church which tourists still flock to see, the district was invisible. It still is. The Bristol Temple Meads Station façade continues to conceal those who need to work from those who enjoy what they produce. If Emily had hoped for some improvement, she was to be badly mistaken. Industrial decline had accelerated during her absence. Barton Hill was a dense, residential district, populated, over-populated, by working-class families who, at that time, were struggling with and against each other to make a living. The closely packed houses, originally built to house the workers who serviced the once-thriving 19th-century factories and businesses that lined the waterfront, were now slipping steadily into some of Bristol's worst slums, blackened and disintegrating back-to-backs fronting narrow streets. Housing was so scarce and so desperately needed that finding somewhere to live meant taking whatever was on offer.

By the time Dad was 13, this was all he had known. As a child, he woke each day to the ugliness of urban dilapidation and breathed in the dirt, pollution and stink of cruel, life-threatening environmental conditions. Despite anxiety about the nation's health, shockingly exposed only a few years later by the poor condition of many men volunteering for war service in 1914, and the patchy attempts to improve child health nationally, in districts such as Barton Hill it deteriorated. As Dad grew from baby to toddler to boy and a global war began to seem possible, unemployment increased, men and boys spilled out from congested houses on to the streets to kill time, to find camaraderie, to fend for themselves. Petty crime, house-breaking, drunkenness and street brawls were familiar dramas of daily life. Barton Hill, no longer the heart of Bristol's prosperity, found itself trapped between the Feeder Canal, the waterway link between the factories and the shipping routes, the dark web of proliferating railway tracks, and confined inside road boundaries. It seemed helpless in the grip of an appalling historical moment.

The end of the war in 1918 was not the end of Barton Hill's troubles. During those difficult post-war years, Dad was old enough to be out on the streets, watching what was going on with the sharp eye of a ten-year-old. For many individual families, of course, there would have been great joy at the safe return of a family member but there was little celebration to welcome waves of demobbed men. They only swelled the population, increasing levels of unemployment, homelessness and social conflict while new levels of sickness and disability added another burden to families and community. Unemployment reached epidemic proportions, prompting a description of Barton Hill streets as in a state of perpetual Bank Holiday idleness as men, girls and boys hung about in the street every day of the week with nothing whatever to do. And unemployment continued to rise relentlessly. The closing in 1925 of one of the district's last major employers, the Great Western Cotton Works, was a terrible blow to virtually every Barton Hill household.

On his walks to school and back, playing street games with friends, running errands or in the first years of his working life, normal daily life for my father meant witnessing the corroding effects of insecurity and desperation. In 1921, when the Prince of Wales, later Edward VIII, was despatched round the country in a post-war propaganda exercise to meet the 'people', Barton Hill, with its heavily congested share of 'the people', was one of the locations he visited. There is no way that Dad could not have known of the Prince of Wales's visit. It is very likely that he was lined up with his class-mates with strict instructions to cheer and wave union flags. Dad, who could have made a great story out of this royal visit, never mentioned it. It was Mum who told us about the good-looking prince who worried Parliament with his populist instincts. In the intervening years, Dad had learned that a prince's visit was mere show and made no difference whatsoever to his 'people'.

Some men and women tried to fight back, to turn the arguments and the anger into action. Impatient with the slowness of change, men of working age began to organise. Barton Hill became a focus in Bristol for the working-class political activity that was also sweeping through other urban centres of the country. There were frequent demonstrations or protest meetings about hunger, lay-offs, factory closures, wage cuts and housing. The groundswell of discontent and deprivation was fertile ground for the embryonic Labour Party, which poured men and resources into the district to build electoral support and overturn Bristol's long-standing Liberal tradition. Dad heard Walter Baker, the Labour Party candidate, speak on the stump in Barton Hill on several occasion over the years as he campaigned for election. He took to heart the promises Baker gave about housing, employment and justice for workers. 'A fair day's wage for a fair day's work' rang around the streets. When older members of the family dropped round he was old enough to voice his own opinions and to take part in vociferous discussions. For the young, hope comes more readily than scepticism and no doubt Dad shared in the sheer excitement about the tangible possibility of change.

It took two general elections for Labour to break through in Barton Hill. On their third attempt and Walter Baker's second, in 1923, against a background of national and local political hostility, Bristol East (as it was formally named in 1950) returned Baker as its first Labour MP. He left Bristol for Westminster, emerging from the belly of the railway arches, striding away from the warehouses and factories, out of the crowded streets to enter Temple Meads Station from the front. He was cheered on by a procession of the unemployed. It was said that he carried with him the hopes of thousands.

It was a long time before I began to realise that my father had been born into poverty and even longer before 'poverty' was more than a word. My father's footballing success is his, unique, but our understanding of it is enhanced by recognising how his distinctive achievement gradually emerged from an interplay of innate characteristics, family influences, and the harsh knowledge thrust upon him by the streets of Barton Hill. A profound aspect of that knowledge was resilience. Perhaps the Hapgood family were astute; perhaps just lucky. My guess is that their locally well-known sense of themselves as socially superior may not just have been inspired by Harry's streetwise braggadocio. After all, when the number of jobs in Bristol shrank in the 1890s, Harry and Emily had taken the bold step of moving to Wales where Harry worked in the mines for over 14 years. Even when she and then Harry returned to Bristol, all their children grew into healthy adults who eventually built stable lives.

The spirit of this beleaguered community endured for over half a century before Barton Hill was finally designated for 'slum clearance'. Desperate as conditions were, Dad grew up in a community and family that cared, that held together and made the absolute best of a difficult set of cards. He was never 'poor' although poverty nearly overwhelmed his family, but somehow, incredibly, not quite. It certainly did not overwhelm their individuality, their determination to survive and to improve.

The Dings still feels cut off. Walking towards it along Cattle Market Road with the railway lines above my head and the Feeder

Canal on my left, I immediately felt isolated. Not threatened, but separate. For a moment I was distracted by the brilliant colours of a mural painted with scenes of children's games which soften the concrete railway embankment and brighten the small patch of green below. In contrast, an iron post, heavy and unadorned, stands at the entrance, at first glance a reminder of the industrial era. On the unpainted iron poster at the top, these words stand out like rough-edged Braille:

WHY DO WE CALL IT 'THE DINGS'?
HERE IN 1626 THERE WAS
FARMLAND 'UPON THE DYNG'.
IN 1610 IT IS RECORDED AS
'BENGS' OR 'BINGS', SAXON
WORDS FOR A GRAZING
MEADOW WHERE THE WITHIES GREW.

The words and phrases are unexpected, for a moment out of place. Perhaps if I had been a casual passer-by, I would not have been so moved by the fiercely defiant claim of a dispersed community to a history that transcends its brokenness. But there would be no casual passers-by to a hidden, forgotten part of Bristol where the withies are reached via Anvil Street, Gas Lane and Bread Street. This dream of history, of a pastoral idyll, was the residents' own sustenance, their assertion of their lineage. Beneath the iron, the bricks, the marshes, the dirt of its industrial past, there lies, and will always lie, an Arcadia of meadowland, of sheep and shepherds, where the willows trail their leaves along the surface of the streams. The words are a testament to the imagination as a weapon of survival.

Mike and I first visited the Dings in 2010, over 100 years after our father was born there, after three phases of 'slum clearance' and a more recent project of district improvement. We wandered around a small square pulled out of shape by closed-off exit streets and past demolition. The houses that remained were quiet but not abandoned; they were the first of those which Bristol City Council hoped would bring a new cycle of regeneration to the district. The day had become grey and gusty. Rubbish fell and lifted around house railings and a recycling bin rolled aimlessly back and forth. We didn't know what we were hoping to understand or what we were looking for until we found it: 2 Union Street had been demolished but nearby in the road, Mike spotted a manhole-shaped iron memorial to 'Eddie' Hapgood. We looked at each other. Our father and Bristol's 'England Footballer' lived here.

As we finally and reluctantly decided to make our way back to town, we noticed a circular drift of words inscribed in the pavement, framed by a series of brick circles rippling outwards. On a day that now had a hint of rain, I knelt down to clear the leaves and cigarette stubs away with my hands and read:

THE DINGS – A COMMUNITY WITH ECHOES OF STREETS PULLED DOWN PEOPLE MOVED AWAY I WONDER WHERE THEY ARE NOW IT'S THE PEOPLE THAT MAKE IT NOT BRICKS AND MORTAR ISOLATION HAS BROUGHT US CLOSER TOGETHER.

The Dings, Echoes, Isolation. I don't know who conjured up these words. I could imagine a group working together offering phrases and words determined to create a community poem that would act as a statement for those parents and grandparents that had preceded them. If the withies of the entrance post spoke of their ancient roots, the pavement memorial spoke of their final loss. The simplicity of these words did not suggest circular harmony but the *huis clos* of the abandoned. It was neither a memorial nor a commemoration, but a final record. There was no one around to notice us and I continued to kneel.

A conversation I had had with my father, perhaps in 1965, came back to me. I realised with a shock that, as we had talked all those years ago when my mother was ill, he would have known that the demolition of Barton Hill, of the Bristol he had known best, had recently been completed, yet his daughter did not even know that such a place as Barton Hill existed:

'It was a bad time,' Dad began. Mum was in hospital for an operation and Dad and I went together to visit her as soon as she came round from the anaesthetic. I don't think she was fully conscious when we arrived. Dad knelt in silence for a long time beside the bed holding her hand, his head resting on the covers. He was deeply troubled by her illness and frightened too. Later that evening, both of us silent and thoughtful, we sat down together to have something to eat when he began talking, his food untouched. I'm not sure he knew I was there, but he talked and I listened. I thought in his anxiety he wanted to talk about Mum, but, for the first time he told me about growing up in Bristol. He spoke quietly, almost to himself.

'It was a bad time,' he said again. 'It was pretty tough where we lived but nothing like some of the places I saw when I grew a bit older. The milk round I did in those days when I left school took me through some of the poorest streets in east Bristol, poor in a way I hadn't ever seen even though I was living only a few streets away. Or perhaps I just hadn't noticed as a boy. In those days, the council gave out milk coupons to the dairy for the destitute and one of the things I had to do was go round, collect the coupons and make sure everyone got their share. Women, it was always a woman even if their husbands were unemployed, would stand at the door waiting for me, hand over the coupons and hold out their pitcher to be filled. It was a kind of nightmare. I'd say, "Good morning," or something, but they would just stand or vanish immediately behind the door. They never spoke to me. I don't think they saw me.'

He hesitated. 'As long as I live, there's one woman I'll never forget. I see her again and again. She was young – but I don't know why I thought that because she looked old – her face was hollow and malnourished. Her hair was thin, her face dead. Her baby was feeding as she handed out her pitcher to be filled. She didn't seem to have any coupons but how could I drive on past? What shocked me was that the top of her breast and her chest were bare, blotches of purple potassium over a rash of wet sores. I knew it wouldn't make any difference if I just drove past her or if I gave her some extra milk for free. In a way she'd stopped living long ago. She'd given up. She couldn't smile. She frightened me.'

After a pause, he went on, 'But I thought I knew everything was going to be all right, after I'd listened to some speeches at the open-air hustings. There was a new chap, a Walter Baker who everyone was getting excited about. He was campaigning for the Labour Party, the party your mother supports.' He paused again but the mention of Mum hadn't interrupted his flow of thoughts. 'It was a very new party back then. He promised that if Labour was returned, housing would improve, everything would change. We all believed him. I thought of that poor woman. I was so inspired, marching around like a pioneer in a new land shouting slogans!'

He smiled to himself. 'But after he was elected, nothing changed. What a lie! The houses still continued to deteriorate and streets were still contaminated by waste and the bits of green penned between marshland, railways, and warehouse sheds ... well, they were dangerous, Mam thought, disease-ridden. There were so many protests.' He shook his head. 'I never voted then because I was too young. I never will vote now. Just tell me' – his voice hardened but he wasn't challenging me, just trying to understand – 'anyone can make a promise, but how can anyone be so cruel as to promise lies deliberately to those who have nothing? How can a prince who had everything come and stare at us and smile to boost his reputation and talk about "his people"?' He shook his head again. 'I never could understand.'

I wanted to say that it wasn't that easy, look how much better things are today, or some platitude to ease the pain of his memories, but I didn't. He had shared with me his first experiences of despair, of treachery, the cruelty of false promises, the casual lack of compassion. This was a kind of human failure he first witnessed in those who ignored the slums of Bristol and the people who lived there but, to his bewilderment, had surfaced and resurfaced in very different situations throughout his life.

Dad never read the words the parting residents had chosen as their legacy, but then he didn't need to. He knew all about the bitter paradox of a pride and solidarity forged from disillusionment and a fighting spirit forged by injustice. As we talked he must have been torn between gladness that his children knew nothing of this and the loneliness of carrying that knowledge, that history on his own. Yet, as we were beginning to realise, it was that knowledge which would forge both his youthful greatness and his mature strength.

3

Blue Skies and Red Horizons

'A fair day's wage for a fair day's work' – this slogan, long adopted by working-class activists, turned out to be a dangerous philosophy in 1922 for a mere lad starting his first job. When he left school Dad joined his older brother Percy at the nearby Great Western Cotton Works. He was more successful than some of his peers at finding a job. He was not so successful at keeping one.

It seems he entered his first workplace like a warrior fired with political enthusiasm rather than sidled in with the appropriate gratitude and timidity of a new boy. A week after he started he put in a request for higher wages. He may have had right on his side but it was hardly the best time to take a stand on what he felt he deserved and definitely foolhardy when he was barely out of school. Dad was not stupid. He knew very well that jobs were precious. He knew that the loss of a week's wages could set a family on the road to destitution, but was inspired by the stirring words ringing out around the Dings and Barton Hill and convinced of their manifest justice. Oliver Twist asking for more couldn't have created more of a furore. Unsurprisingly, Dad was dismissed with immediate effect. No doubt his boss saw the self-righteous young man in front of him as a potential socialist agitator but Dad must have smarted at such a peremptory response.

It was a hard lesson to learn. A young man's mistake, naivety, or simply bravado in trying out his muscle in an adult world? I'm sure there's some truth in each of these explanations but they ignore a crucial point. His impulse was spurred into action because his lived experience had been given words by the dynamic political protests of the time. After all, even the Prince of Wales, visiting the Dings and Barton Hill the previous year, had said something must be done for 'his people'. Dad thought that what junior apprentices were being paid was not a 'fair' exchange for their time and effort, and with the voices of his future king and his own community ringing in his head, he was prepared to stand up and say so.

The confidence to act decisively and with conviction was to become one of Dad's distinctive characteristics. Equivocation never came easily to him. A fierce sense of justice and a readiness to speak out are admirable qualities in themselves but there was also an impetuosity, perhaps a kind of arrogance in him but certainly a loner impulse, which drove him to push back against what he perceived as wrong whatever the consequences and even when he was out there on his own. As a professional footballer, his unshakeable sense of fairness won him friends, profound respect among fellow professionals and the admiration of fans well beyond Arsenal. In his later life he would learn, but never quite understand, that what was praised so highly in his role on the football pitch could, in other situations, be viewed warily as uncomfortable, stubborn and difficult.

All was not lost. As usual the family rallied round. Stella, with typical Hapgood solidarity, co-opted him into the dairy business run by her husband, Jack Sibley. To have a regular job in 1923, and one within the family, was a privilege indeed and fortunately it turned out to be work that, on the whole, Dad enjoyed, giving him responsibility and independence. That Dad worked for the Sibleys delivering milk until he left Bristol five years later is probably one of the best-known facts of his early life. Stella, always very fond of her youngest brother, must have recognised something trustworthy in him. Dad remained close to her and the Sibley family all his life. On my last visit to Burnley before Tony died in 2011, he handed me a large foolscap envelope full of cuttings and photos collected by Stella's son from her albums and forwarded to Tony when she died. He thought there were some I would be particularly interested in. The large shiny photo on the top slipped out easily. I had never seen it before. It was taken by a professional photographer but the mood of the image is happy and affectionate. Dad in his RAF uniform and his younger sister Iris in a dark coat lean towards each other smiling, enjoying the pleasure of a brief reunion before Dad left for war. It was my first and only glimpse of the independent aunt who established her own successful business as a piano teacher.

Another time, another place and Dad might have taken up tennis or golf, both great loves in his later life, but a Barton Hill lad was more likely to kick a ball around and to fall in with footballing mates. He had never had the opportunity to play organised football, so it wasn't being part of a competitive team that he enjoyed in his early teens. The district where he lived was so densely populated that the school playground was a restricted area of tarmac and accessible public playing spaces, to borrow the words of contemporary social commentators, were 'greatly deficient'. Football could only be a local pavement and road game. The advantage of that, of course, was that anyone could play it. No expensive equipment was necessary, no neatly drawn-out pitch, not 22 players, not even five-a-side. Just a ball and some energy.

One of his nephews later recalled that he was remembered for always kicking a tennis ball around. Certainly his own account of breaking a window kicking a football might well have converted him to a small ball. Or, having lost a football, just made the best of it with a tennis ball. Public and grammar schools had a long tradition of organised team sport – rugby, cricket, rowing and occasionally and unusually as at Charterhouse, football – but the school curriculum of early-20th-century state schools didn't include them. This was the story many, many working-class lads of that time would tell their own children yet, extraordinarily, that sense of a working-class heritage still remains powerful today. Liverpool's Steven Gerrard claimed in 2017 that 'all top players come from the street', and even more recently, Héctor Bellerin, Arsenal defender and Spanish international, declared, 'Most footballers come from difficult backgrounds. If your mum or dad is a banker or a doctor, then you're hardly likely to become a footballer.' Even more recently, the young Manchester United striker Marcus Rashford spoke of the food poverty of his childhood in a campaign for free school meals in the summer holidays. Class and poverty still seem to be football's way of acknowledging resourcefulness, independence and survival.

Today, when junior football suffers from over-organisation and is often guilty of raising impossible expectations for its young hopefuls, it is hard to believe that Dad didn't play any form of team football and didn't seem to feel any particular need to until after leaving school. Then he tried a few local teams but if he had to play on his own, then he played on his own. It didn't stop him learning ball skills, he would say, and to prove the point, he would pass the ball up and down and behind his body and along his arms, and on to his head and down his chest and knee to be trapped dead on the ground in front of him – talking all the time. No one would advocate that as the only training for young boys today, but when Dad finally settled into the St Philips adult school club, a well established local amateur club, his street skills were pretty much all he had to take with him. It was 1926, Dad was 17 years old and he was lucky. As the new season kicked off, St Philips was reported to be 'trying some younger blood' and Dad got his chance.

A gloweringly ferocious face glares out from an early photograph of the St Philips team. His springy long crew cut, which appears like canine hackles, dominates but, in fact, the image is misleading. Like many lads growing up in the same social and environmental conditions, he was small at 1.7m (5ft 7in) tall; slight at probably not even 57kg (9st); had neat hands and feet and unexpectedly thin, slightly bandy legs. He didn't present an ideal sporting physique but from the start he was fast, precise, courageous and smart. In boys' football that was enough to mark him out. Percy, three years older than Dad, was, by all accounts, also very talented. Soon after Dad joined the team, Percy dropped out from the weekly demands of playing and training to pursue what the family called his 'man about town' activities. He never lost his love of football but, unlike Dad, he turned from promising player to admiring spectator in just a few years. When Ashley Cole still sparkled for Arsenal in Dad's own position at left-back in 1999, he and Matthew, his younger brother, were interviewed about their early family days. Matthew was the first to admit that, although he was considered as promising a player as his older brother, he was never able to be as committed. Ashley never missed a training session, made sure he kept himself fit and his reward was to be widely considered the best left-back in the world. Percy too lacked that vital spirit of dedication and perseverance that was becoming a distinctive characteristic of his younger brother.

Another striking piece of good luck for Dad was the Bristol Downs League. A freestanding amateur football league, founded 20 years earlier, it provided full-sized pitches for all the youth teams of Bristol. Like the pitches on the Hackney Marshes in London, it was and is an egalitarian space, a proving ground for a number of future sportsmen and the haunt of local scouts. Situated in the far north of Bristol, it required effort and motivation from those who lived in the south of the city just to get there, but for those who wanted to play, the Downs League offered excellent facilities and a new horizon. Gangs of youths roamed the Barton Hill streets – possibly unemployed or perhaps just aimless – stirring up local trouble and local battles. Weapons were anything that came to hand, stones or metal scraps or heavy lumps of wood. You had to have some kind of crazy courage to be involved but you had to have a different kind of courage to opt out. Dad chose the latter path, deciding to give Barton Hill weekend street life a miss. He had decided, whether he knew it or not at that point, to steer clear of trouble. Of course, he still worked at the dairy but as soon as he was free on Saturday afternoons, he headed up to the Downs. Up there, under another sky, playing on the heady heights and sophisticated playground in the heart of affluent Bristol, his talent was beginning to flourish and his confidence to grow.

Occasionally when he was able to get up to the Downs early on a Saturday off, he might arrive in time to watch the Bristol mounted police exercise their horses. The riders in full uniform and the horses under tight control would line up then, in a whoop of energy, the massive horses would be given their heads, thundering across the grass towards the furthest point of the Downs. For a young man, it was a stunning example of discipline and freedom, a vision of power and control he never forgot. Many years later, on one of those story-telling nights, he would reenact how the huge police horses that patrolled Highbury before and after matches delicately sidestepped him to safety with balletic grace unperturbed by noisy chanting and waving banners. On one evening of celebration he had been temporarily separated from his team-mates as they climbed down from the bus outside Highbury. Bouncing gently but steadily sideward, big hooves delicately criss-crossing until its sleek brown coat rubbed against his shoulder, a horse had steered him through the crowd, his hand now holding tightly to its neck harness. Relieved? Frightened? Overwhelmed, he said, by the power and gentleness of the huge creature beside him. Dad was enough of a dreamer to glimpse the possibility of another way of life in what he observed around him but there was no way in a thousand dreams he could have imagined that one day he would be protected by a highly trained police horse.

Of all the distances he was to travel in his life, none, in one significant way, was as far as the distance he learned to cover in his own city. Even today, the distance from east Bristol to the Downs in the north is much more than a matter of miles. The sense of two worlds was and still is palpable. I don't know what shortcuts he took, what bridges he crossed or what fences he jumped over; whether he walked the whole way, cycled or took the new tram up Whiteladies Road to Blackboy Hill at the southern-most corner of the Downs. On those first excursions, he probably accompanied Percy following a well-worn route. Taken up by freedom from work and the anticipation of the moment, did he have any sense that the journey from Barton Hill to the Downs was much more than a journey from one part of Bristol to another or from home to a football match? No doubt he saw what he passed but, in the way of teenagers, looked without seeing and noted without reflecting. I spread out the 1900 map of Bristol rolled up beside my desk, and study it yet again, tracing my finger away from the dark, heavily ruled, too-dense-for-naming streets of the Barton Hill district to the expansive, empty, pale green stretches of the Downs. Something extraordinary had to happen before a working-class Barton Hill lad aged 18 in 1927 could assert a claim to be different, to belong not only on the heights of the city he was born in but to be celebrated in his own right for the heights of his achievement. He had to imagine it could happen and then have the courage to make it happen. Talent, but talent laced with intelligence, self-belief, perseverance, joy – and, of course, a considerable dash of luck. From this distance in time Dad seems like a pilgrim, Everyman himself looking up from the Slough of Despond to glimpse the Eternal City on the Hill. Such an analogy would have been no exaggeration in 1925.

The 1927/28 season, during which Dad turned 18, was to be the first page in the story of his public life. He began it unknown and untried; it ended with his first sporting headline. It had taken a long time for the eyes of professional scouts to turn his way, partly because he hadn't been looking for them. He had none of the exposure of his younger Bristol contemporary Ronnie Dix, for instance, who played for England Schoolboys and made history in 1928 as the youngest player to score a goal in the Football League. It is very possible that Dad had never even heard about Ronnie's achievements. He made his own way in his own way through the local boys' teams. At that time what was most important to him was that he was happier than he had ever been before.

Bristol Rovers, one of the two local professional clubs, were the first to notice him and to offer him an end-of-season trial in their reserves. A result of their interest was his first headline, won on 7 May 1927. Mistakenly listed as A. Hapgood (perhaps because his second name was Albert), the *Green 'Un* announced after his trial, 'THE NEW BACK shows the Eastville Supporters He Can Tackle'. Apparently unfazed by playing for the first time for a professional club in a professional stadium, 'Hapgood, the new lad, time and time again justified his inclusion in the side by clearing his lines like an old stager,' trumpeted the local press. 'New lad'? 'Old stager'? Dad was never any respecter of what he saw as artificial distinctions. He played for Bristol Rovers as he had done all season for St Philips. But he was never to be the 'NEW BACK'. Bristol Rovers immediately offered him professional terms but he rejected them.

Much has been written about what prompted Dad to turn down a tempting wage of £8 a week during the season, a treasure trove in those days. Turn down an offer to play football for a professional club in his home city? Turn down an offer which meant he could continue to live at home and to work at the Sibley dairy during the summer? This is his own account:

'A Rovers director came out to the dairy with a professional offer of £8.0.0d a week, and a place in the first team. I asked what I would do in the summer. "I have a coal business," replied the director, "and I can fix you up driving a coal cart." Gently, but firmly, I ushered him out of the house. I figured there was a social distinction between driving a milk cart and a coal cart.'

Of course he was right about the social distinction between the two kinds of employment, but I think the issue was more subtle than that. Why did Dad bother to ask about a summer job in the first place when one at the dairy was already assured? He asked about summer employment because the club director had not mentioned it, simply assuming that the lad in front of him would jump at the original offer and happy not to pay a retainer wage over the summer. The young man who lost his first job requesting what he felt he deserved clearly objected to his patronising attitude. He was then taken aback or even insulted by the offer of a lower grade job than the one he already had. Dad would never have accepted that lack of respect. Another of his impulsive decisions? In this case, another he would never regret.

When Dad turned down the Bristol Rovers offer, he may already have been confident enough in his own ability to know there would be other opportunities; he had, after all, recently received glowing praise. If so, his confidence and optimism were soon rewarded. Kettering Town, a small non-league club, were interested. He was offered a lower weekly wage than Bristol Rovers, but it had a distinct advantage: the terms of the agreement. His wages would be paid throughout the summer and it was agreed that he could return to Bristol during the summer months to help out at the dairy. What was there to object to? With such a congenial arrangement signed and sealed on 9 July 1927, Dad could not have guessed that his departure from Bristol would be final and that he would never again return to live or work in the city where he grew up. He saw the whole adventure as a huge gamble. No one from Kettering had seen him play; in fact, he had never yet played a professional match! By late summer 1927, he had said goodbye to his family and left to join the 'Bristol battalion' with what I imagine was a light-hearted shrug of his shoulders, a determination to enjoy this latest (well-deserved) turn of events and a certainty that he would be back home the following May. His sudden change of fortune was 'quite remarkable', he commented years later when reminiscing with a journalist for the *Kettering Evening Telegraph* in 1968. The suggestion to sign for Kettering had come up in casual conversation and the local scout, Mr Charlesworth, had persuaded him to give it some thought. And that, he said, was that.

Dad told us the story of his arrival in Kettering over and over again, standing in front of us braced with pretended shock and assuming a face of slack-jawed amazement to convey the depth of surprise and delight he experienced as he discovered he had exchanged the congested, toxic streets of Barton Hill for a small market town in rural Northamptonshire. With his bag on his shoulder and wondering how to find his way to the lodgings the club had organised for him, he approached a nearby policeman. 'Which way to the town centre?' he asked. 'The town centre?' – and he would imitate the policeman's surprised tone. 'This IS the town centre.' That was material enough for Dad to elaborate over the years; how tiny Kettering was, how neat and pretty, with flowers hanging in baskets from the lampposts and a policeman standing around observing the scene with avuncular calm; the implausibility of one policeman single-handedly masterminding a town centre; the sheer absurdity of the destination he had inadvertently chosen for the launching of his new life. How miniature, how dainty it all seemed to the dapper boy from the big city with his urban manners. 'This IS the town centre!' he would repeat in delight. His laughter conjured up for us, not a real bricks and mortar town but a jigsaw box picture of happy children, quiet streets, ladies with hats, a puzzled policeman and Dad, larger than life, which Mum's amused protests did nothing to dispel.

Dad's stay in Kettering may have been brief, but it is there, in 1927, that he enters Mum's story and she enters his. Our father's fragmentary stories had a powerful purchase on our imaginations but they always seemed more part of our present than of his past. Remembering them now, I remember our family gatherings rather than his history. Unlike Dad's stories, our mother's stories never seemed to be casual reminiscences or zestfully performed entertainment. They still seemed fragmentary to us, but fragments charged with meaning, fierce and often poignant, emerging from a hinterland of life. I think that while Dad's memories of Bristol had been temporarily displaced by the events of his football career, her family memories, the sounds, the people, the places, remained the enduring landscape of her mind. She never left Kettering entirely behind and it would only take a word, a poem, a song, an idle question for her to share the memory they prompted. The best times were when she put the ironing board up in the room in the Bath house we called the breakfast room. It was always warmed by the stove and I could lean on the big table with its brown chenille covering or twist the tassels together while she ironed and talked. I am not sure whether we even realised that Dad had brothers and sisters. Mum had an Edwardian novel full of them. One of 11 children, she was the middle in age and companionship to Arthur and Sally – eight, nine and ten in the family order. Mike and I were not aware of meeting any of the much-loved sisters and brothers she told us so much about until we were adults ourselves, yet, as children, we knew them as well as we knew the characters in our favourite books. Each family member was characterised and distilled into a distinctive, unforgettable anecdote or character trait.

Mum didn't meet our father until several years after her own father's death. Boyfriends were, apparently, a delightful mystery to her. These stories were always told with a laugh in her voice, and any questions from her fascinated listeners simply triggered giggles. 'I was such a goose,' was her constant refrain. 'I was such a goose.' This comment was most usually linked to the time she had hidden in the hen-house while her mother sidetracked a young man she had agreed to meet for a walk. 'I didn't know how to say "no",' she would protest when we criticised her callousness. She preferred to dream about safely unreachable heroes, such as the boys from nearby public school Oundle whom she would often see out and about when released from school.

Mum didn't know how to say 'no' to my father either, but that story, a great family favourite, had a happier ending. She was just 18, full of romantic dreams and aspirations when she attended her first and only Kettering Town match at Rockingham Road during that momentous 1927/28 season, shortly after Dad had arrived in Kettering. Persuaded by a friend whose boyfriend was playing, she agreed to go. Dad only played two matches on Kettering's home ground, but the fates had already made up their minds. The ball rolled over the line and into the crowd lining the pitch. It landed at Mum's feet (or so the story went). Running to collect it, my father looked up and saw the face of the girl he would marry. 'Wait for me afterwards,' he had time to whisper before running back out on to the pitch. 'And you did? Mum, that was so bold!' we would chorus.

What had she noticed about him? That he had funny-shaped legs. 'I didn't realise he was wearing shin pads,' was accompanied by a peal of laughter at the young, naive girl who had been entranced by a young Achilles emerging in front of her. No ordinary local boy, but someone altogether more unexpected. Nobody would have bet on Eddie Hapgood and Maggie Althorpe meeting; an outside chance indeed, but Kettering was to be Dad's very own Brigadoon, his professional career and the young woman he was to marry, miraculously (or so it seemed) materialising from a casual decision made one afternoon in faraway Bristol. There must have been something of a dream-like quality for Dad about this life-changing interlude in his life.

If Dad's arrival in Kettering was 'remarkable', what was even more remarkable was that he never completed a season for the club or, still uncertain of his best position, even played particularly well. Like Dennis Bergkamp and Thierry Henry when they first played for Arsenal, the local Kettering paper decided he was not much to write home about. Luckily Arsenal thought differently. That October, a few weeks after he was 19 and after playing only nine matches for his first professional club, he was packing his bags again. What a contrast between his interview with Bristol Rovers and his interview with the Arsenal manager, Herbert Chapman, and his assistant George Allison who had both taken the trouble to travel to Kettering to watch him. The questions he was asked impressed him. Questions about smoking and drinking, about physical fitness, about standards of behaviour. Important, relevant questions. No, he didn't smoke. No, he didn't drink. Yes, personal physical fitness through regular training was vital. Yes, players lived by a code of conduct: to play fairly, cleanly, with heart and loyalty. And then, he was asked if he would like to join the Arsenal. *'Would he like ...?'* The choice was his; an agreement between equals.

Luck was again on Dad's side. Chapman, the recently appointed manager of what was then a very average side, was scouring the country for new players to build an Arsenal team in his own image. He was looking for a balance of youth and experience to implement his defensive football philosophy and his aspiration to create a club known for its stylish distinctiveness. Whatever it was that he saw in Dad that day, Chapman chose him, an untried defender who wasn't yet quite sure whether he *was* a defender, to share in his project. Whatever it was that Dad saw in Chapman, he immediately respected and trusted him. This was altogether another kind of luck. Everything that Dad had learned to value in his young life so far was echoed in the spirit of Chapman's words and substantiated by his forceful presence.

Dad was now a footballer, or at least he had been offered the chance to find out what that meant but I don't think for a moment that he was conscious of such serious matters on that extraordinary afternoon. From amateur St Philips to non-league Kettering Town to First Division Arsenal in a matter of six months. That had to be some kind of record. He had kissed his mother in Bristol goodbye in September. Now, in October, he was saying goodbye to Maggie and Kettering. Awash with happiness, he just couldn't believe his luck or begin to imagine the new path his life had taken. All he could think about on that dizzyingly exciting November day was London, meeting his Arsenal team-mates and playing in front of Arsenal supporters.

But soon, surprised at himself, he was travelling back up to Kettering as often as he could to see the girlfriend whose serious eyes and radiant smile he was missing. He enjoyed being one of her affectionate, easy-going family ('Annie, Maggie, Sally,' he would chant teasingly in imitation of Mam, 'they were always hugging one another.' 'I don't think he minded which one of us he married, he loved our family so much,' Mum would tease back). Soon Eddie and Maggie were officially courting. In 1927, when they had first met, everyone was singing the dreamy love song, 'Charmaine'. While they waited to be together, the words seemed just right for them. Dad was still singing it with energy and feeling in the 1950s as he washed up the dishes from Sunday lunch, splashing the hot water vigorously with his hands:

And I wonder if I keep on praying
Will our dreams be the same
I wonder if ever you think of me too
I'm waiting, my Charmaine, for you.

4

Becoming 'Eddie Hapgood'

On 19 November 1927, with his first Christmas away from home looming, Eddie was selected to play against Birmingham City. He felt he had been a flop in his first match for Kettering and he hadn't been sure that left-back was his best position. At Arsenal there was no doubt. He had been chosen by Herbert Chapman to be a defender and a defender was what he was now sure he wanted to be. For Birmingham fans and sports commentators who were lucky enough to watch that day, he was 'A Wonderful Capture' as one headline ran that same evening, with the report stating:

'Arsenal were a little daring to throw young Hapgood, the Bristol-born player, into the League team so soon ... he not only justified his inclusion, but he showed he is a youth of exceptional promise.'

Arsenal were indeed daring and the crowds very lucky because Eddie was only an occasional sighting from that appearance to his first full season nearly two years later. Even so, from this point in his life my father was on the way to becoming 'Eddie Hapgood', a public face, public property that endured from the day of that momentous debut. He was now a 'footballer', and, although he could never have guessed it, a footballer who had taken his first steps to becoming the player and captain at the heart of Arsenal's First Division and FA Cup successes in the 1930s, the player and captain at the heart of England's international team. The paradox for his three younger children is that any Arsenal supporter, anyone interested in football, any sporting journalist, anyone who reads the sports pages of any newspaper, probably knows as much as we do about his career, if not more. And, if they don't and want to find out, they can access any number of books, articles, lists of statistics and, latterly, Wikipedia and Google searches. It would be hard to add to the specifics of a glittering procession of individual, Arsenal and England triumphs that lit up the 1930s, transformed my family's life and brought joy to thousands of football supporters. If you really want to know about him, it is not hard to answer the question, 'What did Eddie Hapgood do?' A much harder question to answer is, 'What exactly was it that Eddie Hapgood did?'

To try and answer that question means returning to Herbert Chapman, newly appointed manager of Arsenal in 1925. The great Charlie Buchan, who had rejoined Arsenal from Sunderland that same year, is credited with convincing Chapman that Arsenal's defensive positioning needed a rethink. Chapman definitely listened to Buchan's advice but his search for talented players was informed by another over-arching personal vision, a fierce ambition to build a team admired for its finesse, a club associated with culture and respect and, with an eye firmly fixed on the future, a football club that would be a 'People's Palace'.

When Chapman joined Arsenal, he lost no time in implementing his vision of a modern, international football club. No aspiration was too big or practical detail too small to be considered. Chapman was one of the first football managers to take full charge of team selection and management and to have a free hand to shape the identity of his club. He stressed the need for a strict training regime and a healthy diet supported by physiotherapists and masseurs. Drinking and smoking weren't banned but very much discouraged. He engaged the players in discussions about tactics before a match and post-game analysis afterwards, something that Eddie thoroughly enjoyed and energetically contributed to. To consolidate a spirit of team camaraderie, Chapman encouraged them to share companionable afternoons playing golf or tennis after formal training sessions ended. Dad was never a great golfer but many of the happiest photographs of him in these early days show him on a golf course enjoying the spirit of competition in relaxation and sociability with his team-mates. And those traditional tweed plus fours on young men in the peak of fitness seem flamboyantly on trend.

Chapman also had an astute eye for the immediate impact of the club's architecture as a frame for the appearance and behaviour he demanded of his players and the ambitions he held for Arsenal. So much of what he achieved early in the 1930s is well known and forever part of Arsenal history. When Arsenal played Huddersfield Town, his former club, in the 1930 FA Cup Final at Wembley, Chapman seized the opportunity to demonstrate sporting respect and pride by suggesting that both teams walked out on to the pitch together, a practice that is still followed.

Perhaps the 'marble halls' of Highbury may have been a rather inflated description but the redesigned entrance to the former club's home ground of the time was renowned for its art deco elegance and distinction and was certainly intended to create a hologram of cultural sophistication and civic dignity. To increase match intensity, a massive clock was mounted on the newly built south terrace of the West Stand to heighten anticipation and excitement as the minutes ticked away. The all-red shirt, familiar from Woolwich Arsenal days, was brightened by white sleeves to dazzle the eyes of fans. Introduced in 1933, Eddie was one of the first 11 players to wear the new kit against Liverpool. In fact, 1933 was the year when Arsenal became not simply somewhere you went to watch your team play a football match. When the nearby Gillespie Road Underground station was renamed 'Arsenal', it became a London destination. By 1934, the stadium was dubbed 'Golden Gates', 'for the money taken each week at the turnstiles had made the club one of the richest in the country'. The club's aura began to spread beyond its own gates and to influence the very meaning of football across the country.

While all this is familiar evidence of Arsenal Football Club's undoubted glamour and success from season to season in those early years, each external flourish a visible pointer to the building blocks in the club's history, Chapman wanted even more, something far less tangible. He wanted an identity that endured, one that outlasted any meteoric moment which could be extinguished in an instant by a crushing defeat, any one season of success which another club could displace in months with just a few more goals, a few more points. Kits and clocks, stations and stadia are crucial symbols but to endure requires something qualitatively different, as several Premier League clubs have discovered in recent years in their new but soulless grounds, 'more of a tourist destination than a place of communion'.

Becoming 'Arsenal' would necessarily involve a kind of metamorphosis – from man to myth; from club to legend. Whether or not in these early days Chapman would have articulated this ambition so specifically or so consciously, he certainly recognised the paradox in his ambition. Myth-building requires a kind of permanence, a consensus of mystery and wonder between players and fans, but a football club depends on the daily practical activities of training and playing, winning and losing, players arriving and players leaving. Surprisingly and perhaps disturbingly, Chapman recognised with astute commercial insight that it is possible for a myth to be fabricated knowingly and strategically by money and management but, with true footballing insight, he knew that to take root, to suggest immortality, it must also be animated innocently and joyously by players and fans alike.

The new player who arrived from Kettering towards the end of 1927 to help Arsenal fulfil their destiny was callow, exuberant, a tad arrogant but above all else, young. 'Bliss was it in that dawn to be alive, but to be young was very heaven,' he might have said if he had ever heard those stirring words. The poet William Wordsworth was writing about the euphoric early days of the French Revolution; Eddie had been chosen to be part of Chapman's revolution. He was signed to implement the new defensive strategy for a club which, at that time, was drifting towards the bottom half of the table.

He was also signed for his character. Chapman famously required his footballers to be respectable, 'to break away from their traditional cloth-cap image'. The talented newcomer with a friendly, outgoing manner who didn't smoke or drink in an era of heavy smoking and drinking, who according to Chapman was 'as happy as he is good', fitted that agenda too. The nicknames 'Happy Hapgood' and 'Happy-go-Lucky Hapgood', which had emerged first in Kettering Town match reports, were hardly subtle spin-offs from his name, but his personality – his infectious gaiety, his delight in what seemed an extraordinary turn of events, his ready laughter and irrepressible energy made them seem appropriate. Eddie, enthusiastic and full of anticipation, was ready to believe that he and Chapman were in it together, partners-in-football, partners in creating Arsenal's future.

So Eddie was there at what could be called the beginning, one of the earliest, youngest members of the new Arsenal that Chapman dreamed of. But it didn't turn out after all to be the easy beginning he had expected when he had sung his way home a few weeks previously. It was a beginning that might have deterred someone less obstinate, less driven by a growing conviction of his own talent. He was shocked to realise he was lonely and at times the long-term implications of his decision to move to London weighed heavily. In London, he lodged with the recently married Joe Hulme, so he wasn't strictly alone, but the arrangement was only temporary until the club had decided on his future or Eddie had made arrangements of his own. He travelled to Kettering whenever he could but he missed Maggie and the comforting affection of her family. In addition, he had arrived at Arsenal mid-season in the winter hardly aware of what professional football involved and stepped on to a stage already occupied by a distinguished group of players, almost all of whom were significantly older than he was. An unfit, untried 19-year-old and the youngest player in the squad, he found himself training and (when he got the chance) playing alongside luminaries like his landlord Joe, Bob John, Charlie Buchan and Tom Parker. These were players with established reputations on whom in those early days he relied for advice, support and encouragement. He was clearly the minnow in the pool and although he was grateful for the generosity of their welcome and the ready support they provided, there were times he found it hard to feel he belonged. He had to focus hard on fostering the belief that he was good enough to be one of them and on driving himself to realise that belief.

There were low moments when, feeling isolated and underachieving, he was tempted to chuck it all in and return to Bristol rather than confront and overcome the hardest test his courage and confidence faced, the frailty of his physique. Although he had been careful to keep fit since he was 16, in the testing crucible of elite professional football, his general condition was poor enough to prevent him from regular selection for two impossibly long seasons and to keep him week after week on the training ground or playing for the reserve team in the London Combination. He had arrived at Arsenal expecting to play every match but played only a demoralising three times in the remainder of that first season. Chapman may well have originally intended him to play every match. He had, after all, selected him for the first match after his arrival when Eddie had given an excellent performance. His debut at Birmingham had lit up spectators and pundits as his games on the Bristol Downs and his single appearance for Bristol Rovers and nine for Kettering Town had done. But the euphoria wasn't to last. To Chapman, watching him with an expert eye, it was clear that this young lad was as physically vulnerable, as unfit for the hard slog of a professional season as he was lightning swift in the moment.

Eddie's vision of himself as a regular Arsenal player gradually gave way to the hard graft of daily training and more training, of recognising what needed to be done and doing it. His well-known habit of training alone dates back to this time. When sessions were over, he would often stay to put in the extra hour or return to Highbury later in the day to work out in the gym. It is a remarkable tribute to both Chapman and Eddie that neither of them stopped believing that he would come good and that what fans and pundits glimpsed in him would come to fruition. This slow maturing was to be a significant element in his development. His boyish arrogance and urgency to compete gradually changed to a slow-burning steel of certainty in the alchemy of Chapman's unwavering faith in him.

A retrospective article in *Reynolds News* some 16 years later, as the war came to an end, gives an account of playing against him in the 'lost' seasons of 1927–29. Realising immediately that he was 'an England back in the making', the writer remembers, 'There was, however, one snag. Once in nearly every game Hapgood played, he fell unconscious after heading the ball. Though he revived in a minute or two, something organically wrong was suspected. Chapman could not take the risk of putting this frail youngster of 19, who had "International" stamped all over him, in the League side.'

Joe Hulme, already established in the Arsenal team when Eddie arrived, also recorded his anxiety about the damage the new recruit might be doing to himself:

'Particularly did I admire Eddie for the fact that he refused to shield his "soft head" when the necessity for a header arose. Yet it was nearly certain that if Hapgood put his head to a heavy ball driven hard in his direction, he would immediately go down for the count.'

Given the number of times he passed out after a header and the awareness of team-mates of his vulnerability, he was lucky not to suffer some form of brain damage. Concussion has finally been recognised for the danger it is and research is getting closer to establishing a definitive link between heading a ball and dementia. Jeff Astle of West Bromwich Albion, who died in 2002, is the first player known to have passed away from chronic traumatic encephalopathy. Eddie, ignorant of the danger, refused to let the problem stop him. Quite the opposite; his desire and ability to head a ball was to become a defining characteristic of his flamboyant style. The first 12 months at Arsenal were devoted to building up his strength through a combination of intensive training and a special protein diet designed to bolster his stamina and resistance by Arsenal's trainer Tom Whittaker. Chapman demanded everything of his players; Tom cared for them. By 1927 Eddie had reached his maximum height and still weighed only 57kg (9st). After a playing career of over 11 years, his small, light frame continued to draw comments. 'By tape-measure standards,' wrote the journalist Eric Stephenson in 1938, 'he ought to have been a winger not a full-back at all.'

Despite only occasional appearances, Eddie's footballing skill, honed in lonely perseverance on the streets of Barton Hill and refined on the Bristol Downs, was always recognised as exceptional. There was some initial surprise that he wasn't on the team sheet when the 1928/29 season opened but new players being tested or having to wait their turn was not unusual. Arsenal had a poor start that September, drifting steadily down the table with a disastrous run of ten defeats, eight draws and only six wins as Christmas came and went. Then Horace Cope, the incumbent left-back, was injured. In the carousel of a footballing life, one player's misfortune is another player's opportunity. Eddie burst on to the scene in January and Arsenal promptly went on an unbeaten run of ten games. Despite his impressive debut the season before, he was already so forgotten that journalists got his name wrong again. 'Is Albert Hapgood the real mascot of the Arsenal team?' asked the match commentator.

Eddie played 17 more matches that second season before Cope, fighting off injury, briefly, but only briefly, reclaimed his place. It didn't take long for him to be noticed again. Alex Jackson, Huddersfield and Scottish international, one of the original 'Wembley Wizards' who trounced England in 1928, came up against Eddie in his first full season, playing in the 1930 FA Cup Final. He selected him as the kind of defender who is the hardest to play against. 'When the shoulder charger is beaten he is hopelessly beaten,' Jackson wrote. 'But when a back like ... Eddie Hapgood of the Arsenal, is beaten in one move, he is still in front of me wheeling across to tackle from another angle!' Eddie's talent was beginning to alert strikers throughout the Football League.

From his earliest days at Arsenal, despite Eddie's personal inner doubts and struggles, it was the contradictions and drama of his personality as well as the skill of his football that the pundits loved and which inspired their writing. The contrast between the austere dedication of the young man on the field and the light-hearted and noisy young man off it was beginning to be noticed. Their lively copy began to shape Eddie Hapgood's 'persona'. On the pitch, the business of winning controlled his mind and body; off the pitch, he relaxed with ease. 'His Arsenal comrades only have one thing against him,' one journalist wrote that season. 'Hapgood sings a lot and while he is musical he is not quite as musical as he thinks he is.' Singing was his family inheritance and he never stopped doing it. But if his singing and the fact that he didn't smoke or drink gave him the idiosyncrasies essential for capturing public attention, something else had also been noticed in those early years, something that Chapman might have hoped for but could never have been certain of: Eddie's uniquely unwavering attention for every second of every match on the movement of the ball and the shape of the game.

At last, the 1929/30 season put Eddie at centre stage. He was joined that year by the 17-year-old striker Cliff Bastin, and in 1930/31 21-year-old defender George Male and Alex James who, at 28, was the final piece in this perfect jigsaw of experience and youth, of sagacity and enthusiasm, of positioning and speed. Vying with powerful competitors in Liverpool, Derby County and most threatening of all, Aston Villa, the following season Arsenal won the First Division for the first time, triumphantly breaking the league record with 66 points. In an extraordinary race for supremacy against Villa, Arsenal scored 127 goals – Jackie Lambert netting the most with 38 – but Villa notched up their own spectacular record, scoring 128.

Yet it was during this season of glory for Arsenal's strikers that journalists were struggling to describe what was different about the playing style of the new defender Eddie Hapgood; what was mesmerising, what drew curious neutrals to the stadium to watch him. They described him as an 'artist', 'exquisitely smart' with an 'intuitive gift' and in an extraordinary accolade, as 'one of the principal reasons why the lovers of artistic football flock to Highbury'. Artistry on mud, in heavy kit and manoeuvring a leather ball? How could his movements be elegant, artistic? What mysterious inner vision could possibly bring physical toughness and graceful balance together? Those were the questions the pundits posed, the fans revelled in and which evoked despair in opposition fans.

Behind the scenes and out of the public eye, Eddie had already proved that he had the patience to build an infrastructure for his brilliance through the daily physical drudgery of training and the daily mental discipline of total concentration. Long before television, social media and Twitter could catapult an individual to instant stardom, it had taken a mere 15 months after he found a place in the Arsenal team for journalists to introduce the opening of his first full season with an article discussing 'How Eddie Hapgood Found Fame'. 'If he puts the work in and does not let himself down in terms of effort or strategy, he can leave the result to the football gods,' it declared.

But there was always a parallel story waiting to take over, to tweak the triumph and spoil the fun. The 1931/32 season, which everyone expected to crown Arsenal's new supremacy, opened with a dismal 1-0 defeat at home to West Bromwich Albion. Deprived of the pleasure of the seemingly inevitable win Saturday by Saturday, scrutiny turned on the defence as everyone began to ask, 'What's wrong with the Arsenal?' 'Everybody was feeble,' was another argument, and Arsenal's indomitable defence had crumbled. 'Why did Hapgood fail so often?' was often asked.

Down but not, as it transpired, out. That year Arsenal fought back to come in second to Everton. Brave, determined? – yes – good enough? – no. Challenging for the league title is exciting, winning it is better, but Arsenal aspired to winning magnificently, incontestably, and that is quite another matter altogether. And there was always the threat of psychological disasters, injury or complacency along the way waiting to trip up their sense of superiority. While self-confidence and entitlement inspired worship at home, it also inspired burning ambition in lesser clubs who fostered their dedication to scupper the big boys in the once-in-a-lifetime chance offered by the FA Cup. During the magnificent 1932/33 season, when Arsenal romped to the championship with 25 victories and eight draws in their 42 First Division games, they encountered Walsall. Their defeat is the substance of one of Arsenal's most famous stories. In the dark days of January in the Black Country as the year turned, Third Division Walsall's team of part-time pros and amateurs trounced

Arsenal 2-0 in the third round proper. The fact that Arsenal went on to win the championship for a second time did not eradicate the sense of diminishment which continues, even now, to run deep in the club's collective consciousness.

Although injury prevented Eddie himself from playing in or even seeing the Walsall match, he shared the team's wretchedness and learned a bitter lesson. 'It's harder to beat a team below you than a team above you; they have nothing to lose and you have everything to lose; they have the glory of an unexpected victory and you have only humiliation; never underestimate the underdog,' was a piece of wisdom we children were often given. I didn't realise how heartfelt it was, that this was wisdom watered in tears over years as the result of a single match that had torn Arsenal's sense of pride to shreds. The *Daily Mail* rejoiced in reporting the 'widespread feeling of schadenfreude'. Myth-enhancing journalists seized with glee on the David and Goliath theme of 'Walsall's Wonder Win'; class-conscious local journalists revealed the exotic secrets of the Arsenal regime which 'trains its players on ozone, brine-baths, champagne, golf and electrical massage in an atmosphere of prima donna preciousness', while 'Walsall men eat fish and chips and drink beer'. While such comments were primarily inspired by a nose for a good story fired by resentment and envy, they embodied political and social truths. The deepening crisis that was to lead to the Depression would hit the Midlands and the north much harder than London. Eddie, who a mere handful of years before had been a witness and victim of the poverty of Bristol's industrial decline, was now seen as a member of 'the unseeing and condescending south'. And he was now a fixture in the most prestigious, wealthy and dominant club in the First Division.

This was the time of the first version of the 1930s Arsenal team, the first wave. These names – George Male, Eddie Hapgood, Bob John, Tom Parker, Cliff Bastin, Joe Hulme, David Jack, Alex James, Jackie Lambert, Herbie Roberts – are names that occur and re-occur whenever the club's history is rolled out. This season coined many of the phrases journalists continuously repeated throughout the decade – 'Arsenal's artistry', 'toe-to-toe passing', 'the sinuous dribble', 'the crafty footwork'. These descriptions were the work of the *Sheffield Daily Telegraph* in January 1929 as the newspaper lamented The Wednesday's (later Sheffield Wednesday) attempt to match Arsenal, let alone stop them. Eddie emerged with flying colours as he 'proved to be one of the best and most defiant backs in the game'. As Arsenal's reputation grew so did Eddie's belief in Chapman's vision, his influence and his sense of team responsibility. Young as he was, he unconsciously took upon himself a commitment to help realise his manager's ambitions. For Eddie, youth, admiration but most of all being part of the creation of Arsenal was a heady cocktail which assured him that legend was not the future identity of the club, but his very own metamorphosis. In his heart and body, player and manager, man and club became indivisible. He was, at last, well on the way to becoming 'Eddie Hapgood'.

From our vantage point today, the wide sweep of 1930s Arsenal achievement seems a whole picture to be admired and wondered at even as the triumphs, scale and meaning mystify. A great arc of inexorable narrative spans the years from mediocrity to greatness and the titanic struggle of wresting supremacy from the formidable giants of the Midlands and the north. Inscribed in the records, this epic tale and Eddie's role in it seems simple and inevitable:

1927/28 First Division: Arsenal 10th; Eddie: 3 games

1928/29 First Division: Arsenal 9th; Eddie: 17 games

1929/30 First Division: Arsenal 14th+ FA Cup winners; Eddie: 38 games

1930/31 First Division: Arsenal champions; Eddie: 38 games

1931/32 First Division: Arsenal 2nd; Eddie: 41 games

1932/33 First Division: Arsenal champions; Eddie: 38 games

For Eddie and the players who lived it with him, the experience was different. They knew that the individual moments and personal contributions created the energy and urgency of the whole event. Every strike, save, goal, sprint, tackle or leap may be the vital touch that makes the final picture a victory of genius. Equally, a single flaw will surely destroy, if not necessarily the scoreline, certainly the magic it has the potential to create.

How often do we read a post-match analysis such as the one regretfully lamenting 'England triumph over Kosovo despite defensive lapses' as a recent headline summed up England's 5-3 victory in a European Championship qualifying group match in 2019. Such comments would have spurred Eddie on to work harder, to eliminate those offending 'defensive lapses'. He built his

Arsenal campaigns like a craftsman might create a mosaic, each successive 90 minutes the arrangement of finely etched seconds. In his mind and body, however often he and his team-mates may have fallen just short of their ideal, victory through footballing perfection was always the aspiration; football as art. Arthur Hopcraft put it this way, 'What happens on the football field matters. It has conflict and beauty, and when these two qualities are present together in something offered for public appraisal, they represent much of what I understand to be art.'

But – was the promising Eddie a hero or a villain? A catalyst for creativity or a blocker of it? There was always the gripe that Arsenal only won because they valued defence over attack. No team should have brilliant strikers AND brilliant defenders. That bordered on unfairness. The 1933/34 season provides another example of a story told again and again about a match Arsenal shouldn't have won, and almost didn't win, but even so notched up another victory. This on 25 November 1933 again against Huddersfield, a long-term and worthy enemy, still smarting from an FA Cup defeat in 1930 and a home defeat to Arsenal a year previously. Under pressure from a hungry and determined side, Arsenal were on the defensive. As 'Hapgood headed from under the bar when the ball was flying through', the crowd howled 'Lucky Arsenal!' and the 'phrase was shouted at every corner'. It was a scrappy match, apparently, with Huddersfield the better side, but the defence had triumphed against the odds, with reports stating, 'Hapgood appeared the best footballer of the 22.'

On that occasion, Arsenal's defensive strategy had worked again to frustrate an opponent's ambition. But that was not always the case. A journalist writing up an account of the Stoke v Arsenal match in the following March obviously felt cheated as he wrote glumly that Arsenal 'have lost something ... Male and Hapgood were just Male and Hapgood'. But on other days that same season, when Arsenal were in full attacking flow, the defence took up a supporting role to the brilliance of the strikers: of Jackie Lambert, of Cliff Bastin, of Joey Hulme. This was truly a team, one for all and all for one in the best heroic fashion. In this triumphant season, Leslie Compton gave testimony to the team's attitude and Hapgood's role in creating it. 'What a back,' Compton wrote in 1933. 'His speed when he covers me is marvellous!' Defence and attack: attack and defence; equally essential; equally respectful of each other's contribution. A startlingly new concept of team dynamics had been born. The different elements of Eddie's character flow towards each other and merge as the seasons pass: his remarkable talent, his determined, grinding battle to get fit, his joy in the team's success, his undeviating focus on the moment, his deep dedication to excellence.

Weaving a tapestry of words and comments from those who watched him, those who played with him or against him, his own stories, journalists who wrote about him, images of those early days begin to form:

For more Saturdays than he can count, Eddie Hapgood runs down the tunnel from the dressing rooms and out on the Arsenal pitch at Highbury and the pitches of great clubs around the country. He knows he has done this every Saturday in the history of his life and he knows that Saturdays will always be this astonishingly surreal experience as some strange alchemy transforms confidence, training and skill into a joyous force of nature. He revels in the glorious store of energy youth gives him.

For much of his career, he is the first to appear from the tunnel on to the pitch and he surfs the wave of sound that rises from the crowd as they see him leading out their line of heroes and watch with anticipation as they scatter into position around the pitch. The noise is so thunderous, resonating ever more powerfully as year follows year and as the new stands embrace the sound and send it back down amplified. The players plunge into it as into a new element, terrifying and elating in turn. Hands are shaken; a coin is tossed; the noise dips in expectation; the referee's whistle is a call to arms. Packed together shoulder to shoulder, the crowd metamorphoses into a single entity. It sways and stills in unison with the movements on the pitch; it cries, it howls, it sings, it chants above a continuous roaring undertow like a spring tide on a pebble beach.

The thousands – 50, 60, even 70 thousands – of flat caps rake downwards in a steep grey slope shading the single focus of the eyes that stare from under their peaks towards the pitch. They have the power to raise their thumb or lower it; the power to raise a hymn of triumph, a howl of derision or the silence of shocked despair. The tumult smashes back and forth ... stuns you, and leaves you gasping for breath. And the opposition fans? They do their best but they are mere pretenders hoping without hope to silence the reverberating shouts of, 'Come on Arsenal! Come on Arsenal!' left, as the stadium empties, to whimper their way back to the scheduled football trains from St Pancras and Euston. For Arsenal is now pre-eminent, even threatening to displace clubs as prestigious as Aston Villa or Sunderland or Everton and, aspiring season by season to an ever higher position in the football hierarchy.

From Saturday to Saturday Arsenal will win. Carrying the weekly expectation is the players' responsibility, Eddie's allotted role is to defend but with his speed and agility he might be a winger or a forward, dribbling up the wing, beating one opponent after another or helping the attack as much as the defence. In a crisis, his substitute role is goalkeeper and he revels in those rare moments when he has to pull on the goalkeeper's shirt and precise footwork gives way to the theatre of leaping and diving.

He is always a fully focused left-back, but from his position he observes and plays every position on the pitch. He sees the pull and tug as teams battle for territorial supremacy. He moves up with the surge of the Arsenal attacks and the wild encouragement of the fans, holds his position as the pace slows to a steady ebb and flow, notes the patterns the players make as they press for space on the pitch. He is back when the opposition pours forward, falling calmly into position as the roar tightens from ecstasy to apprehension. Eddie watches the opposing striker running at him and waits, waits for the fraction of a second when he knows his opponent, with the ball still at his feet, is sure he will score. But when he kicks, the ball has vanished – stolen! – and the Arsenal attack is surging forward again. Exhausted, dirty, bruised and battered, at the final whistle Eddie heads for the dressing room and a steaming bath. He is happy with a simple intensity that can only be fired in the deep magic of Highbury. So total is his experience, he remembers every kick of every Saturday, of every game, to the end of his life.

In truth, though, is it possible for any writer or enthusiastic fan to capture in slow, linear words the frantic tumult of an encounter that resolves itself in a flash of movement that cheats the eyes even of spectators craning forward in suspense? Somehow Eddie finds a wrinkle in time within the seconds they all share, typically on the goal line. The forwards, the goalkeeper, the defenders and the ball are seemingly suspended in the stillness of a Grecian frieze when Eddie 'pops up from nowhere' and sweeps the ball clear. Yet again, the despairing opposition fans chant 'Lucky, lucky Arsenal' and the sports papers, already waiting for the final whistle and the printing presses to roll, pick up the chorus. Lucky? Joey Hulme, his long-time team-mate, doesn't think so. 'That [the clearance] wasn't luck. A full-back can't head the ball away from under the bar unless he has taken up that position. He is there by design, not by accident.'

He was right. Eddie's timing was not the magic trick it could appear to be in the heat of the moment but a cool appraisal of a situation precisely executed. His greatest gift was in his head or as Jens Lehmann, Arsenal's goalkeeper from 2003–'08 was to ask rhetorically years later, 'What is the fastest thing on the football field? A thought!' Eddie knows that a straight line may be the shortest distance between attacker and defender but not necessarily the best one. Here is Eddie's explanation in his own words, 'I want to see the ball all the time, not to lose sight of it by rushing into a bunch of players and trusting to luck. I prefer to wait for the ball coming out of the ruck and deal with it then.'

It is strange, how ignorance of time is the corollary of such intensity. Did Eddie hear when Herbert Chapman declared in 1933 that it was 'time to rebuild'; could he have imagined in 1933 that anyone, much less Chapman, might think that 'the team had played itself out'? Would he have even understood if he had heard? Rebuild when they had hardly begun? 'Played out?' Who? Would it have occurred to him in 1933 that Tom Parker was all of 36, the elegant, intelligent David Jack whose transfer fee to Arsenal in 1928 was the first five-figure deal, had mysteriously become 34 and the prolific record goalscorer Jackie Lambert was 31? Impossible.

It is strange that all the players seem unaware that the 1928/29 season has moved silently through the years to 1933/34, from September 1929 to May 1934. Yes, there have been changes. Some players have left, some have arrived but the Arsenal team through some powerful alchemy is unchanging. No matter how many Saturdays pass, the players are forever young. They train hard in the mornings and play on Saturdays with all their hearts. It has become a habit for Eddie to stay behind for an extra session on his own in the empty stadium, kicking the ball up the ridges of the standing areas and trapping it dead as it bounces hectically down again. 'If ever there's a ghost at Highbury he'll probably look like me,' he later wrote.

The rest of the time they play at anything and everything. They are talented in more ways than one. Golf – they can play on their own, in groups, in friendly challenges. They play cricket too, tennis, table tennis, head tennis – anything with a ball. They can play them all. They play too at life with unflagging exuberance; they don't know whether they are celebrities or schoolboys, heroes or local lads. On one occasion, Eddie records, with no time to bath and afraid of missing the last train to King's Cross, they race back from playing Everton in the north-west, towels wrapped round their dirty kit. What does it matter? Anything goes. And when the season is over, the summer still lies ahead. If he was asked how it felt to be a footballer, he wouldn't have had an answer because, after all, he didn't *feel* like a footballer, he *was* one. It would be as absurd as saying he was a human being.

As Eddie began to assume the shape of 'Eddie Hapgood', he found himself having to deal with the tensions of what almost seemed a double life, to balance the problems, decisions and joys that lurked out of the public eye with the glamour and drama of Arsenal life. He and Mum had married in 1929 and Tony, the oldest of the four Hapgood children, was due in June 1930, at the end of Eddie's first full and, as it turned out, triumphant season. As soon as the last game was played, they had arranged to travel to Kettering where Mum would be able to rest, surrounded by the reassuring and interested conversations of her mother and siblings. She must have longed to be in Kettering as the birth of her first child drew nearer. As it was, she was 21, feeling far from family and friends. There's no escaping the sense that these early years of London and parenthood were the forcing ground of two very different sets of concerns.

It was a life-changing moment for both of them when Eddie, now 22 years old, won the FA Cup for the first time and Mum, heavily pregnant, was waiting impatiently for the football season to finish. Somehow, to Mum's frustration, everything in their lives suddenly seemed to have become about Eddie. The Monday after the cup final victory, instead of heading for Kettering, he was enjoying his first taste of official pomp at the civic reception held at Islington Town Hall. After the reception, an open-top bus made its way slowly back to Highbury stadium through streets thronged with cheering crowds as north London erupted with triumph and excitement. Dad, taken by surprise, stared amazed and incredulous at the spectacle, at the colours waved ecstatically up and down, round and about, at the police on gleaming, curvetting horses opening the way, hearing the rise and fall of voices nearly hoarse with excitement, everything somehow mingling with the memory of the whoops of mounted police galloping across the Bristol Downs. Was it only five years ago? Meanwhile Mum, nursing her own anxieties, could only listen to the radio accounts and later try to enter into his overflowing excitement. Only recently, she had faced another uncertainty, a decision to be made as Dad was selected to play for England for the first time on the summer 1930 European tour leaving in May. She had held her breath dreading that she could be on her own for the birth of their first child, that Eddie might miss those first miraculous moments. Dad, clutching the letter in his hand, had read the words again. He was now an international player – for England. For the briefest of moments he was utterly overcome. Then, as single-mindedly decisive as ever, he had written a request for leave to the Football Association. He knew that being selected was little short of a command. He knew he could be wrecking his chance of an international career. He had no idea whether such an opportunity would ever come his way again.

When they arrived in Kettering, the final weeks moved with inevitable slowness. Once Mum was transferred from the car to a wheelchair and vanished down an apparently endless, impersonal corridor, Dad was ignored, left to wait and wonder in a frenzy of anxiety like any expectant father in the 1930s. Now everything was about Mum and the new baby. On one occasion, and I cannot remember what prompted this confidence, she told me how terrified she had been when Dad's fingers slipped from hers, 'I didn't know what was going to happen. Anything I had ever known or guessed just vanished.' Screaming with pain and fear as she was wheeled into the labour ward and lifted on to the labour bed, a firm slap on her cheek stunned her into momentary silence as the midwife told her brusquely to stop making a fuss. 'I didn't want him to be born that day,' was a later comment to me that revealed the shock she had experienced. 'Friday, 13 June isn't a good day to be born, is it?' she asked as if in some way fearful of what she had bequeathed her new baby. More happily, glowing with the memory of her first child, she described the glorious weather of that June and how the maternity ward was festooned with sweet williams of every colour. 'At first I wanted to call our new baby William,' she told me, 'but that idea faded away and we christened him Edris Anthony.'

Now there was a new baby, there had to also be a new house away from the noisy bustle of Finsbury Park. During the 1931 summer of sun and triumph, Dad, Mum and Tony moved house to West Finchley. It was Mum who had first encouraged Dad to think of moving. She missed the familiar beauty of Northamptonshire's level agricultural landscapes, the freedom to walk wherever she wanted, the exploration of woodlands, villages and pathways, the freedom to breathe in clean air. And Tony would soon be walking. There were schools to think about; healthy places free from traffic and urban jostle that it would be better for him to grow up in. So they drew a circle on the north London map. West Finchley, teetering on the dividing line of town and country with gentle walks to nearby Mill Hill through unspoiled countryside and unfolding towards the limitless wilderness of the north up the old toll road, seemed perfect. What's more, London and Highbury were as near as they ever had been. The house they chose at 13 Hutton Grove was a five-minute walk from a tiny station that had been opened only the previous year to serve the new housing developments in the area.

All round it was a good decision, for practical reasons, for domestic reasons and perhaps, above all, for reasons of personal security. Not so very long before, a home of their own had seemed beyond all rational ambition. Both of them had lived with the insecurity of temporary rented accommodation, and in Dad's case its often degraded condition. Perhaps for them, there would be the good fortune of something different. With growing excitement they planned and shopped. They organised their new home and imagined the garden that would emerge from the conventional stretch of lawn outside the stable-style back door. The old familiar song that both of them used to hum caught the mood at that moment exactly:

A garden of Eden just made for two
With nothing to mar our joy
I would say such wonderful things to you
There would be such wonderful things to do
If you were the only girl in the world
and I were the only boy.

But it was going to be better than any old Eden. The West Finchley Eden included Tony and was 'just made for three'. Somehow, unexpectedly, they were also joined by a cream-coloured pedigree Samoyed dog, a fashionable house-warming gift from a wealthy Arsenal supporter.

Mum often found it difficult to deal with Eddie's growing fame. However exciting, almost fabulous, their new life seemed to observers, at times she must have felt terribly adrift, even alone. Before she met him she had only travelled away from Kettering once, to enjoy an exhilarating weekend with girlfriends in Blackpool enjoying the beach by day and the Tower Ballroom in the evening. Like most young women she had lived in the family home she loved before leaving for London and a life with her new husband in 1929. While living in Kettering, she had supported Eddie through his early struggles and self-doubts at Arsenal, the possibility that it would all go wrong, but now she was on the sidelines, watching her husband happy and heady with success being lionised by a world she knew nothing about. She must have occasionally yearned for the reassurance and support of the familiar.

A measure of her aloneness when she first moved to London is her friendship with Mabel Cope, the wife of Horace Cope, whose place in the Arsenal team Dad made his own. Mabel was several years older than Mum, but she kept an eye on her in those early London years. Mum's gratitude was profound. We children used to receive what we thought were horrid-looking gloves and socks every Christmas and were required to write 'thank you' letters to a woman we had never met. But Mum would stand no jokes, moans or complaints. She never forgot that Mabel had every reason to resent the arrival of a young player who signalled the end of her own husband's career but who was always welcoming and supportive. As her own spirit was gradually drained by what she discovered was the cut-throat nature of the footballing world, so her recognition of Mabel's good-heartedness deepened.

The death of her mother in 1933 contributed to Mum's sense of being stranded and vulnerable. Mam had been a vital and loving support during those early married years as Mum found her feet in London. She was not able to travel to Kettering when her mother died. 'They thought she had slipped into a coma,' she told us. Then one of my brothers said, 'She's going,' and Mam opened her eyes, just for a moment, and murmured, "Life is very sweet."' As we children grew older, in Mum's family stories, Ada Althorpe became a perfect mother with deep reservoirs of unconditional love, a gold standard Mum strove after and never, in her own mind, achieved. And so reminiscences would run, 'Mam never went to bed, however tired or cold she was, before kneeling by her bed to pray'; 'Mam loved children so much that she always said that she would have as many children again'; 'Your father loved the way Mam would hug him when he came to the house'; 'Mam would always find something for the odd-job boy who was a bit simple to eat'; and, heartbreakingly about Tony, 'She thought it was her fault for giving him the wrong food.'

Not long before Mam was hospitalised, two-year-old Tony had had an accident while staying in Kettering. At first, he had just seemed bruised with some stomach pain. During the night after their return to London, he woke up convulsed and screaming. Dad later described the culminating emergency as he rushed into the street carrying Tony and looking for a taxi to hail when, by some wonderful accident of fortune, Tom Parker, Dad's Arsenal colleague, drove past and stopped to take them on what must have seemed an interminable three-mile drive to Great Ormond Street Hospital where Tony was admitted for an emergency operation on a ruptured intestine. He was lucky to survive, but his recovery was slow and the shock took its toll on them both. Mum was particularly affected. She grieved that she had not been able to reassure her mother that the little bowl of nuts she had given Tony was not to blame for his suffering as her dying thoughts and wandering mind had convinced her.

I think Mum was slightly resentful of Dad's life, which often seemed very remote from her. She sometimes felt that she was always on the margins listening in to Dad's tales of friendly gossip from the Arsenal training ground and footballing hopes and fears while she remained at home. Mum hadn't seen Dad play very often she told me once (a comment Dad disputed) and during the season she saw very little of him although she didn't say why. I remember being surprised. The most likely reason was that for many of those early years she had a young child to look after but much more significant was that footballing culture in those days quite specifically excluded women. The existence of players' wives was barely acknowledged. The startling explosion of the WAG (wives and girlfriends) culture at the 2006 FIFA World Cup entranced the cameras which followed Victoria Beckham, Coleen Rooney, Cheryl Tweedy and other glamorous young women around the elegant German town of Baden-Baden but was darkly thought to be the reason why England didn't win the tournament. Women are, after all, a distraction.

Players' lives were nearer the monastic than the decadent in the 1930s. My father stayed with the team in hotels the night before important matches even when they were being played in London and would travel on alternate weekends and sometimes midweek for away matches. Fixtures were organised as much as possible to minimise travel so a midweek away match in Manchester might be followed by a Saturday match in Sheffield. Christmas Day and the new year period were footballing hot spots. Correct diet and sound sleep ruled out family celebrations and certainly visits to Kettering or Bristol to catch up with the family. One marathon challenge at Christmas in 1932, for instance, involved matches at home on 24 and 26 December, and away on 27 December to Leeds United. When friends and family were relaxing, Dad was playing and that often meant travelling. Mum would take the train up to Kettering with Tony during Dad's frequent absences.

It was a simple journey. From St Pancras Station in north London to Kettering took less than an hour.

From another perspective, their family life was astonishingly full of leisure time and privileged beyond the wildest dreams of the average working man and woman in the 1920s and 1930s, privileged beyond the dreams of other professional football players contracted season-by-season to smaller, less wealthy clubs. The day was theirs from when training finished around lunchtime. Summer stretched from early May to pre-season training in early August; sometimes it seemed it would never end.

Dad never joined in conventional pub socialising, preferring to spend time at home with Mum and Tony when he was relaxing. Mum must have welcomed such domestic security. Gradually the private inner world of a shy, thoughtful and inexperienced young woman aligned itself harmoniously with the external glamour, affluence and public exposure of Dad's world. She grew to love London's West End, the shop windows, the theatres and cinemas, the clothes, the sense of being at the heart of things. She discovered fashion, Elizabeth Arden cosmetics and silk lingerie and although she never entirely lost her shyness, she took easily and gracefully to the elegant conventions of banquets, civic receptions and fine dining celebrating Arsenal's successes. She listened and learned about education, manners, received pronunciation versus dialect. It was here in London that she learned how life could be, what other objectives could be aspired to, what other people took for granted.

Mum may sometimes have been a bewildered and occasionally intimidated witness of my father's world but she had a sharp eye for social pretensions. She instantly recognised the sly and covert patronising of those who cosied up to the famous. What she understood with a clarity Dad was never able to grasp was that their place in this world was very possibly transient. On the outside looking in she rapidly became conscious of the superficiality of their lives in society and the high risks of the football world. Much of Dad's brilliance on the other hand derived from an insouciant confidence that inspired him to believe that football was the alpha and omega of life, making sense of the harshness of his past, interpreting the present and shaping the purpose of his future. He had glimpsed what could be achieved if he didn't give up, had evolved an indomitable will to overcome difficulties, had learned a grounded self-belief, had fused mind and body into a finely tuned instrument.

He was also beginning to understand that being a footballer wasn't just a set of on-field skills but somehow an expression of the kind of man he was and wanted to be. This was the holistic footballing ideal he now pursued. He was also a husband and father of a son, with new and unexpected demands on his emotions and his time. But for Dad, everything could be carried on a tide of exuberance. It seems that every experience, every emotion, fused into a source of energy that burned at its most intense on the football pitch. Pain and grief, fear and loss were not experienced any less deeply by him than by my mother but for him, for a time, they were contained within the context of a glorious present. In love and in their different ways riding with the tide, together they sang the beguiling American songs that filled the radio waves, the films, the new shows and somehow lingered in the memory and in the memories of their children decades later:

EDDIE HAPGOOD FOOTBALLER

Night and day you are the one
Only you beneath the moon or under the sun
Whether near to me or far
It's no matter darling where you are
I think of you night and day.

5

England v Italy 1933 and 1934

Italy. From Barton Hill to Bristol to Kettering to London, onwards and upwards. ITALY! Beyond the wildest dreams of Eddie's imagination and certainly beyond his knowledge. Italy. In fact, Italy v England, Rome, 14 May 1933. Waiting on the platform at London's Liverpool Street Station for the dawn train to Harwich, his suitcase packed and strapped with sticky labels marked Roma, Italia safely stowed in the luggage coach, Eddie was excited but uncharacteristically apprehensive.

The team photograph shows a confident, fashionably dressed line of young men but apparently no Eddie Hapgood. I wondered whether the faded caption underneath had got the date of this international tour wrong. Impossible. Or whether *he* had got the dates wrong. Impossible. And then I spot him at the very back of the group, a sliver of his face peering over the shoulder of a team-mate as if questioning his right to be in such company. When Arsenal's triumphant championship-winning season, the second in three seasons, closed in wild celebrations, with barely a second to switch tracks and refocus

Eddie was packed and ready to go. It was his first tour as an England player.

The British Home Championship competition and the international summer tours of 1931 and 1932 had come and gone without Eddie Hapgood's name on the squad sheet. In fact, it was three years after the Football Association had first noticed him that he was finally selected to play for his country again. His decision to put his wife and new baby before his first selection in 1930 did not go down well with the football bureaucracy. To the selection committee his attitude must have smacked of arrogance or casualness, both unacceptable characteristics.

Despite his disappointment every time the international programme was published without his name, he was sure his opportunity would come. He knew he was up against fierce competition, hoping to dislodge the extraordinary, tried and tested Sheffield Wednesday defender Ernest Blenkinsop. Perhaps, back in 1930, the Football Association was looking to the future since Blenkinsop was some six years older than the emerging Eddie but then England went on a successful run, conclusively bagging the Home Championship in 1931 and trouncing France 5-2 in 1932. Eddie was forced to wait in the wings. Even so, early as it was in his international career, it was this apparently routine match against Italy that would sketch the outlines of what was later to describe elements of his footballing distinctiveness.

The roar that greeted the teams as they plunged from the cool, dark, narrow entrance tunnel into the broiling heat of Rome's massive Stadio Nazionale del Partito Nazionale Fascista was beyond anything Eddie had ever encountered before. There was a moment he felt overwhelmed, his face stiff with tension captured in a photograph as he ran out behind the captain, Ray Goodall, and standing rigidly to attention like a schoolboy as the national anthems rang out. But that was only the beginning. Once the referee blew his whistle, the players found themselves swept up in an extraordinary theatrical event as a crowd of some 50,000 Romans, eager to witness a gladiatorial contest, kept up a drama of sound throughout the match, chanting, cheering and drumming in a frantic rhythm of celebration. When their hero, Giovanni Ferrari, still recognised in the historical records as one of Italy's greatest players, opened the scoring, the crowd's ecstasy overflowed. They were 'storming the barriers', as Eddie later wrote in quasi-revolutionary language, as fans flooded on to the pitch to embrace their scorer, present him with a bouquet and escort him back to the centre spot while massed fans tossed more flowers from the upper tiers.

Somehow Eddie and the England team regained their concentration. A magnificent goal in the second half from an inspired Cliff Bastin, at 21 already an experienced international, rescued England's reputation, levelling the score at 1-1. That evening an elaborate reception was organised for the England team at Mussolini's official residence, the Palazza Venetia. An official group photograph was taken for the Italian press and, in a display of graciousness, Mussolini later signed a copy for each player. It was the very photograph that would spill out on to our sitting room carpet for our entertainment one war, one assassination and 22 years later amid gales of laughter as Dad performed his Italian impersonations.

More revealing of Eddie himself than his performance that day or the immediately colourful, noisy events of a match played in sweltering sun at an electric pace – or even the result – is the way that accounts and then memories of his contribution were shaped in jokily complimentary anecdotes which acknowledged not just his skill but the force of his presence. The English players were well aware of Mussolini's status but, with Anglocentric confidence, hardly impressed. Eddie, an international beginner, was the player who became associated with two of the best known comic perspectives on the Italian dictator. Have you heard the tale of a wild clearance he supposedly made which soared above the heads of the crowds into the VIP box and hit Mussolini in the stomach (or, according to some accounts, his chest)? Who knows who first started this one rolling? A team-mate allegedly.

Eddie related this story in his autobiography. I suspect that he did so partly because he couldn't resist a good story himself, but mostly because, by 1944 when he was writing, whatever the truth was, it had already become part of the myth of his career. The joke may have been an entertaining one, but more interesting are the political assumptions behind it. Making a fool of a Mussolini inflamed by fascist pretensions must have been inspired by his presence at the match and in his own account this is the angle Eddie took, 'Musso, sitting in profile with his chin at the angle favoured by all dictators since Nero, failed to see the ball coming and it crashed against his tightly fitting uniform, just above his lunch.'

The awkward style, the patronisingly self-conscious diminutive 'Musso' and reference to 'Nero', the colloquial 'lunch', has nothing of the humorous fluency of Dad's storytelling. It is more likely exaggerated by editorial flourishes. The whole story seems extremely unlikely or even completely fictional. It was hardly possible in the grander stadia of the time for the ball to travel that far and if it did, to land with such an impact. Eddie, a player 'who got angry with himself if he even put a ball into touch', was renowned for not wasting balls with aimless kicks but for always turning a defensive move into a counter-attack. But then, who knows? The previous season he had been noted for being a 'tear-away defender' with 'a remarkable "scissor-kick"', his ability to get a full-length kick from all sorts of difficult positions makes him an interesting back to watch'. Taking the wind out of Mussolini's sails (aka stomach), however, would be an excellent footballing riposte to a trumped-up caricature of a dictator. Whatever the facts, the important point is that it became Eddie's role to be seen to have taken the Italian dictator on. Bastin scored on the pitch but it was Eddie who scored the moral victory. As with many anecdotes hatched in casual conviviality and matured over the years, it pointed to some truth about Eddie's personality, if not his skill. 'Mussolini? Who's he?' as fans would chant today. 'Eddie Hapgood? He's ours!'

Mussolini was also the butt of the second joke. It is true that he invited British ridicule for his aggressive jaw-jutting stance but it really isn't true that Mussolini walked around with his chin in the air because he wanted to be seen to have as good a jawline as Eddie or that he looked at Eddie 'with jealousy in his eyes' as team-mate George Male claimed. The signed photograph of a puffed-up Mussolini in the centre-back of the group (and at some distance from my father), was familiar from evenings around the suitcases but the stories it provoked were not inspired by politics or football or Eddie's supposedly impressive looks. Rather, they were hilarious evocations of the 'Englishman in Italy', told with all the fun and energy of a man remembering his first experiences of another culture and one so markedly different from his own. There were the comic pitfalls of continental travel and voluble cod-Italian laced with comic (as we thought then) Italian footballers' names, like Pizz-i-o-lo, Con-stan-ti-no, Ber-to-li-ni and Ferr-ar-i pronounced with an exaggerated lilt and air-cleaving Italianate hand gestures.

However, in the eyes of his team-mates and the press, even as early as 1933, Eddie's first appearance for his country highlighted two characteristics of his football persona; he was no respecter of persons and he had the look of a leader, a glamorous one at that. And thriving in the atmosphere of international competitiveness and growing political hostilities, the two stories to prove the point flourished. The following year, his team-mate Alex James described how Eddie had finally won his position in the England team from Blenkinsop in 1933. 'Now,' he predicted, 'the boot is on the other foot and it looks as if any great left-back … during the next few years will have to take second place to our Eddie!'

International matches always arouse passionate feelings but as it turned out there was an unusual intensity of national pride at stake for both countries in this encounter. When the England team arrived in Rome, Mussolini was already busy preparing to host the second World Cup the following summer with every intention of winning it in front of home crowds. The Football

Association had short-sightedly chosen not to enter the inaugural 1930 World Cup in Uruguay, openly dismissing it as a competition for also-rans, for embryonic nations not yet ready to play in the European arena and certainly not worthy of swelling England's international programme. British officials were also resentful and wary of the growing profile of the Féderation Internationale de Football Association (FIFA) and the threat it posed to the status of a mature football nation. So embedded and unquestioned was England's belief in her own sporting superiority, a view Eddie naively supported, that officials lacked the vision to understand that advances in competitive football in the pre-war years across Europe, the vigorous ambition of South American countries and the steady shift from amateur to professional status were setting new standards. With the advent of the World Cup, previously unrecognised nations were drawing considerable attention to their flamboyant games while the English, Welsh and Scottish national teams were in danger of drifting to the sidelines of international football. Mussolini looked forward to being the one to topple them.

The date the match was played, a year before the second World Cup in 1934, gave it a particular footballing significance. Benito Mussolini, Italy's self-styled dictator, watching from start to finish, was apparently unconcerned that Italy had failed to win and were quite content simply to peg English pretensions back. As far as he was concerned, he had achieved his objectives: to play host and to impress; to be seen as equal on the European stage with a world empire. As he made quite clear, this match was after all just a friendly, a useful preparation for the more important task of winning the World Cup which he was hosting the following year. The date also added an explicit political punch to the importance of the occasion. A fascist dictator of a poorer, less influential country, committed to extending its power and influence worldwide, Mussolini also saw the match against England as a useful opportunity to provide his still divided country with a splash of glory and a common sense of identity on home soil. With a firm eye on proving that England's isolationist sporting position was a metaphor of declining imperial strength, he was dedicated to using football to assert Italian supremacy and bring the so-called 'founding fathers of football' to heel. It was only 1933, still early in a decade which few people guessed would end in the second European war in 25 years. Now, Mussolini had explicitly locked politics and sport together, putting his personal stamp on the importance of the match by attending. May 1933, when the euphoric rookie Hapgood lined up with the supremely confident England team at Liverpool Street for an official photograph before travelling to Rome, was an attractive public relations image of what a supposedly enduring state of affairs might look like. It is only with hindsight that we are able to realise that this enthusiastic, youthful team was effectively being offered up as a sticking plaster over growing fears of the vigour of European fascism.

The Italian story didn't end with the trip to Rome and neither did Eddie's Italian adventures. The return match in 1934 was to be explosive. True to Mussolini's dream, Italy had won the World Cup earlier in the year with the very players who had played against England in Rome the previous year when they had only just been held to a draw. Italy had opened the tournament with a triumphant 6-2 thrashing of France, a record score by a host country not equalled until Russia beat Saudi Arabia 5-0 in Moscow in 2018. It was obvious that this time, the match would be qualitatively different. England was not asserting but defending her superiority against the legitimate champions of the world.

With astonishing arrogance, the Football Association, determined to prove that England still deserved her singular pre-eminence, unilaterally decided that England v Italy should be regarded as the 'real' World Cup Final, a 'battle for the unofficial championship of the world'. The match began to assume a significance that appears to have taken even the players by surprise. On 10 June 1934, Italy had won the World Cup. The following November, the Italian team arrived to play England, who thought the World Cup an inferior competition. Eddie was selected for his first captaincy for England against the newly crowned world champions determined to consolidate their reputation. In fact, Eddie was selected to lead out the England team in the defence of national superiority.

The anticipated arrival of the Italian team had stimulated debate in England about the political and moral implications of fascism. Mussolini was looking more dangerous, no longer a bombastic one-man band who had been around long enough to be mocked. Rumour had it that he was preparing to invade Ethiopia and reclaim the 'Empire' lost in 1923. He was a potential German ally, being drawn, if rather reluctantly at first, into the slipstream of the new man on the block, Adolf Hitler, chancellor of Germany. Fascism was out and about on the streets of London as Sir Oswald Mosley, the founder of the British Union of Fascists, intensified the group's campaigns. The *Daily Mail* had named Mosley 'the paramount political personality in Britain' and in June 1934, just months before England v Italy, hecklers who dared to challenge Mosley's politics at the Olympia Rally were forcibly removed by his Blackshirts.

One way or another, England v Italy was a match being defined on all sides as an ideological battle, 'pregnant with a significance that outstripped simple sport'. For their part, the Italian press upped the political stakes. They declared that England was an enemy of fascism and publicised negative propaganda depicting the English as 'imperialists and gluttons' – although the connection between the two insults remained mysterious. For Mussolini, the English tour represented yet another opportunity to consolidate, through Italian football, a national identity, a national myth of achievement 'intended to accelerate the regeneration and nationalisation of the masses' that he craved. This time, on English soil, he wanted to win, and the players were reputedly offered huge bonuses to encourage them, including an Alfa Romeo each but also indefinite exception from military service. Perhaps the latter 'bonus' was gleefully fabricated by the British press to emphasise the Italians' desire for the good life but not the patriotic life. At the last moment Mussolini was not able to attend. When the match kicked off he was in Berne with an increasingly dominant Hitler demanding his attention. He had no alternative but to hang on to the telephone to receive updates from the Italian commentator Carioso, whose immense popularity, fired with patriotic fervour for Italy and with visceral loathing for England, meant, 'The whole of Rome was listening.'

The catalyst for the mayhem that followed was a tackle by Ted Drake, about to become Eddie's colleague at Arsenal, on Luis Monti, which broke a bone in the Italian captain's foot. This foul triggered what must be one of football's most unforgettable stories. Both men were known for their hard tackling but, in this case, the rights and wrongs are obscured by any number of conflicting accounts. No matter. The Italians, resentful even before the game began, now felt they had been thoroughly stitched up. Against the wishes of their manager, Vittorio Pozzo, the match was being played not at the national stadium at Wembley, but at Highbury, Arsenal's home ground; they were refused permission to train on the pitch before the match; they faced a team of no less than seven Arsenal men, and in the second minute their captain was deliberately injured (as they saw it) and they were down to ten men. They felt they were being treated without respect as a second-rate team, and it isn't difficult to sympathise with their point of view. Perhaps the insults had been deliberately engineered by the Football Association. They let rip. In the second half England retaliated in kind as Wilf Copping, one of the Arsenal contingent and in his element, laid into the Italian players with his characteristically fearsome tackling. And so the famous 'Battle of Highbury' was fought, if not to the death, with no hostage given. 'AFTER THE BALL WAS OVER' ran a headline the following day, with this detail:

The most serious English casualties at Highbury yesterday were
Hapgood, broken nose
Brook, arm X-rayed last night

Bowden, injured ankle

Drake, leg 'nearly cut to ribbons';

Barker, left hand in bandages

Copping, bandaged from 'left knee to top of thigh'

Although the injury tally was remarkable, not all British or Italian newspapers recorded events with the same sensationalism. The final result, a 3-2 England victory, is in the record books but when the furore died down, it seems that the footballing honours were even. The consensus of the English press was that the foul on the Italian captain had not been deliberate and England had dealt bravely with an unprecedented level of retaliatory violence that called into question whether international games such as this should be played at all. In language used to describe a war zone, Ivan Sharpe wrote in the *Sunday Chronicle*, 'Things happened that day I never want to see on a football field again,' before adding, 'The Highbury dressing rooms afterwards were a glimpse of blood, sweat and tears.' Pathé News called the affair 'unique' and 'a match of absolute madness'.

Despite the extravagance of the language, it was generally agreed that England had not played a team of mere thugs. In fact, under the headlines, most of the newspapers conceded that Italy had played magnificently, particularly in the second half, and that England had been severely tested. Back in Italy, they told their own story. Defeat was translated into a win with the press declaring that 'defeat was worth twice as much as victory'. Italy had played with the odds stacked against them and showed courage and tenacity in 'a theatre of international war'. At the final whistle the Italian players had proudly given the widely known fascist salute in honour of their country and had emerged as 'the lions of Highbury'.

On that gloomy November day, not now in the blazing heat of a May day in Rome, but rather in the heat of Italian anger in London, Eddie's reputation matured into legend. This contentious and controversial match was a tough introduction to the captain's role but the publicity it created and its immediate aftermath confirmed and enhanced his growing reputation. It had taken him only one international season to win the captaincy and it remained his for most of his career. A deliberate jab of the elbow by the Italian captain Attilio Ferraris had 'carefully' caught him on the face with full impact, broken his nose and briefly knocked him unconscious. He was stretchered off the field but ran on 15 minutes later to complete the match. He was still captain and not prepared to risk England losing their lead. Eddie shored up resistance to the Italian fightback in the second half which had brought the score to 3-2, and in the final minutes 'saved his team with a splendid tackle on Meazza' to prevent a hat-trick. The footballing public decided that this was the kind of man to lead England and confront a team created for and by a fascist dictator. Eddie's only comment to the press was, 'It was a hard-fought game to the end.'

It was the moment after the final whistle was blown by the Swedish referee Otto Olsson that clinched the tag 'immaculate Hapgood', which came to define him. As the Italian team lined up to give the fascist salute, one journalist noted under the sub-heading 'Hapgood's Gesture' that at the end of 'the most violent football match ever played', the 'nicest thing was when Hapgood, captain of England, ran up to the referee and shook him heartily by the hand'. That such a gesture was sincere and appreciative is testified to by the *Daily Telegraph* the following day, which also congratulated the referee for handling 'a most difficult match firmly and with quick decision'. Later that night, with a throbbing headache and his nose heavily strapped, Eddie again felt that his duty as captain was to attend the traditional Football Association banquet for visiting international teams. A provocative grin from his assailant Ferraris as they passed each other was ignored; in Hapgood's own words, 'He wasn't worth it,' an act of 'diplomacy' much applauded by the press the following day. 'But retaliation was never in his armoury,' as Brian Glanville put it many years later.

It was a magnificent, selfless and brave performance, and the one that Arsenal chose to commemorate on the Arsenal wall of heroes at the Emirates Stadium in 2011: 'Eddie Hapgood was both brave and remarkably even-tempered; not reacting even after a brutal challenge broke his nose.' A style of playing inseparable from a way of being.

Eddie's entry on to the international stage opened the floodgates of publicity. Suddenly, it seemed, everything that Eddie did was worth photographing and commenting on. It was at this time that the first of the popular photographic essays of Eddie at home began. Published in October 1933, there is an intriguing one of him, wearing snappy, wide-legged trousers while tuning in a radio. It may have been a gift given to all the players, either club or international, or perhaps a special gift to celebrate Arsenal's First Division title, won a few months previously in May or, perhaps an acknowledgement of the BBC's increasing commitment to live football commentary. Since George Allison, Chapman's *aide-de-camp*, was one of the BBC's resident presenters, that seems very likely. Whatever the provenance, the radio is large, impressive and up to date for the time.

Tony, now nearly four years old, became something of an Arsenal icon. Dressed in Arsenal kit and wearing tiny but authentic leather boots made to measure, he was photographed kicking a ball with some style as Eddie, Alex James and Frank Moss, the Arsenal goalkeeper, watched. Published on the front cover of *News Illustrated*, it sold out the same day and had to be reprinted. The combination of Eddie and Tony became irresistible publicity. It was lucrative too, landing Eddie his first celebrity endorsement well before they became run-of-the-mill. He signed a contract with Mars to advertise the famous chocolate bar. There, Eddie and Tony sat in football kit as if in a changing room after a match, relaxed and smiling and munching Mars Bars with the floor around them littered with wrappers. One version of the Mars advertisement specifically acknowledged the 'Battle of Highbury' with a shield-like plaque on the wall behind their heads announcing 'Eddie Hapgood CAPTAIN OF ENGLAND against ITALY'.

When I stand on the Arsenal concourse in front of the instantly recognisable image of him that towers above me, I begin to understand how he achieved such a unique place in the history of the turbulent 1930s. 'Why,' I recently asked a lifelong football writer whose memory of my father stretches back over 60 years, 'did you worship a full-back? Hardly the most glamorous position to attract a boy's attention.' The answer was simple and final, 'He was the captain of Arsenal and England.' That answer also helps me to understand something that has always puzzled me: why did Arsenal choose to celebrate Eddie through an international event rather than a club one on the wall of their new stadium? One answer perhaps is that in the 1930s a captain was more than just a player and the England captain more than the property of a single club. In those days the captain had a singular role in organising, advising and encouraging his team, far more responsibility than a current-day captain who can be swapped from week to week and sometimes seems little more than a technical requirement. In the 2016/17 season Arsenal were actually punished for forgetting to name a captain after the usual armband-wearer, Laurent Koscielny, was substituted – both actions unthinkable in the 1930s. In fact, his attitude to the captaincy has been a weakness in Arsène Wenger's philosophy of the modern team. Wenger was criticised for using the captain's armband as a bribe to keep star players such as Robin van Persie at the club 'rather than identifying a proper leader in the mould of Eddie Hapgood, Joe Mercer, Frank McLintock, Tony Adams or Patrick Vieira'. What a formidable list.

Giving Eddie his first captaincy for what turned out to be such a volatile and politically sensitive game, in which he suffered a serious injury, gave him the stage for a kind of public transformation. Together with his team-mates, he was unarguably a great footballer, but, as the press applauded him for his physical bravery and tough but diplomatic leadership, he was well on the way to being imagined as a popular hero. His atypical fusion of physical elegance with indomitable mental toughness, physical bravery with fineness of spirit and courtesy of manner was, perhaps, particularly admirable in such unpredictable times. I knew without doubt that Dad was proud to play for Arsenal, indeed that Arsenal were who he was. Perhaps, I now wondered, was it the other way round? Were Arsenal proud to be able to claim that Eddie Hapgood, captain of England, played for them?

As children, we were never told about the disputes, the violence, the nationalist agenda, and never a word indicating Dad's excitement about captaining the England side for the first time or how difficult it had been. He told us a different story with typical brio. 'My nose was broken,' he told us, wobbling it from side to side to demonstrate it was possible that, even now, it might fall off, 'and covered with heavy plaster to protect it and to speed up the healing process.' But that footballing fact spiralled far away from the football pitch (although the bald statement was always emphasised by an elbow being lifted purposefully and jabbed into an imaginary person behind him so that we all caught our breath and winced).

Over the following days, he became aware of an unpleasant smell in the house. 'I can't smell anything,' our worried mother told him, checking out every possible source. They searched round the house as if they were spies in a movie (much acting involved at this point). Is it a blocked pipe under the sink? Is it a scrap of old garbage clinging to a dustbin? Is the kitchen door creating a disgusting draught from the outside drains? Has a piece of meat fallen behind the kitchen cupboards and begun to rot? Is it (heaven forbid because my mother was terrified of mice) a dead mouse behind the skirting? Mum, unable to smell anything unusual, was distracted by his insistence and after several days was at breaking point. Time to return to the ground and have the plaster removed and the nose inspected. And there, in the Arsenal changing room, the source of the smell emerged. A fresh blood flow after the dressing had been applied had coagulated and grown stale. 'Urrrrgh!' we howled in disgust. 'Ah yes, but there *had* been a smell,' he said glowing with triumph, 'and your mother refused to believe me!'

6

Changes at Arsenal 1933–1935

Between May 1933 and November 1934, Eddie's world was so profoundly transformed he could hardly grasp the whirligig that life now became. The two matches against Italy bracketed an extraordinary change, not in how Eddie saw himself but in how football supporters and the football world saw him. The first match marked the thrilling triumph of his selection for England against Italy in 1933. He would never forget travelling on that mind-spinning journey with roars of victory for yet another Arsenal championship success from the previous week still ringing around his head and heart, to be plunged into a searingly hot, colourful Italy where everything, it seemed, took place in a tumultuous explosion of noise. Afterwards he felt as if he was treading the landscape of another earth.

He had played seven more internationals, three in the British Home Championship against Wales and Scotland, four more against Switzerland, Hungary, Czechoslovakia and Ireland, his head full of places and people. Perhaps enjoying the adulation of all who met and cheered them, he was alight with success.

The future? He had no need to think about it. What could be better than now? He had been selected as captain for the return match against Italy in November. And with one First Division title already won, he couldn't wait for the new season to begin to help Arsenal win another. He revelled in the confidence of continuing success, of building a history that would be enhanced by every match at Highbury. He anticipated with delight the challenge that would be thrown at them by other clubs, from the mighty Sunderland in the north to the determined Portsmouth in the south. And the whole football community, enjoying the emergence of a new hero, was with him every step and kick of the way.

When Eddie had signed back in for pre-season training in August 1933, it seemed to him that nothing and everything was changed. But then something happened he couldn't possibly have prepared himself for. The unexpected death of Herbert Chapman at the age of 55 on 6 January 1934, the night before a home game against Sheffield Wednesday, sliced the season in half. Chapman left behind him a team of talented players in the fullness of their success, a vision of football others would respect and adopt, a story that would colour football history to the present day – and a title race only half completed. He also left behind him a young man whose football potential he had recognised and whose character he had steadfastly understood and appreciated.

For Eddie, the shock went too deep for consolation. He had lost a mentor, a staunch supporter and the nearest to a father he had known. His grief, as it turned out, was to be transformative and determining. Eddie's greatest personal triumphs were to come after Chapman's death, fired by what he felt was his new role at the club. All his team-mates, signed and shaped by Chapman, would instinctively and wholeheartedly honour his legacy. For Eddie it was a personal legacy, and one he would be incapable of betraying. From the moment he helped carry Chapman's coffin into the church for the funeral, along with his team-mates David Jack, Joe Hulme, Alex James, Jackie Lambert and Cliff Bastin, he poured his whole self, his training, his matchday faith into fulfilling Chapman's ambitions and fighting to defend his style and values. He knew that Chapman had chosen him as a defender on the pitch but now he was also a self-appointed defender of Arsenal's future and if Eddie had anything to do with it, Chapman's spirit would live on.

An article Eddie wrote at the beginning of the 1934/35 season is a pre-emptive strike against any football chatter and negative punditry that might question Arsenal's ability to do the impossible and win the championship for the third consecutive year. To me it is clearly an open letter, almost a challenge, to George Allison, who would take over Chapman's role. The headline 'CAN ARSENAL HOLD?' runs over the subheading 'Secrets Behind the Champions' Consistency'. The 'secrets' Eddie divulges are a fluently argued summary of Chapman's approach: play every game with full respect for your opponents; don't think back or look forward – the match you're playing is the one that matters; keep key men consistently in the positions that matter most; play to a definite team policy discussed before each game – tactics are designed on the blackboard; matches are won on the pitch.

Eddie's final, intriguing claim, based on Chapman's vision of an organic team ethos, that each player must act both as part of a 'machine' but also as an 'individual', leaves conventional football advice standing. Was any inspirational individual, such as Alex James, David Jack, Ted Drake or Eddie himself, really able to see himself as a cog in a machine? Was such a team chemistry possible without slipping into pedestrian mediocrity? *The Times* had thought it was, way back at the end of Arsenal's title-winning 1932/33 season when it declared that they had triumphed because, 'The various players have sunk their individuality in the team and each has taken his full share in promoting the fortunes of the club.' Eddie always saw it as a kind of metamorphosis into the spirit of Arsenal, 'There was a feeling that once you put on an Arsenal shirt nothing could go wrong ... outsiders called it the "Arsenal atmosphere" but we knew it was "team spirit".' Nearly 60 years later, asked to explain Arsenal's impossible snatching of the 1989 First Division title from the rampant and brilliant Liverpool under the very noses of their fans at Anfield, Tony Adams, Arsenal's captain, tried to find words for what he experienced as a similar phenomenon. 'The unit was bigger and better than the individuals,' he finally said. Today the modern transfer system makes such unity increasingly difficult, if not impossible. An individual player's 'selfish agendas', as former Tottenham Hotspur manager Maurizio Pochettino recently lamented, undermine a team's security and 'the right dynamic takes time to recover'. And if it doesn't recover the team loses its way.

But Arsenal *could* 'hold it' as they clinched their third consecutive First Division title. The team Chapman built stormed home to the championship in 1933/34, finishing at a sprint in the final matches. For Eddie, that success was a joyous vindication of

Chapman's philosophy and a tribute to the two men, Chapman's *aides-de-camp*, Joe Shaw and Tom Whittaker, for whom he had profound respect and trusted as fellow members of the Arsenal family. He was ready to give the same total commitment to both these men he had always done to Chapman.

Then a new recruit, Ted Drake, had exploded on to the Arsenal scene after Christmas like a force of nature whipping up the vitality and courage of a team in shock at Chapman's death with an explosion of goals as if in homage to the club's ideal. 'Allison put his signature to Ted Drake's transfer,' Dad always pointed out, 'but Ted was actually a Chapman target. Allison only dealt with the paperwork.' In his view, the league title certainly didn't belong to George Allison. Even so, it was Allison who formally took over as manager in September 1934. He continued to leave much of the player side of things to the skills of Shaw and Whittaker to carry on as before and turned instead to do what he did and had always done best: to focus on 'celebrity', on enhancing Arsenal's glittering reputation, on publicity, on media events, on cultivating figures in the media who would sing Arsenal's praises across the country, on making sure that the Arsenal story was always more than just a series of match results.

Despite all the elation, the 1934/35 season was a difficult, transitional time for Eddie. He never forgave Allison for not being Chapman and for not being able to be Chapman. In this first season under Allison's full managership, Eddie struggled to accept that the team would be run differently and that he would have to forge a new and different relationship with his manager. Gone, he felt, was the respectful equality he shared with Chapman, the readiness to be advised, the encouragement to contribute. 'Allison wasn't a football man,' Dad would say to us firmly. 'He didn't know who to sign and when he'd signed them, he didn't know how to use them. He tinkered and that just upset the balance of the team.' It would not be surprising if Allison was as wary of Eddie as Eddie was of him. He would have been fully aware of Eddie's devotion to Chapman and his criticisms of his own approach. He would also have been aware of Eddie's growing status among the other players, his possible influence over them and his rapidly accelerating national reputation since his headline-grabbing performance in the recent 'Battle of Highbury'. If Allison felt the need to stamp his own identity on the team and its new arrivals, he may well have seen Eddie as a good place to start. There is no doubt that their relationship was fractious and that Allison occasionally took the opportunity to put Eddie in his place. Eddie himself certainly thought so.

Was Eddie right? Surely Allison's strategy was working? Arsenal had, after all, won the championship again despite the tragic disruption of Chapman's death and the occasional pundits predicting doom. So surely Arsenal were good? No, exceptional – a team for history to cherish, for football to mythologise. Perhaps, but the pundits still couldn't resist quibbling, 'Are Arsenal really that good? Perhaps no other team is up for the challenge? Perhaps Arsenal is only as good as Ted Drake?' While the lure of the new and the desire to write exciting copy for your paper is understandable, the season's achievements were ridiculously underestimated. When the list of 'key men' of 1934/35 is written out, doubts seem laughable as names and statistics burst off the page into excited life again: Frank Moss, Eddie Hapgood, George Male, Wilf Copping, Jack Crayston, Pat Beasley, Ray Bowden, not to mention Alex James collecting and distributing with lethal precision; Joe Hulme steadily hitting the back of the net week after week; Ted Drake, ripping the back of the net with his powerful kicks; Cliff Bastin, who held Arsenal's goalscoring record for an incredible 60 years until Ian Wright topped it in 1997. In May 1935 Arsenal were still, undeniably and unquestionably, a magnificent team.

Even so, the commentators were right in spotting something although they couldn't quite put it into words. A subtle change in atmosphere? A lessening of desire and drive? Whatever it was, there was definitely a shift that season, an indefinable spiritual slackening of which the players themselves might not have been aware. After all, if you have won the title for the third consecutive year and the fourth time in five seasons, answered the doubters, coped with the challenges thrown by other powerful teams hoping to topple you and the stress of staying ahead at all times, it is surely possible that complacency or fatigue might become an invisible problem. At the very end of that incredible record-breaking season, on 4 May 1935, by chance Eddie glimpsed it. Because of a minor injury he was unable to play the final match, at home against Derby County. Watching, as the game drifted to its conclusion, he suddenly realised with a cold shock that for a moment made him sit rigidly upright, that he was watching a team who knew that they had already won the title. In front of their home crowd, Arsenal recorded a meaningless 1-0 defeat to a Derby side who finished sixth in the table.

What was it Chapman had always drummed into them? True, the 'key men' spine of the team was temporarily broken by injuries to Eddie, Copping and Bastin. That wasn't the point. Even with brilliant and committed strikers such as Frank Hill, Ted Drake and Alex James on the field, the team seemed drained and unfocused. Afterwards there was a lap of honour, rousing celebrations, crowds spilling into the north London streets, and, later, a luxurious and triumphant banquet and speeches full of compliments galore. Yes, they had won; yes, they had achieved a consistency that seemed almost impossible, the stuff of legends; yes, Arsenal had made history and added fuel to the myth of their immortality; but, as Eddie saw it, one of Chapman's fundamental principles had somehow, without anyone realising, been sacrificed along the way, 'The match you are playing is the one that matters.'

On 16 May and fit again, Eddie travelled to Holland on international duty, the sudden stab of personal disquiet about Arsenal's direction happily forgotten. Back home in London with yet another victory for the record books, fired by the excitement of the moment and light-heartedly surfing the waves of success, Mum and Dad bought a car and within a couple of weeks of his return were heading to the West Country and to Cornwall. If Italy and Switzerland were sun-drenched fantasy lands, even more so was the discovery of Fistral Beach, his and Mum's and Tony's very own adventure.

Today's GPS gives five hours as the distance from London to north Cornwall, and that's on motorways, in cars that have defeated the basic dangers of the combustion engine and dodgy electrics. In the 1930s, factories inspired by the American model rolled cars off the production line ever more cheaply even though ownership was still way beyond the reach of the majority. In an era of hardship, protests, and the lowering Depression, Eddie joined the new pretenders as they grabbed their opportunities, bought a car and hit the roads, hooting cheerfully at other cars sporting an AA badge in highway camaraderie. He had never driven a car when he dropped into the local garage to buy the Austin 8 he had had his eye on. With his new registration number, BYE 408, a brief lesson on the forecourt, a promise to drop the salesman home in exchange for a second lesson on the road, and that was it. He managed to find his way only by overriding any reason, however pressing, for stopping and drove entirely in first gear, the car roaring in pain. Eddie eventually passed the newly devised driving test; Mum began learning. All they had to do was put Tony in the back seat and bundle essentials into the boot and drive until they didn't want to drive any further, and then stop. Where they stopped in June 1935 turned out to be Fistral Beach.

As a child, Fistral Beach sounded a fairytale place to me. The very name seemed strange and it was a long time before I learned that it meant 'dangerous waters' because of the violence of the tides and the massive waves that rolled up the beach breaking the silence with hisses and thunder. This was their first visit, but for summer after summer in the mid-1930s Mum and Dad had Fistral to themselves. Few people were holidaying in June, and even those who could did not choose the wild, deserted openness of the north Cornish coast. Here, Mum came into her element. She loved to walk the trackless infinity, or so it seemed, of the golden sands and to plunge into the sea and swim beyond the waves. She surfed in an idle way, giving herself to the surges, ebbs and flows, so different from rural Northamptonshire and urban London. Where Mum learned to swim so well was always a mystery. The beach stretched into a distant haze and even on sunny days the wind whipped up in unpredictable gusts. Here, there was just them. Dad played football, beach cricket, built sandcastles, climbed up the sandbanks and jumped back down again with Tony. He wrote 'ARSENAL' in huge letters with a stick in the firm sand, and 'TONY' – 'so if you get lost someone will see it and rescue you'.

They all explored the numerous rock pools which, like Christmas stockings, yielded up surprises such as popping seaweed, tiny crabs, immoveable limpets, abandoned shells and wavering reflections of a blue sky. There were no cafes and no cinema, there was nothing to distract from just being there and shouting or singing loudly into the wind if they happened to feel like it.

On the drive down there was a stop at Bristol to visit Dad's mother Emily, Stella's family and to catch up with Percy and Iris if they were around. Then, on the second leg of the journey, there were picnics on the roadside sitting on a rug with the car pulled up on a grass verge; and, later, on the beach, tucked into the hollows of the dunes. There were chopped ham sandwiches, cheese sandwiches, tomatoes to be dipped in a little mound of salt, cucumber with pied skins of dark and palest green, crunchy on the outside, cool and moist on the inside – and tea. The milk was in a glass jar; the sugar screwed up in a paper bag and the flask, hot and steaming as Dad opened it and poured the tea out in carefully measured amounts into plastic cups in a familiar ritual. 'It is a very good English custom, though the weather be hot or cold,' Dad would half chant, half sing in imitation of the popular Jack Buchanan's lazy drawl; then triumphantly, joined by Mum, 'Everything stops for tea.' On later holidays, picnics were packed neatly into a large woven wicker hamper, a present from Glasgow Rangers to each of the Arsenal players after a friendly match. We were still using it many years later when, Dad's career in football at an end, he and Mum rediscovered Cornwall with all of us, their four children, Tony, Margot, Mike and me together again. But not on Fistral Beach. As far as I know, they never visited Fistral again after war broke out. Perhaps it had only ever existed in a story we were told.

7

Highs and Lows at Arsenal 1935–1937

Eddie's lurking doubts about George Allison's loyalty to Herbert Chapman's ideals were triggered again when the 1935/36 season was well under way in January 1936. An informal photograph of the 'Golden Line-up' – of Male, Drake, Bastin, Hapgood, Bowden and Crayston – taken at the beginning of the season, seemed so familiar, so inevitable, so unchanging that it had seemed just possible that the turbulent aftermath of Chapman's death had been calmed. For now, Eddie was in good spirits, amused that the pre-season league table had not been published according to tradition in alphabetical order with Arsenal firmly first. 'This must be seen to,' he wrote, only partly in jest, but then added lightheartedly, 'It is good for the game in general that affairs should go all topsy-turvy. Indeed if I weren't a member of the Arsenal I could argue to the extent of a whole column that it is good for the sport that the honours should go round.' But the calmness was deceptive. As the new year period came and went, Eddie couldn't deny the currents of change that were surfacing ever more persistently to challenge the continuity he was fighting to defend. If you don't watch time passing with the care you would watch a ball at a striker's feet, it is easy to get caught out because, like a brilliant striker, time rarely announces its intentions.

Unfortunately, things going 'topsy-turvy' seemed likely to come true. By Christmas, Arsenal had fallen sufficiently far behind those fighting it out for the title at the top of the table – Sunderland (way ahead), Derby County (never giving up) and Huddersfield Town (always lurking) – for another championship to be unlikely. The trouble seemed to be with the forward line. As the season wore on, Cliff Bastin was off top form much of the time; Alex James, with numerous fitness problems, was only occasionally available; Ted Drake, although the most prolific scorer, was susceptible to injury. Allison's team 'tinkering' became ever more frenetic. Did he have a strategy? It wasn't clear whether his primary motive was to replace Chapman's 'key men' strategy with what we now call squad rotation; to make more use of home-grown talented players such as Leslie Compton, whose careers had been overshadowed by their established colleagues, or a long-term vision of a new Arsenal, gradually easing out the older players and refreshing the team with new signings. Whatever his policy, week by week the team's identity shifted.

Disaster was kept at bay by the defence, which remained as consistent as injuries allowed. Just like the previous season, the number of goals scored against them was the lowest in the league. Whether the pundits enjoyed the spectacle or not, as the year reached its end, there was general agreement in the press, with one report reading, 'The defence was near impregnable with

England's George Male and Eddie Hapgood, Jack Crayston, Herbie Roberts and Wilf Copping.' But Allison now, incredibly, decided to abandon the chase for the title. After three consecutive championships but with vanishing hope of a fourth, he decided to maintain Arsenal's national superiority by focusing on the FA Cup, making it to Wembley and winning it as the season closed. Relying on the judicious selection of players for specific tasks and grading matches against one another according to their importance to a final outcome, he was prepared not only to break up the 'key men' but to sacrifice 'continuity'. Inevitably this involved 'resting' and 'saving' players. Taken by surprise, Eddie may never have noticed Allison's strategy if it hadn't been for the way he deployed Alex James during the second half of the season when the cup ties began.

The first fixture didn't alert him. It was played post-Christmas as usual and included lower-league teams who had made it to the third round. Arsenal were drawn against Bristol Rovers. In the light of later events that season, this match, insignificant on paper, was for Eddie to become part of the emotional fibre of the unsettling 1936 FA Cup campaign narrative. He was returning for the first time in eight years to play against the club in his home city that he had turned down all those years ago. The *Daily Herald* recounts the event with delighted bemusement. We can enjoy the gentle comedy of the account but be moved at the pride and delight of the Hapgood family as they turned out in numbers to celebrate Eddie's success:

'Another cameo was Mr and Mrs Hapgood, parents of England's captain, congratulating their son after the match and posing for a picture with nine or ten other Hapgoods in a family group outside the dressing room.

'Bristolians through and through, Mr and Mrs Hapgood wore the Arsenal colours. Arsenal "fans", I doubt if they have seen the Highbury team more than half a dozen times, but Eddie's fame makes everything O.K. – even to wearing the Arsenal colours at a match in which Bristol Rovers are interested.'

Alex James was not selected to play in this match, which Arsenal won 5-1. There would have been no questions asked about why he hadn't been selected. It was to be his penultimate season. As brilliant as ever and with a positioning sense in the middle of the field that linked defence and attack to deadly effect, he had been struggling with ill health for some time. When his fitness allowed, he was still more than capable of generating the moments of magic that could seal an Arsenal victory through the finishing boots of Bastin and Drake, but he could no longer do it week after week.

James, however, was selected to play the remaining six cup matches (they had a replay in the fifth round) as Arsenal moved through to the final. The records look odd. Alex played against Barnsley in the quarter-final on 29 February but was not selected for the following four league matches. He played in the semi-final against Grimsby Town on 21 March but in only one of the following eight league games. He was then selected for the FA Cup Final against Sheffield United on 25 April. With the FA Cup safely won but the championship lost, James ran out for the last two First Division fixtures, dismal echoes of the match against Derby the previous season. This time it was Arsenal who were to finish sixth.

It is hard not to conclude that Allison was 'nursing' James's skills, relying on his occasional flashes of genius to win cup ties while crucial league matches were downgraded, a very unusual strategy in those days although much more familiar today. Ironically, Arsenal were fined that season, not for 'saving' players but for 'resting' them. The players in question were Eddie and George Male, and the matches were the two in the First Division prior to the FA Cup Final. 'The Golden Line-up', playing steadily week by week, might well have felt resentful of this negative approach. No less than four league matches (and very probably more) had been deliberately marginalised. Such cynical pragmatism, as Eddie saw it, was anathema. It exposed a purely mercantile attitude to the honour of the sport and he was sure it would have a demotivating effect on the players. Even the usually reticent Bastin was to comment ironically, 'Possibly we may have striven a little harder in the tail end of the season we won the cup.' To Eddie's dismay, any remains of Chapman's philosophy had finally bitten the dust, and he had been part of it, instructed to sit matches out to conserve his energies.

These football worries were pushed to the back of his mind by two family crises. In the weeks running up to the FA Cup Final, Eddie was living with the knowledge that his mother had been ill with cancer for several months. Now, while he was involved in pre-final training in Brighton, a telegram arrived with the news that Emily had been rushed into hospital in Bristol for an emergency operation. Racing first to London to collect some clothes and to tell Maggie and Tony, he left as soon as he could for Bristol, arriving in time to be with her in hospital. Exhausted and emotional, he was reassured that she had come round from what appeared to be a successful intervention. The following day was one of relief and happiness as she rallied but he was desperately reluctant to leave her and return to London for the final – suddenly remote and less important – to be played, and anxious team-mates waiting to know what had happened and whether he would be back. Emily encouraged him to go, promised to follow on the radio, wished him luck, called him her champion, but, in fact, there was never any way that he wouldn't have returned. An irresistible sense of duty and hard-wired determination had been imparted to him by Emily herself. He had to be there. He arrived in London late on the Friday evening and ran out with his team the following afternoon, psychologically drained and tactically unprepared, but up for the fray.

Having made the difficult decision to leave his mother and travel back from Bristol, Eddie had no idea what team had been selected for the match or, if he was in, what his role would be. He knew that he might not be picked, that Allison might choose not to play a man who had missed the final training days and whose mind might be distressed or, at best, elsewhere. The *Daily Herald* certainly reported that Leslie Compton was being held in reserve in case Eddie was not able to return. There was also the question of Alex James's fitness. Eddie had captained the previous four league matches because James was unfit so that if he was selected to play, it was highly possible that he might also have to assume the captaincy. His uncertainty on both counts was banished by a radio announcement he heard on the morning of the match. He was selected, and so was James. Perhaps Eddie had no right to be hurt that Allison had not inquired how things stood, whether he was back in London or spoken to him personally, but he was.

Of course, nothing like this could happen today, all of 70 years later in our caring society, could it? It takes more than personal grief to interest your club in your wellbeing and just occasionally we glimpse the tragedy on the other side of some football event. Trapped in the slow demise of lowly Bury in 2019, Harry Bunn learned from the television that the English Football League (EFL) had expelled his club and that he and all his team-mates had lost their jobs. 'The first time we hear anything,' he said, 'it's at the same time as everyone else.' No job. No wages. No information.

The 1936 FA Cup Final was a tremendous success for Arsenal. Nearly 100,000 spectators packed Wembley's terraces as the match was filmed from a helicopter and presented by Pathé News as a spectacle, an afternoon of light entertainment. It was the subject of the first experimental radio commentary and men sported sandwich boards proclaiming Allison's role as commentator. Joe Hulme was celebrated as the man of the match (although no such formal accolade existed then), George Male won plaudits in defence and Alex James transcended his poor fitness to perform brilliantly against Sheffield United, earning tumultuous roars as he climbed the steps to collect the FA Cup with its cascading red and white ribbons from the new king, Edward VIII. Eddie mounted the steps behind him and grasped the hand of the man who, as a young and apparently promising Prince of Wales, had visited the Dings and Barton Hill 15 years previously and declared himself shocked at the conditions he witnessed. It was to be the

Emily Hapgood, a mother with 'strength and self-respect'

Pavement memorial of 'Bristol's England footballer' in the Dings where Eddie was born

ENGLAND FOOTBALL CAPTAIN
EDRIS ALBERT 'EDDIE' HAPGOOD
BORN 1908 IN UNION ROAD
TWENTY ONE TIMES

The Dings FC mural brightens the railway embankment and keeps up the football tradition

Ada Althorpe, Maggie's 'perfect mother'

Maggie Althorpe, 17, was entranced by a 'young Achilles' who turned out to be Eddie Hapgood

1930 Kettering. A new life!
Eddie Hapgood 'the dapper
young man with his urban
manners'

1930 Young Eddie Hapgood in
his Arsenal shirt 'had international
stamped all over him'

1935 *Dedication. Eddie
and Ted Drake train
in the snow for the
Christmas Day match
against Liverpool*

*'Artistic' tackling in the
winter mist at Highbury.
Eddie takes the ball off
Bud Maxwell's foot 'in
typical fashion'*

1936 George Male, Eddie, Joe Hulme and Alex James relax after training for the upcoming FA Cup Final

1936 Butlins opens its first holiday camp and Eddie and Cliff Bastin get a taste of celebrity!

THE ORCHESTRAL STAGE

Butlin's HOLIDAY — CAMP —

OPEN to the PUBLIC on SUNDAYS
10 a.m. till 7 p.m.   (No Admittance after 6 p.m.)

✕ CELEBRITY SUNDAYS
In aid of the GREAT ORMOND STREET HOSPITAL

SUNDAY NEXT   AUG. 20th

EDDIE   CLIFF

HAPGOOD & BASTIN

The Famous International Arsenal Footballers
Will judge the Parade of Bathing Belles at 2.30

DMISSION to the Camp 1/- includes inspection f Main Buildings and Grounds, use of Tennis ourts, Bathing Pool, etc., & the EVENTS of the ay. Children accompanied by Adults FREE.

NTIRE PROCEEDS in aid of the Hospital for ck Children, Great Ormond Street, London.

THE VIENNESE BIERGARTEN

1937 George Male and Eddie lark around on the tennis court after training

May 1938 Arsenal team-mates, Bastin, Drake and Hapgood, change into England shirts for the infamous summer tour to Germany

1939 Eddie at home. He and Maggie wave son Tony off to school from Hutton Grove

1939 Eddie and Tony display Eddie's record number of international caps

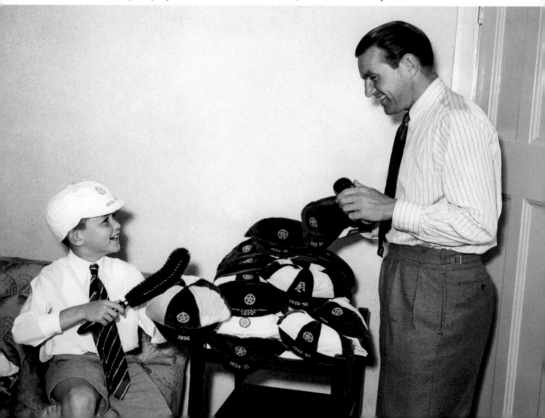

1939 Eddie Hapgood, Arsenal and England —
'a leader who could encourage his team-mates
to rise to their greatest heights'

only football match the king would watch and the only time Eddie and he would meet.

Before the year was out, Britain would be shaken by a different kind of crisis, one that struck at the heart of the established monarchy. Edward VIII abdicated on 11 December, professing love to be incompatible with the responsibilities of power. If a working-class footballer's dilemmas can be compared with a king's – and I think they can – then I would claim that the opposite perspective was true for Eddie. On that bright May afternoon in north London, there is little doubt that nothing could have been further from the king's mind than either football or his national duty; for Eddie facing a similar dilemma, it was his duty to football, to Arsenal, to his team-mates that won out over personal feelings.

James was Arsenal's captain on that cup-winning day. There really isn't any mystery about who was the captain of Arsenal despite later discussions framed as 'The Captain Debate' (James or Hapgood) and 'The Forgotten Captain' (James). The 1934/35 season had started a run of three campaigns when Alex was officially named captain but the role in public understanding was assumed to be Eddie's. In match accounts and articles during these seasons, journalists often referred to him as Arsenal's 'skipper'. The *Sheffield Independent*, full of FA Cup Final coverage on the days running up to the clash with Arsenal printed James's comment, 'I think I shall have the honour of leading a victorious team at Wembley,' but referring to Eddie's possible absence, it reported elsewhere in the same edition, 'There was good news yesterday for Eddie Hapgood, the England and Arsenal captain.'

The newspaper's assumption seems to be that Hapgood was captain but that if he was not able to play, James would lead the team out. That was quite the reverse of the truth. As James's struggle for fitness continued and his career neared its end, Eddie running out of the Highbury tunnel first was to become a regular sight for the rest of the decade. In the mind of press, public and fans, it is not surprising that 'captain of England' and 'captain of Arsenal' seemed to merge. However, the confusion, or the deliberate obfuscation, was to lead on that FA Cup Final morning to what Eddie saw as a slight that he felt deeply and which drove another wedge between him and Allison.

There is a distinct difference between *being* a captain and being *named* a captain, although of course they can be one and the same. There was always something about the captain in Eddie's personality, not because he identified himself with a formal position, but because inspiring his fellow players to cohere and create to the best of their ability was an instinctive footballing and moral position. I think this can be recognised in the speeches to the press after Arsenal's victory. James, Arsenal's named captain, was interviewed after the match for the *London Evening News*. He paid handsome tribute to Sheffield United, but for Alex, the game and its details, were all:

'I thought Pickering and Barclay as good as ever they were. In regard to Dodds, I had heard a lot about him, and there was rather a difference of opinion about his play in what I heard. But on this form against us in the Cup final I am sure he is going to be well in the running of having his ambitions realised of playing for Scotland one day.'

In contrast, exuberant and triumphant, but, as he later wrote himself, 'weighed down by grief and anxiety about my mother', Eddie's response to journalists after the match shows his natural inclination on a big occasion to speak up for the virtues of his sport and for all footballers:

'It was first and foremost a real game played in the spirit of sport. Let this cup final give the lie to the suggestions, sometimes made, that when there is anything real at stake the footballer does not mind how he wins so long as he does win.

'In stressing this point, there is a pat on the back of our opponents particularly, and they played so well that I wish they were coming back to the First Division next season. They would be a credit to the top class.'

Both responses are interesting – perhaps James's comments on specific players more so at the time – but the tone and the objectives are markedly different. Stanley Matthews didn't fudge his judgement, 'His [James's] approach to life and football was in as sharp contrast to that of Arsenal team-mates Eddie Hapgood and Cliff Bastin as Falstaff to Henry IV.'

During the unfolding of the FA Cup Final, there was another frightening problem for Mum and Dad to face. Tony's health had unexpectedly deteriorated. Over the winter breathing difficulties had caused sporadic problems but in the new year they had become more severe, visits to the hospital more frequent. There had not been a specific diagnosis yet, but there was a possibility of a tubercular gland in his throat and neck. This is a condition which can begin in the womb, a possibility Mum learned about later and which she linked in her mind with the ominous Friday, 13

June date. There were anxious days and nights with Tony in pain, his breathing laboured and his temperature flaring and falling, wondering what they should do, wondering what the matter was, asking themselves whether their young son was in danger. What they hoped was nothing worse than a heavily congested chest was finally confirmed as the result of a tubercular throat gland, a serious but common condition at the time and routinely resolved by the removal of the diseased gland.

It may have been medically routine but the surgery Tony underwent as a small boy is considered today as 'monstrous and disfiguring'. When the surgery was first carried out, apparently it left a savage scar but by the time I was about six and Tony 19, the long, deep cleft in his neck had taken on his own skin colour and was as much part of him as his smooth-skinned hands and curly hair. As Eddie played his way from Bristol to Liverpool to Newcastle and Wembley in pursuit of the FA Cup, Maggie watched alone by Tony's hospital bed and, full of relief, was at last able to bring him home as the season ended.

Four weeks after Tony's operation and months of mounting anxiety, two weeks after Emily's operation and the frantic rush to Bristol and back, two weeks after the FA Cup Final and all its hectic celebrations, two days after the last match of the season against Leeds United, it was 4 May 1936. Time to leave for the international summer tour. Eddie, quite simply, wasn't ready. There was no time to catch his breath with his family, no time to assess and prepare for the task ahead in Europe, and no time to make the journey back down to Bristol to see his mother before he left for Austria. For the first time in his life he wished the world would stop, that football would stop, if only for a few days. Life was surely good and he was surely still lucky but, for the first time in Eddie's life, the demands and stresses of playing for so long at such a high level of professionalism with so many expectations from club, country and fans, were draining him. His family desperately needed him and he had no time for them. The tour was a disappointment. England lost both matches, the first 2-1 to Austria and the second 3-2 to Belgium. The reputations of both continental sides, particularly the Austrian *Wunderteam*, were flourishing. Eddie blamed himself for the poor results. Later he called it his unhappiest tour, and well he might.

Although glad to be home at last, the summer break now carried its own strains. Mum and he had decided a summer trip to Cornwall was impossible. Instead, as soon as he returned from the tour, he collected Emily from Bristol and brought her to London to stay, to give her what he hoped would be a holiday, a chance for them both to rest and recover. With the summer break reaching ahead, he had hoped to spend time with her, to talk, for her to enjoy her grandson who was recuperating well and, with Maggie, to spoil her a little.

For one reason or another it hadn't worked out. In one of the very few real-life glimpses I had of Emily, my own mother confessed she was overawed by her mother-in-law and that she had found her cold and stern after her own loving and affectionate mother. 'I realised later,' she told me, 'what a struggle she'd had and how that had drained all softness from her.' I think she felt some regret at the fact that she had not been able to be more sympathetic but perhaps she needed more sympathy and support herself as she coped over the months of Tony's illness and recovery. Sometimes it seemed as if she and Eddie had had time stolen from them. The frictions and tensions had been tiring and saddening. Emily felt she would be happier at home. Before the new season began, Eddie drove her back to her Bristol family, reluctantly agreeing that she would feel more comfortable surrounded by her daughters who all still lived nearby in Bristol.

When pre-season training began in August, Eddie was still tired and unprepared. Then, in October, another blow fell. It was totally unexpected, a rupture in his life that felt like physical pain. Eddie lost his place in the England squad and his captaincy. He was sure the selection committee's decision must have been prompted by the poor results on the summer tour. He felt that he had failed to ignite his team or mount a cohesive response to either the Austrian or Belgian sides, but at that time, it had never occurred to him that his international career might be under threat. It was a judgement he simply hadn't anticipated. Although the loss of his captaincy was the inevitable corollary of losing his place, it seemed a double verdict on his failure.

In fact, it is unlikely that all the blame was heaped on his head alone. In a wave of panic over two consecutive losses in Europe following average performances in the British Home Championship, the Football Association had decided that a big shake-up was needed. Grumbles had been surfacing about the number of Arsenal players in the national team. Six on the recent European tour and never fewer than four seemed a lazy transference of an excellent team into a surrogate national squad. There was pressure to give more opportunities to the burgeoning but often overlooked talent from the north and Midlands. Eddie was dropped but, with the exception of Cliff Bastin, so were all the Arsenal contingent. Even so it took two men to replace Eddie. Ted Catlin of Sheffield Wednesday took over at left-back and Jack Barker of Derby County was appointed captain.

Then two weeks after watching England vanquish Hungary 6-3 at Highbury, Eddie was dropped from the Arsenal team. At first, it was just time out for a seemingly minor knock during a home defeat against Manchester City, but that injury refused to respond to treatment. The arrival of Christmas, usually crammed with football, crowds in festive and holiday mood and a passionate desire to end the year with a flourish, seemed like a punishment. Even when he was fit again, he was forced to watch as Arsenal trounced Chelsea 4-1 on 19 December, pummelled Preston North End 4-1 on Christmas Day, dashed to Everton on Boxing Day and held them to a draw, then travelled across the Pennines to meet Preston again and bring the Christmas season to a triumphant conclusion with a 3-1 victory on 28 December. In case of injuries or unforeseen events, Eddie had travelled north with the team as 12th man like so many lesser-known players before him. He was selected for the last match, standing in for George Male who had himself suffered a knock against Everton, but was then dropped again. He had become a useful 'spare man'.

The sudden disappearance of Eddie from the public gaze – as it seemed at the time – caused concern and questions. More seriously, rumours began and judgements emerged in their wake. He was 28, no longer young. He was getting slower. 'Was he, and let's face it, it happens to all football players at some time, over the hill?' the punters and pundits began to ask. 'He's had a good run.' His name was still absent from the team sheet as Arsenal began their FA Cup campaign against Second Division Chesterfield on 16 January 1937. 'Although travelling, Eddie Hapgood who has taken part in so many Arsenal Cup battles is unlikely to be included,' intoned the *Birmingham Daily Gazette*. In the public view, he had become an official reserve, not as a substitute would be used today, but a man in case of need before the referee's whistle blew to start the game. The *Daily Herald* saw it differently. Clifford Webb, a journalist and long-time admirer of Eddie, was mystified. Eddie's absence just didn't make sense. Under the sub-heading 'There if Wanted', Webb attempted to explain the mystery in terms of Eddie's loyalty and his unquestioning commitment to his team rather than to himself:

'Hapgood, I'll hazard, doesn't like being idle, as he was on Saturday – a mere spectator. Nobody with the Hapgood spirit likes that sort of thing. But Eddie was there if wanted, and so far as he was concerned that was all there was to it.'

Webb rightly recognised Eddie's founding football principle of total loyalty to his team but it certainly wasn't the whole story of that moment. Whenever Eddie watched a match, any match, any team, he was completely involved. He played every position in his head. Like a chess player, he tracked each move, anticipated possible responses, kept his eye on victory. Like a mathematician studying a page of geometry drawn by a combination of intelligence and intuition, the players' positioning would be seen and understood. Chapman had valued his observations and it was the job that had helped keep his spirits up since being dropped.

Watching the Chesterfield match was different. Arsenal were so superior and Chesterfield players so overwhelmed, it was hardly a football match. Eddie had time to think. He knew that he was good enough to play. He knew he had something to contribute that would improve Arsenal's performances. He knew the club needed him.

Later that month he discovered a possible reason why he had been benched even after he had regained fitness. Somehow he had become a commodity. Leicester City had offered Arsenal an £8,000 transfer fee for a player whom managers' gossip, triggered by the anomaly of his sidelining, agreed had 'four or five years of good football left in him yet'. It was the first time Eddie had been assessed as livestock in a market or that any club had even considered trying to move him – to do so would be 'something akin to the removal of Nelson's Column from Trafalgar Square' as one wit commented. Webb mused on the oddity of the situation. Was it that Arsenal already felt in line for a possible fifth championship title with their current team that they could leave such talent on the bench? How could that be so when Arsenal's squad was small with little margin for absences or for injuries? Allison's immediate and unequivocal response to Leicester City, 'that there wasn't a chance of Hapgood leaving Highbury', enlightened nobody. If he was such a fixture, why wasn't he playing? However, when Eddie read the end of that sentence in the national press, it confirmed what he had, in fact, already guessed. 'There wasn't a chance of Hapgood leaving Highbury although he had temporarily lost his place to Leslie Compton.' A wave of grief hardened into a sense of injustice and anger.

'Mr Allison dropped me from the team. No discussion, no reason,' he told me some 30 years later but still with barely repressed grief and anger in his voice. 'That couldn't be right. To say nothing. *And* he discussed a transfer to Leicester with their directors. Not with me. No explanation. Players were supposed to make an appointment to see him but I ran upstairs to his office, knocked on the door. He said he still wanted me in the squad but he was considering different formations, making room for different skills. "Skills?" I queried. After we'd talked I said to him, "You know you'll have to play me. I'm too good to leave out."'

There was bravado in his gesture but the words were simple truth. Players were not allowed to go directly to the manager's office in those days but while Eddie was a respecter of people who deserved respect, he was not a respecter of arbitrary authority, of a man who couldn't be bothered to check on his players' injuries or inform them of his decisions. The particular nature of his self-belief echoes down the years through advice he gave to all us children. 'It isn't arrogant to know your own value,' he would say. 'You should be proud of what you can do and be brave about standing up for yourself, to expect respect.' As a child, I simply took his words as a parental truth. As I grew older, I thought such advice to daughters in the prim days of the mid-1950s, well, that was one amazing piece of faith he was asking us to have in ourselves. With maturity I realised it was a recognition of his rights, as a person and as a footballer, that he had felt compelled to defend. Sitting there week after week watching and analysing, he knew that he should be part of that team, that – yes – he was necessary to it. 'You'll win your place back. Say nothing,' Mum advised. But he hadn't listened.

This confrontation with Allison lingered in Dad's memory and resurfaced again and again over the years but we only guessed at the depth of his feeling as late as the mid-1950s, a memory marked by Slim Whitman's recording of the popular song 'Rose Marie'. As we children tried to copy Whitman's exuberant yodelling with high pitched squeaks, he told us that he had heard the song first one Christmas when Mum had persuaded him to see a new film starring Nelson Eddy and Jeanette McDonald to cheer him up – although he didn't tell us why he needed cheering up. He told us Eddy's version was much better than any other new-fangled version, and demonstrated the fact vigorously until we were all singing:

Of all the queens that ever lived I'd choose you
To rule meeeee my Rose-e Marie-e -e -e

As it turned out, he told us after he had finished the story, Allison had had to agree with him. A few weeks later, he was selected to play against Sheffield Wednesday on 13 February and played every match for the rest of the season. It was too late. For the first time in seven years it seemed that Arsenal were diminished, a once great team being allowed to drift needlessly towards mediocrity. Their season finished without the title, without the FA Cup, without even an appearance in the final and with a squad of restless players. Temporarily, the incident was forgotten, but the mutual wariness now took on a tinge of distrust. Eddie knew his action and his words that day had been some kind of watershed but he never understood what the plot was and was always baffled by the meaning of this unhappy period of his life.

Eddie's challenge to Allison was not triggered simply by being dropped, however upsetting that was. What hurt him was not being given the chance to discuss his position despite seven years of holding a regular place, his loyal commitment to the team and his unstinting work rate. What hurt was that an injury had been used as an excuse to shunt him aside. What hurt was the lack of support, of faith in his ability when Allison knew grief and anxiety had threatened his form. It also hurt that Allison discussed his position with the press and not with him. Painful memories came flooding back. His first employer at the Great Western Cotton Mill had dismissed him on the spot for implying exploitation. The Bristol Rovers director had expected to take advantage of his inexperience to buy his skills cheaply. Walter Baker, voted in as the Labour MP by the people of the Bristol East constituency on a promise of jobs and houses, provided neither. For Eddie, the common denominator between all these experiences of his early Bristol life was lack of honesty and respect, an honesty and respect he felt were his right and the right of all his team-mates. The years of happiness at Arsenal suddenly had a question mark over them. He felt he was on the defensive in more ways than one.

A week after regaining his place in the Arsenal team, a fan letter arrived for him that raised a smile. The musical *Home and Beauty* had opened at the Adelphi on 2 February 1937. A fan, well informed by the press that Dad was teetotal but consumed gallons of tea, welcomed him back to the team by sending him a record of Binnie Hale's song:

I like a nice cup of tea in the morning
For to start the day you see
And at half past 11
Well my idea of heaven
Is a nice cup of tea
I like a nice cup of tea with me dinner
And a nice cup of tea with me tea
And when it's time for bed
There's a lot to be said
For a nice cup of tea

It became a family joke and we all continued to sing this silly, tuneless song with mock London accents for many years.

A few weeks later, returning home from training in late March, Eddie let himself into a silent house. Tony had recovered well from the difficult operation on his neck and was back at school. Mum had left a few minutes previously to collect him. Before leaving she had propped a letter addressed to Mr E.A. Hapgood on the hall stand, a letter embossed with the words 'The Football Association, Lancaster Gate'. With a shiver of joy Eddie knew immediately what it would say. He was back as captain and defender in the England squad for the summer British Home Championship and the close-season Scandinavian tour. A nightmare of fear, grief and loss that seemed to have twisted a whole year out of shape and raised more questions about who he was and what he could be than he knew how to answer, was over. The happiness of that summer of 1937, so different in every way from the dark summer of 1936, was profound.

8

England v Germany 1935 and 1938

As the decade progressed, so did the ludicrously misguided flirtation of the Football Association with Europe's fascist powers. Football, under the colluding hand of the Foreign Office, was slowly but steadily appropriated as a useful tool in the government's barely acknowledged appeasement strategy. An invitation was duly issued to Germany to play England in December 1935. It turned out to be an altogether strange affair; a football match in which football was the least important element, the players necessary but unimportant participants. It was an event to be managed, an event which had 'unintended consequences' as politicians like to label their ill-considered actions or their outright mistakes. This one was to hand a diplomatic coup to Germany.

The Italian matches of 1933 and 1934 begin to seem like straightforward playground dramas in the light of the unpleasant combination of moral cowardice, political sleight of hand and massive incompetence displayed in equal measure by the Home Office, the Foreign Office and the Football Association in their dealings with England's two international fixtures with

Germany in this decade. The political landscape had changed again; it had become darker and nastier. Germany posed very different questions than Italy and promised to make completely different demands of England and its now established captain, Eddie Hapgood. Mid-decade, in a period of rumour and fear, of deliberate political obfuscation and uneasy public ignorance, the match was organised, planned and monitored long before the players ran out for the kick-off on 4 December 1935. The spokesmen of the British government and the Football Association stood shoulder to shoulder to roll out the cliché to the public that sport is a politics-free zone while they were all busy playing out another kind of 'sport' in meetings, across desks of the Foreign Office, around tables at the Home Office and on the telephone to the German Embassy.

A wave of public protest met the announcement that Germany were to play England and what's more, it would be at White Hart Lane, the London home of Tottenham Hotspur. Spurs always had, and still do have, a strong Jewish following. If the FA had wanted to be deliberately provocative, its officials couldn't have made a better choice of venue. It is more likely that they remembered the Italian protests in 1933 about playing at Highbury against a team with several Arsenal players and thought they were playing safe. They were completely taken aback, dismayed and anxious by the unexpected response, an anxiety rapidly shared by the Home Office as the possibility of the match being the focus of anti-German protests began to emerge. Jewish communities joined the protests and *The Star* ran a headline proposing that the match be called off.

The only organised voice of the protest was that of the Trades Union Congress (TUC), backed by the left-wing paper the *Daily Worker*. The vacuous and dishonest 'debate' that followed continued to deny any relationship of sport to politics. The TUC was told by Sir John Simon, Home Secretary at the time and seeking to disguise the real political situation, that the match had no political implications at all. Although none of the German players were known to be formally signed-up members of the Nazi Party, they were now coming to England as representatives of Hitler's National Socialist regime whether or not they agreed with their country's determined path towards ethnic cleansing and totalitarianism, or even knew about it.

The TUC's last-ditch formal request to the Home Office to call off the match was rejected but it prompted the Home Office to implement a damage limitation exercise of extraordinary proportions. In what is possibly the largest package tour ever devised, and with the total support of delighted German officialdom, 10,000 German fans were provided with fleets of coaches and taken to see the sights of London until they were deposited at the last minute at White Hart Lane. Drawn up in long lines at the turnstiles, many of them were more than a little late for the kick-off. Despite all the precautions, none of the threatened protests actually took place. Jewish fans, many of them refugees from earlier eastern European migrations, made up a significant section of the crowd on the day. Both British and German national anthems were sung without any disturbance. One famous and never-to-be-forgotten gesture was perhaps the most moving. The *Daily Mail* recorded a swastika flying over one of the White Hart Lane stands, which someone had managed to cut down, although later the rope was repaired and the flag re-hoisted. After the match, during which the German fans had behaved impeccably, they were swept off into coaches and deposited at Victoria. Other than a small, jostling group at the station, a disorganised mixture of Mosley's fascist Blackshirts, communists and anti-German protesters, everything, as far as both sets of officials were concerned, went according to plan. No doubt with heartfelt relief the British contingent must have been delighted that this peacetime diplomatic operation had worked so well. No protests had been visible enough to remind players or crowds that the occasion was anything other than an international football match in a stadium packed to capacity. The result was pleasingly true to form as England won by three goals. Job done.

What did the England players think about all this? Those travelling to the match from outside London were very probably unaware of the local situation. This was a fixture scheduled during the regular season programme, in winter and near to Christmas. They were travelling to London from Sunderland and Stoke, from Birmingham and Bolton. The players did not meet up as a team until the evening before the match when many of them would have been tired from their journeys and ready for a bath and a meal. There wasn't even time for them to train together. What did the London-based players think? What did Eddie Hapgood think? Were they aware of the doubts swirling around, the questions being asked, the negotiations taking place at the highest political level, the possibility of cancellation? More than that – had they absorbed the news flowing from Europe that was the source of all this unease?

Some facts can help to shape the context. Despite being captain, Eddie was never consulted or, after the plans had been made, informed about what had been decided. He had no knowledge of the direct involvement of Cabinet ministers or the weeks of backroom planning. He certainly did not know that the German ambassador was summoned by Home Secretary Sir John Simon to discuss the management of the team and the German fans. However, four players – Eddie himself, George Male, Cliff Bastin and Jack Crayston – played for Arsenal and lived in north London. They not only knew each other well but lived in close proximity to the local protests. Eddie's new house was on the rural edges of Finchley, the home of long-established Jewish communities. It is very likely that they knew of particular campaigns such as the TUC's attempt to have the match called off and surely it would have been impossible for them not to know about local neighbourhood disturbances.

However, whatever each member of the team knew or thought individually, there would have been precious little time to discuss it or to be briefed before assembling at White Hart Lane the following day. If there had been a manager perhaps that would have been a possibility. Absurd as it may seem, the English team did not have a manager; selection was made by a Football Association committee and team management handled by administrators. Once he had been named captain it was up to Eddie, in the short time he had, to try and marshal his group of individually brilliant players into a smoothly functioning team.

Whatever anxieties or unease individual players were feeling, whatever political and moral vacuum Eddie felt caught up in, for him there could only be one task in hand: to lead his team out of the confusion and on to the pitch with professional pride in their excellence, and to fire them with the desire to play as well they were able and with a determination to win magnificently.

The full political significance and meaning of this match became shockingly clear to the players only at the post-match banquet, a suspiciously congratulatory and uncomfortable ritual of mutual admiration. As Eddie and his team-mates listened to the after-dinner speeches, organised well in advance in committee rooms and no doubt written by civil servants, they could not have failed to realise how their sport and their personal efforts had been used. The speeches specifically included a condemnation of the TUC's 'unpatriotic' protest and, after a toast to King George V, glasses were enthusiastically raised to Chancellor Hitler. The following morning, the players who lived outside London left with their expenses paid and £4 in their pockets while Eddie and his London colleagues had already made their way home the previous evening. The Football Association had done its work and delivered England's best players as diplomatic stooges. The government, led by Stanley Baldwin at a time when it was still just about possible to divert public concerns away from Hitler's ambitions, had been successful in maintaining good diplomatic relations with Germany.

The defeat didn't ruffle Hitler at all. Like Mussolini before him, he already had his eye on much greater triumphs envisaged for the following year at the Berlin Olympics. Indeed, when he was informed about the protests which had threatened the England v Germany match, he had even offered to cancel it to ease the situation. For him that would have been preferable to spoiling the political image which it was his aim to project. He had got what he wanted. English officialdom had shown its support of fascism by hosting the team, generously organising the fans and graciously acknowledging him as Germany's Chancellor while the match and the faultless behaviour of the German fans had provided him with excellent publicity.

Of all the internationals that Eddie Hapgood was called upon to captain, this was the match where his role was effectively nullified. Only at the last minute on the pitch was he able to exert any influence. Eddie's own memories of that day were divided. A creditable victory, yes, but an international game played as if it was an exhibition at which the players were mere spectators of a disturbing diplomatic dance. Eddie and his ten team-mates had been made ciphers by the invisible powers-that-be and their front man, the recently promoted referee, FA secretary Stanley Rous. Inevitably, with something of a sour taste, he was tempted to conclude that the result was 'Goals three [George Camsell scored two, and Cliff Bastin the other] – football nil'.

But zoom in on the match itself, the players and the fans, and as usual a different story emerges like a picture from behind an accumulated patina of grime. Eddie was proud that as the accounts rolled off the press that night, it was generally praised as a fast-paced, cleanly played, good game. The Germans had not expected to win and they were hampered by the surface of the pitch, which cut up badly after recent heavy rain. They were no match for England's individual skills but even so, they fought to the final whistle with considerable vigour and determination volubly supported by the numerous German fans. Under the headline '"Master and Pupil" Game at Tottenham', one account records the forward Fath, heading towards an open goal with the ball at his feet, see it vanish as if by magic, as 'Hapgood dashed across and kicked the ball off his toes just in time'; Hapgood and Bastin combining to pick out Camsell who, outjumping the German defender, 'sent the ball flashing past Jakob – a great goal'; Cliff Bastin sealing the Germans' fate even as 'they were valiantly repelling the rampant English forwards'. Final result in spite of the framework of history: England v Germany, football integrity – equal honours.

In 1938 came Eddie's 12th match as captain, another great occasion and a magnificent win. English football was at its most exciting and creative in Berlin against Germany on 16 May. The match itself has long been lost behind an endlessly reprinted, tell-tale black and white photograph of the England team performing the Nazi salute in Berlin and the political machinations that surrounded 11 young, working-class men who found themselves assigned with the responsibility for saving Britain from war. But the game itself is where I will begin because what happened did *not* change the course of history. When all is said and done, it was a football match and Eddie Hapgood was a football player. So back to the beginning in as much as there is a beginning to this end-of-decade event. Eddie's own words sum up the febrile and ambiguous atmosphere the players were collectively caught up in back in England before the tour even began:

'I can recall the excitement which seemed to suffuse the whole of the English soccer world. I can't explain how I felt at the time, but although we are professional footballers, we also have human feelings like other people. We read the papers and listened to the wireless, and I fancy most of us had the same thoughts where Germany was concerned. We remembered the happy, laughing fellows from Austria who had given us such grand games at Stamford Bridge and Vienna, and what had happened to their country and to them, since. And so, although it was with mixed feelings we awaited the announcement of the names of the players who were to take part in this game, it was also ... with mounting excitement.'

The Austrian team, the *Wunderteam* of the 1930s, was officially disbanded after Germany annexed Austria and their players were required to play for Germany. Austria were allowed to play their last match as a national team against Germany on 3 April 1938 in Vienna, just six weeks before England arrived in Berlin. Before that final game kicked off, it was made clear to the players that scoring a goal against Germany would not be approved of. The Austrian hero and captain, Matthias Sindelar, the adored leader of the *Wunderteam* for his paper-thin slightness, his brilliant footwork and goalscoring ability, waited until the last minutes of the match, and then scored. His skill was such that he could choose his moment. He further stamped on German pride by celebrating when the final whistle announced an Austrian victory. Five years Eddie's senior, Sindelar tragically lost his life to the Nazis just two years later in 1938. His crime? To celebrate his goal against the German national team. Eddie played only once against the magical Sindelar when Austria defeated England in that sad summer of 1936, and now, barely six weeks after the gesture of defiance that would lead to the Austrian's death, Eddie was with the England players in Germany, in Berlin.

Out on the pitch, the formalities over, the spectre of National Socialism temporarily stilled, political propaganda temporarily set aside, the referee blew his whistle and what Eddie had always known and believed became clear. When he recalled the event some ten years later, Cliff Bastin agreed in his characteristically ironic manner, 'There must have been a large amount of anti-British feeling ... but, if there was, I, for one, did not notice any!' The surging crowd of 110,000 fans, the largest crowd he and his team-mates had ever played in front of, were not a hostile gang, ready to jeer and revile, but devoted football supporters.

It turned out to be one of those matches when two opposing teams and those who are watching come together to turn sport into art; effort, enthusiasm and joy into moments of sublimity. Who knows what temporary relief that day may have given to the thousands of working people from the violence, the poisonous fear and repression that had gripped their nation? Eddie knew that the German crowd had gathered to see a great England football team in the flesh, to identify their heroes, to see for themselves the skill and courage they had heard so much about, and that it was his job to inspire the team to rise to this momentous occasion. It was like British ballet lovers queuing all night for tickets to see Russian Rudolf Nureyev dance; Wimbledon tennis lovers to glimpse the Swede Björn Borg's bewitched embodiment of concentration or athletics devotees willing Jamaican Usain Bolt to crown his retirement with a magnificent win.

Of course, the crowd wanted Germany to win; of course, they cheered their team on and went wild with excitement as two lucky goals challenged England's pre-eminence. But that was not the whole point. When Len Goulden scored England's sixth goal at the last minute with an unstoppable flying volley, the crowd burst into appreciation of his brilliance and Eddie said that he found he too was jumping up and down in sheer amazement. At the final whistle according to the *Manchester Guardian* the crowd rushed on to the pitch, cheering everyone. 'Without the fans, it's impossible ... with only 11 players it's not possible,' Pep Guardiola declared recently. Final score, Germany 3 England 6. Football honours – even.

Crowds had gathered around the station to welcome the England team as they arrived in Berlin. Crowds celebrated them as they clambered down from their coach before their appearance at the stadium and after it was all over, more crowds gathered to cheer the England team off as they left for Switzerland on the second leg of the tour. Something akin to happiness and pride managed to burn brightly that day on both sides despite the stifling oppression of the political agenda. Back in England, the *Daily Echo* recorded, 'Everywhere praise is bestowed on the visiting team, some praise is almost ecstatic.'

It hardly seems possible but so joyous was the atmosphere and so appreciative of the sporting spectacle they had witnessed from both teams that the German equivalent of the Football Association produced a commemorative booklet congratulating the 'English who showed how football should be played'. 'It was,' the review continued, 'perfect football.' Sporting rivalries can create respect and sometimes even friendship. In different times, that may well have been the outcome of this match. Eddie's counterpart, Fritz Szepan, the German captain, wrote, 'In a hundred years' time I could be just as enthusiastic about the English achievement as I am today. I have often dreamt football should be played like that.' His comments were syndicated the length and breadth of Britain.

Dad often wondered what happened to those he played against and those who watched that day during the dark days of war and its aftermath. 'They would never forget Len's goal anyway,' he would say with a smile. Indeed, the fans came back for more. One of the most touching facts of this 1938 England tour is that, astonishingly, the stadium was packed to capacity for a second time the following day to watch an Aston Villa team that was touring Europe. But nothing in those days was ever straightforward. The Football Association had refused to play the national team against a combined Germany/Austria XI in protest against annexation but had ordered the players to give the Nazi salute. Aston Villa, on a club tour and Arsenal's current rivals on the domestic front, agreed to play against the combined opposition but indicated their disapproval of Hitler by refusing to give a Nazi salute, although they had saluted without question on their previous tour games. However, as if to prove their credentials as football fans pure and simple whatever the political circumstances, German supporters turned out in their thousands to both matches.

Sadly, there is no escaping the fact that Eddie was also a player in a parallel match. There were two very different stories at work on that electric, sunny afternoon. Although he didn't know it at the time, it was not the FA but the British government that had sanctioned the fixture and was involved from the start in an exercise of cultural propaganda in a desperate attempt to maintain stable international relations. Government strategy had moved from the half-anxious, panicky reaction of 'coping and doing our best' (as against Germany in London in 1935) to a specific approach of appeasement in which sport, football, club and international were requisitioned to play a part. The simple, sole reason why the England team, and other British club sides, were allowed, even encouraged to tour Europe that summer in a time of such dangerous unpredictability was the result of a political decision. In footballing terms, the whole sorry mess came to a climax in the decision of the England team, captained by Eddie, to give the Nazi salute before the match. The whys, the hows, even the wheres of the process that led to that decision are as smudged by conflicting accounts, conflicting attitudes, bureaucratic silence, by the Chinese whisper effect of information recycled again and again over the years as a photograph is by water.

The bare bones of the story are simple. The keynotes of the official account issued to the press by the Football Association are calls to patriotism and the nation's security; the proud contribution of the players in demonstrating the former and upholding the latter. Eddie's personal account gives the story a different emphasis. After the players had arrived and settled – they had a couple of days in Berlin before the match – he was called to Stanley Rous's hotel room for the usual pre-match discussion. Eddie was instructed that the players' behaviour must be exemplary, and that it was important for the football to be excellent to impress the German officials and fans. To Eddie, such words were irritatingly irrelevant and patronising. Why on earth would their behaviour *not* be exemplary? When had it been anything else? However, as the conversation concluded, Rous added as an apparent afterthought that he had recently spoken to the British ambassador, Sir Nevile Henderson, who had decided it would be a good idea to salute Hitler at the beginning of the match as a mark of respect. Taken by surprise, Eddie pointed out what Rous already knew, that such a salute was unnecessary, that, of course, they would all stand to attention during the German national anthem as was usual in football protocol against any national team. 'And anyway,' Eddie added, 'we salute our country and Empire, not theirs.'

The surprise was genuine. Although discussions about the Nazi salute were a growing irritant, they tended to be resolved on an ad-hoc basis. They had never before become a major issue for a national team except when Hitler himself was involved as at the 1936 Olympics. Perhaps the rumour that Hitler would be attending the game was the source of the sudden pressure for a redundant gesture. Characteristically, it never occurred to Eddie that he was being *ordered* to salute. As on other occasions in his life, and with a dash of naivety, Eddie considered that he was being *consulted*. This possibly lost him the initiative. Rous, apparently nervous because of his experience at the Berlin Olympics, something he had confided to Eddie on an earlier occasion, was already one step ahead, advising Sir Nevile that the salute would be a good idea '*in order to get the crowd in a good temper*'. It was another phrase that surprised Dad and he italicises it in his autobiography. Their arrival two days previously had been enthusiastically welcomed. He had no reason to think that the crowd was anything other than excited about an international fixture. In the more fractious atmosphere in London in 1935, the German fans had created no trouble, enjoying the match and accepting their defeat in good spirit.

When Eddie recounted his conversation with Rous later to the other players, there was a general sense of unease and some strong opinions were voiced. Only the players know how Eddie reported the news when he rejoined them, how they responded, or how the matter was finally resolved. The following day, when they gathered in their changing room, high up in the Berlin stadium before kick-off, they were joined by Stanley Rous as well as Wreford Brown, the tour manager. Anxious that they could not rely on Eddie to carry out what they considered to be orders or that he would be reluctant to overrule any dissident players, they emphasised the importance of pleasing Chancellor Hitler and repeated the need to keep the crowds calm. In direct proportion to the rising anger of a significant number of the players and Eddie's own surprised objections, they upped the threat level. The players were told that their protests showed they didn't really understand what was going on behind the scenes and that failure to salute could be 'the spark that could set Europe alight'. The die was cast.

An hour later, Eddie led the team out and, together, they lined up and performed the Nazi salute just once towards the VIP stand where Sir Nevile was sitting with Joachim von Ribbentrop,

Joseph Goebbels, Hermann Göring and Rudolf Hess. It is an odd fact that British officials appeared to be fascinated by Germany's rising power brokers. Sir Robert Vansittart, from the British Foreign Office, 'liked Goebbels and his wife at once', we are told, and Henderson spends a chapter of his memoir enthusing about Göring and confessing, 'I must frankly say that I had a real personal liking for him.' The German team then saluted to the other three sides of the stadium. A historical footnote: Hitler did not attend the match. 'If he thought there was any chance of Germany being beaten, he wouldn't turn up,' Eddie told the journalist Derek Henderson in 1972. 'To him, Germans couldn't be beaten.'

Many years later, Tony filled out another part of the story for me. As the first son, born when Mum and Dad were very young and sharing the growing stature of Dad's career with them, he was the natural confidant as they grew older and he more mature. Of the notorious 1938 match, he told us that on one occasion Dad had talked about how he was faced with a final decision only a short time before kick-off. After discussing it with Eddie, the players had agreed that they would not salute. The salute seemed to have become a far more serious business, he said, than in previous years. When extra pressure was put on the players just before the match, he had asked himself just how dangerous the situation was. It was a question he couldn't answer. At short notice, he had been faced with a choice he hadn't felt equipped to make.

He told Tony that he had very briefly considered refusing to lead the players out, a decision he felt the players would probably support although he couldn't be sure. However, he felt he had to trust what he had been told and take the decision, not as an individual but as England captain. He decided that he was prepared to take upon himself the responsibility for the salute but not what it stood for, and to lead the players out in the only way within his control – to a great vindicating victory. As Eddie stood there in the stadium, waves of sound rolling down from the stands and his arm pointing upwards in the Nazi salute, he reluctantly supported his country as he had been instructed by acknowledging the power of Germany in their own land but he and his team-mates would play the best football the crowd had ever seen to celebrate their own country. The stage was set for football v fascism. It seemed the best he could do. They would play cleanly and fairly. They would defeat the inexperienced but fit, strong, talented, state-sponsored opposition. The result was a brilliant match and the triumphant 6-3 victory. Some 15 years later, Jack Crayston paid testimony to the influence that Eddie had had on the team that day in an interview with the *Daily Herald*. What he remembered about the Germany match, he said, was how Eddie had kept them focused, 'Eddie Hapgood's inspired captaincy … We had a team conference at half-time with Eddie "in the chair" …. Eddie's remarkable soccer brain helped us to work out how best to exploit the German defensive weaknesses. The plan worked perfectly.'

Dad only once talked about the incident in any detail with me. I had given him an LP called *Churchill's Greatest Speeches* for his birthday, perhaps in the early 1960s, and it must have triggered a train of thought. As he pondered over the past, he said, 'Nevile Henderson told me after the match that he had received a telegram from the Foreign Office ordering the salute.' He was musing, talking aloud. He had never mentioned before that he had met the ambassador although he certainly would have been introduced to him at the post-match banquet. However, it seems unlikely that Henderson would have made such a statement, ambassador to footballer, at a formal social occasion. On the other hand, Henderson knew from Rous about the unhappiness of the players and shaking the England captain's hand, it is very possible that he could have indicated (wishing to exonerate himself) that higher powers had made the final decision.

At the inevitable banquet, in a relieved, private conversation with Rous, Sir Nevile apparently dubbed the players 'football ambassadors', in this context a dubious accolade that was passed on to Eddie by Rous at a later date. No wonder Henderson completely failed to mention an incident that had apparently been so politically important only two years before in an embarrassingly self-justifying book, published in haste in 1940, and rather appropriately titled *Failure of a Mission 1937–39*. He had to blame someone. He chose to blame the press for his difficulties.

War is inevitably the telescope through which different versions of this event are perceived. At the time, *The Times* played along with what officials wanted the public to know, commenting that the salute 'made a good impression'. In fact, British club teams on European tours had been giving the Nazi salute in both Italy and Germany throughout the decade. As early as 1934, for instance, Derby County had saluted before each of their four games. When war was declared, any public disquiet died down as football was suspended and journalists turned their attention to the plight of clubs, stadia and the sad dispersal of great players to the armed forces. It was only after the war that the press woke up in outrage at 'the shameful salute', 'the national disgrace' which, looking through the other end of time's telescope was exactly what it seemed. When the war ended and victory in Europe (VE) was celebrated on 14 May 1945, the players who had been involved looked forward to demobilisation and the joy of peace but also back over six lost years of their footballing lives. That would be the first time they saw Germany whole. Like the astronauts of the 1960s, who discovered, 'We came all this way to explore the Moon, and the most important thing is that we discovered the Earth,' so they remembered being instructed to save Europe from war only to discover with hindsight they had played a unifying and joyous game of football.

It was not until then that they realised just how deeply they had been betrayed – pawns spuriously deployed to flatter the ambitions of von Ribbentrop (convicted and hanged by the Nuremberg court in 1946), Rudolf Hess (captured in 1941 and sentenced to life), Hermann Göring (condemned in Nuremberg but committed suicide in 1945) and Joseph Goebbels (committed suicide in Hitler's bunker after poisoning his six children). Those names had been barely known to them in 1938 but were now resonant with evil, the instigators of a calamitous and tragic upheaval of much of the world and many of its peoples. And they had saluted them, as the Foreign Office had instructed, 'as a mark of respect'. Eddie remembered that match, the magnificent win they had been proud of then, the delighted fans, the celebratory atmosphere, the political chicanery, the morally flawed instruction, and grieved.

His account of the game, its prelude and aftermath as it filtered down over the years, is a patchwork of vividly remembered experience, troubled recollections, and sudden, unexpectedly prompted memories. What happened over the few days the team was in Berlin was never entirely absorbed into his consciousness as part and parcel of his career. It was always liable to be recalled and pondered over. But the triumph of the match itself was never forgotten.

Immediately after the war, in 1945, Eddie's autobiography, *Football Ambassador*, was published. He chose to put his account of the 1938 match out of chronological order at the beginning of his book. As he set about writing the story of his footballing career, the first player to do so, he clearly felt the need to address that match before anything else. Or perhaps that was an editorial decision. Certainly there is a strange two-tone effect in the account. Apparently playing to understandable and powerful post-war prejudices, the German team are described as stereotypical Aryan giants in the power of the state. Yet he gives a sober and unembellished account of the match and the events surrounding it and describes with pleasure the welcome the team received from German fans. There certainly seems to be more than one hand at work in the account. Stanley Rous endorsed Eddie's autobiography with a complimentary preface implicitly accepting the truthfulness of Eddie's account. 'In this brief foreword,' Rous writes, 'it would be impossible to pay adequate tribute to the part which Eddie Hapgood has played in the development of Association Football during recent years. I always stress that they [professionals] should strive to behave on the field as a model on which young players can mould their play and conduct. That, Eddie Hapgood has done.'

After Eddie's death, he contradicted that position entirely and in 1978, now as Sir Stanley Rous, he claimed that there was no conflict about giving the salute, that Eddie understood the situation and conveyed it to the players who were proud to help their country in any way they could. According to this revised version, the players 'all agreed they had no objection, and no doubt saw it as a bit of fun rather than of any political significance'. Yet, despite this unpleasant and specious backtracking, the trail of responsibility is clear. Rous, anxious because of hostility to the Great Britain team at the Berlin Olympics in 1936 and informed that Hitler was planning to attend the match, suggested a salute to Eddie. Because of Eddie's obvious reluctance and, possibly his own added anxiety that Eddie might influence the players, he contacted Sir Nevile Henderson for his support and told the players that Henderson was the instigator of what was now an instruction. When the players responded in dismay and anger, Sir Nevile was contacted, and made last-minute contact himself with the Foreign Office. In its turn the Foreign Office duly sent a telegram – plus a threat.

Other than Jack Crayston's praise for Eddie's captaincy in difficult circumstances, only two other players wrote afterwards about what had happened. Cliff Bastin's account was published in 1950 and Stanley Matthews's much later in 2000. Bastin's version gives the impression that he was not particularly concerned about the outcome of the discussion but this might simply reflect the fact that British teams had quite often given the salute on international tours previously. I feel that some of his diffidence might be put down to his worsening deafness. Dad used to say that Bastin often coped with noisy banter and argument by falling silent. It is certainly possible that Bastin switched off as the argument and emotions surged round the changing room, relying on his team-mates to make the right decision. He does, however, add a point not mentioned by any of the other players and for which there is no photographic evidence, that after the Nazi salute the players gave their own military salute.

Matthews's account agrees with Eddie's but is written many years later with an eye for the drama of an event which was, by then, finally slipping away from public consciousness. The major difference is that Matthews implies that Eddie had definitely decided *not* to give the salute. He emphasises the suddenness of the order and the subsequent surge of emotions. He particularly notes Eddie's uncharacteristic anger. Interestingly, he suggests that 'an FA official' rushed out of the changing room and later returned with instructions to salute within minutes of kick-off. This must refer to an emergency contact with the Foreign Office in the face of player hostility, and be the source of the instructions Henderson claimed to have received and that Dad confided to Tony and me.

As the event passes into deep history, so facts become more distorted or plain wrong. A few other players, including Bert Sproston, Stan Cullis and Frank Broome, have had comments attributed to them. Cullis apparently protested vigorously but more recent accounts which claim that he refused to salute and was consequently dropped were probably prompted by the fact that, as a reserve, he had not been selected to play. However, he told his son at some later time that all the players protested vigorously, including Eddie. Broome, rather oddly, is attributed Matthews's account on the Aston Villa website. Most entertaining is a 1998 60-year anniversary 'Memory Lane' account in the *Kettering Evening Telegraph* in which Eddie becomes again the local lad under the sub-heading 'The Poppies Player Who Upset Hitler'. In this account, the performance of the England team led by their captain Eddie Hapgood 'so enraged the watching Adolf Hitler that he stormed out of the stadium before the final whistle'. Well, it's a good story!

Context is all. Prime Minister Neville Chamberlain was not thinking about football when he made the momentous radio announcement on 2 September 1939 declaring war on Germany, almost a year to the day after he had flown in from Berlin to announce to a relieved nation, 'Peace for our time.' A small part of his speech, however, goes a long way towards offering an explanation about how England's international football team became entrapped in an unpleasant propaganda exercise that appears to the present day a notorious and unhappy marker in football history. What Chamberlain said was:

'You can imagine what a bitter blow it is to me that all my long struggle to win peace has failed. Yet I cannot believe that there is anything more or anything different that I could have done that would have been more successful. Up to the very last it would have been quite possible to have arranged a peaceful and honourable settlement between Germany and Poland, but Hitler would not have it.'

He might have added, 'Perhaps another football match might have done the trick.' However, the worsening persecution of Jews which had provoked popular protests four years previously, the annexation of Czechoslovakia in March 1939 and the invasion of Poland the following September had extraordinarily *not* been stopped by requiring 11 football players to salute before a football match. All perspective, it seems, was lost. As Chris Brasher wrote 50 years later in relation to the Moscow Olympics, 'Since trade continues apace, and people still come and go, there is considerable resentment that young sportsmen and women are being used as the government's guns and soldiers.'

But of all the threads woven like an intricate web around this match, one of the most extraordinary is the complete lack of moral condemnation delivered by history on Eddie's decision and the players' compliance. The salute was seen as disgraceful but the players themselves were never condemned, emerging from the debacle as exploited heroes, 'more sinned against than sinning'. It was recognised by press and public that yet again, playing a football match had meant that they had to walk a tightrope across a quicksand of moral ambiguity. They survived perhaps because the victories they won on the pitch acted on the public mind and in their own hearts as a kind of joyful expiation.

Eddie was well aware of the growing symbolic significance of the matches and their role as shadow wars (against Italy) and diplomatic events (against Germany) in the looming European conflict. Even so, and even as the decade moved from crisis to crisis, would it have been remotely possible for him to imagine that he was playing a part in the grand arc of history, or that history would play its part in what he himself was to become in the public imagination? Unlikely. Such an insight needs the long view, the retrospective view, not the real-time intensity of a football match or a few outings wearing national colours. Even so, these four matches, two against Italy and two against Germany, however paradoxically and counter-intuitively, were to bestow a kind of immortality on him.

Dad would claim that every kick and every run he ever made was important, but these particular matches against Italy and Germany had the effect of pulling the contradictory aspects, the strengths and the weaknesses, the failures and successes, the certainties and the doubts of one man together into a single identity – captain of England. Surely as the journalist had predicted in 1930, the football gods would favour the Achilles my mother had seen materialising in front of her and allow 'the stamp of greatness' later identified by his team-mate Cliff to be fulfilled. If any of the gods had indeed marked Eddie out for greatness it must have been Clio, the muse of epic poetry and history.

By a coincidence of timing, both home and abroad, he was valued not just as a great footballer among other great footballers, but, as captain of England in a time of political turmoil, a true defender of the best of England's efforts. It seems that he became a necessary arsenal of national values, a necessary symbol of strength, necessarily victorious. It is certainly true that as the years rolled by, legends began to attach to his name as barnacles to a rock, legends that grew more detailed and elaborate year on year, progressing through hope from facts to myth – not a remote myth of the heroic age but myth as words, stories, what men say to each other and what men write, a pattern that men see emerging.

9

'And Then There's Eddie Hapgood'

There is no one word that can sum up the 1937/38 season. The *Daily Herald* captures the joy and anticipation right where it begins with the simple statement, 'Tomorrow's the day! Round about 3.30 p.m. is the time King Soccer will become crowned once again.' It is 27 August 1937 and Eddie is back in training for the opening of the season and ready 'to take the limelight from cricket' again, even from the great Denis Compton. He is 29; it is ten years since he joined Arsenal and he is absurdly happy.

The journalists who had mourned his absence from Arsenal in the barren months of early 1937 and were mystified by his disappearance from the international scene, woke up and went into action, carrying his name and reputation back into the headlines as an ancient hero might be carried in triumph on the shoulders of his troops from a great victory. They had nearly lost him once to what they felt was the dubious judgement of his manager and the Football Association's selection committee. They were going to make sure he was never sidelined again.

'The Man Who Came Back' trumpeted one headline with a quasi-mythical suggestion of rebirth. Magically, mythically, from August 1937, there was definitely a change. Fans not just of Arsenal but of football, journalists not just from London but those filing their stories across the regions; players not just from Arsenal but from the north, the Midlands, London and the south, joined in the plaudits. It wasn't just Eddie's longevity at the highest level of the sport that commanded their interest and respect. It was because time in the guise of injury, of loss of form, of personal grief, of age had nearly defeated him. But not quite. On behalf of all sportsmen and women, he had defied the rules of sporting decline and he had come back.

As with so much of the story of Eddie's career, a straightforward personal tale of footballing glory is charged by the invisible pulse of a dark and tragic decade. The high-octane excitement which exploded as the 1937/38 season kicked off was a surreal time in which the national sport, its national heroes and its loyal supporters somehow created a separate sphere for themselves as a bulwark against the oppressive mood of a deeply apprehensive and unhappy country. You might not support a particular club, you might not be able to name your local team, you may never have kicked a ball in your life, but nobody could help knowing that, like the chimes of Big Ben, Saturday football was comfortingly regular, that Arsenal more often than not won, that the England team was admired throughout Europe and that, thank goodness, your country's captain, Eddie Hapgood, was back.

At the beginning of the 1937/38 season there was something about the consistency of his distinctive style and sporting integrity, about a mature identity in which his captaincy and his football skill had become fused in the popular imagination, about the power of his influence on the field and yet the slightness of his physique that encouraged journalists to focus on him. They wrote as if his just being on the field was all you needed to know, that his presence inspired the performance of the whole team and the energy and colour of their writing. Perhaps something similar was happening recently when the tragedies of a pandemic turned us hopefully towards the youth and unity of today's England team playing in Euro 2020.

To his credit, George Allison had added the icing. Then as now, Arsenal was the club of choice for the literati, for film stars, for media darlings, the facilities of choice for great cricketers such as Denis Compton and great tennis players such as Fred Perry, the desirable location for football-themed glamour. Perhaps Eddie was even in danger of becoming something rather more mundane than a great footballer – a celebrity. Anna Neagle, the famous actress of the 1930s, was delighted to be photographed with him, leaning flirtatiously towards him as he kneels at the side of her chair, and to sign it too. I had no clue who this strange woman was when she turned up at my school in 1960 to watch our production of *Sixty Glorious Years* in which I performed as Prince Albert and to shake the hand of the headmistress who couldn't stop beaming. I still don't know how her visit came about. Mary Pickford, the influential and famous film actress was 'quite taken with him' when she met Eddie at Highbury, but 'it wasn't the first time that Hapgood's looks had got him noticed by the rich and famous', Ted Drake commented later. Fred Daniels caught that look in his studio photographs which the National Portrait Gallery bought and one of which adorned its staircase until the 1960s. Years later, the gallery used the same photograph as a wrapper on souvenir chocolates. Much amused, we bought dozens of them for Christmas presents but then decided they would mean little outside the family and ate the chocolate ourselves before it went stale.

He is almost glamorous in the carefully posed images modelling men's coats for Burton, which show him slightly turned, looking back over his shoulder. He is reassuringly domestic mowing the lawn and drinking tea with Mum in an *OK*-style 'Day at Home with Eddie Hapgood' spread in the *Illustrated News*. Public interest encouraged journalists to keep the spotlight on the man as well as the footballer; his achievements and his demeanour seemed to give people inspiration in the troubled mood of the times. Proud and delighted, he surfed it all in a light-hearted spirit, full of laughter, spinning everything into material for the stories he would tell his children. Tom Finney was to write later, 'Footballers may not have been celebrities back then, but they were heroes.' Eddie succeeded in being both.

The season began with Arsenal defeating Wolverhampton Wanderers 5-0; an excellent start. Alex James, recently retired, wrote, 'By 1937 nothing had changed. Arsenal's defence, as a whole, was so good – and Hapgood is the coolest of them all so Joe Hulme and Jackie Milne are able to focus on going forward because Hapgood is always protecting their backs.' Away to Chelsea in October, for a 2-2 draw, 'Too much work was thrown on Hapgood, Compton and Roberts. They came out with flying colours. Hapgood is the finest left-back in England at present beyond the shadow of doubt!' In November, Grimsby defeated Arsenal because the strikers were leaving too much to the defence, 'Every time Grimsby pushed the ball down the middle either Compton or Hapgood was forced to act as a cover for Joy.' Charlie Buchan, whose great career with both Arsenal and Newcastle was now over, wrote about 'The Decline of Arsenal' and noted, 'Both Hapgood and Compton played powerfully at the back and it was well for Arsenal that those two … were in great form.'

By the turn of the year, Arsenal had played 22 matches, winning ten, losing seven and drawing five, with 41 goals for and 26 against. After a blistering start to the season, they were rapidly losing ground. By the end of February, after a dismal 0-0 draw away to Portsmouth, the pundits decided that Arsenal had blown it. 'And we all kind of sniffed and snorted about Arsenal's championship possibilities because as they played at Portsmouth, this Arsenal side looks as much like a title-winning team as I look like one of the seven dwarfs,' was one colourful analogy. By April 1938, defensive strength and attacking weakness prompted the familiar old question. No team could win a championship by preventing the opposition from scoring goals while scoring very few themselves. Could they? After another dreary 0-0 display against Birmingham at home on 16 April and with the title now heavily contested, a frustrated journalist complained, 'If the Arsenal do get away with this championship, special medals should be struck for Hapgood, Male, Bernard Joy and Copping.' The tension mounted for the penultimate match of the season against Liverpool at Highbury. Somehow or other Arsenal scraped a 1-0 win, earning the headline 'Swindin, Hapgood Save Arsenal' as 'once again the spotlight falls on that indomitable, highly skilled organisation – the Arsenal defence' by keeping out a relentless and brilliant Liverpool attack against the odds.

Incredibly, as if living a dream of success, Arsenal did win the league title that season with Eddie, their longest-serving player, now formally named their captain. They clinched the championship with a magnificent and conclusive 5-0 win over Bolton Wanderers on 7 May in what turned out to be an extraordinary climax on the final day of a very difficult season. The race could hardly have been more evenly balanced. Arsenal were one point behind Wolves who, despite their trouncing at Arsenal's hands on the first day of the season, had somehow caught up and overtaken them. For Arsenal to win the title, they had to beat Bolton at home and Wolves had to lose to Sunderland away.

The Wolves match had kicked off about ten minutes earlier than Arsenal's. With no mobile phones to update the crowd, 'On the strike of five o'clock, when there were seven minutes to go and Arsenal were leading by 4-0, a man dashed out to the results board at Highbury with two white-numbered squares under his arm.' It had finished Sunderland 1 Wolves 0 and Arsenal had won the league for the fifth time in eight years. The crowd roared their excitement. Bernard Joy recalled years later that he had spun round to share his delight with Eddie only to find him still focused on the game, unaware of the noise around him or of the now clearly signed scoreboard. '"They've lost, Eddie!" I shouted to Eddie Hapgood. So intent was he on the game – one of the marks of his greatness – that he did not realise what I meant for a moment or so!' But, as Eddie knew, there was still time to net another goal, and it finished 5-0. The match you are playing is the one that matters.

This triumphant match, which crowned Eddie's comeback and his Arsenal captaincy, was also a moment of glory for another Eddie, 21-year-old Edward Carr, who had scored the final two goals against Bolton and sent the crowd into rapturous demands to celebrate him. Fans, wrapped in red and white and delirious with excitement, broke police cordons and milled across the pitch as the chants of 'We want Carr' grew louder. Finally, to avoid crowd trouble and to celebrate the youngster's brilliance, Eddie made a decision. If the crowd wanted Carr then they should have him, and he duly appeared with his captain in the directors' box. For several minutes the two players were cheered continuously. Sadly, in one of those too frequent football tragedies, Eddie Carr played only one more game for Arsenal. At the beginning of the following season he suffered a serious knee injury.

For the older Eddie, the season had demanded the very best of him. Perhaps it was because he had overcome his own struggles and disappointments or because of the harshness of the criticisms some of his team-mates suffered throughout the season that as defender and captain he rose to the occasion. The 1937/38 season gave his particular range of skills and his particular personality at the peak of his footballing maturity a glorious, retrospective showcase as the 1930s drew to a close. 'Well,' the *Daily Herald* concluded, agreeing with everything that every other paper was writing, 'we must hand it to Arsenal!'

I never watched Dad play but I shared the vibrancy and urgency of these match-by-match moments as the 1937/38 season built to its climax, while working in an office deep in the Arsenal Museum behind, bewilderingly, a life-size photographic image of my father. He is standing composed, arms folded, with a slight smile. The background, the skin of his face and arms, his hair are washed in red, testament to a man red to the core. The whiteness of his collar, sleeves, badge and shorts glow as if under an infra-red lamp. The image is part of the museum's display, but unnoticed, to the left of his waist and at my shoulder level, is a Yale lock. When I insert the key and push the door open, it is an eerie moment. I feel as if I am entering my father's consciousness, experiencing an intense and immediate encounter with the past that has so significantly shaped my siblings' and my own present. The piercing recordings of radio and television commentators of the past, the sudden roar of the crowds and the voices of visitors that resonate round the museum echo through the door and embrace me in the reality of a football match.

Behind that door I also discovered the circle of his career. Back in 1930, Dad's 'artistic football' had caught people's attention. Now, in 2014, I read a handwritten note under a photograph taken on 11 December 1937 when Arsenal defeated Preston North End 2-0 at home. It wasn't taken by a press photographer but by a freelance journalist and fervent young Arsenal supporter, Harry Homer, an Oxford graduate who had attached himself firmly to the team and kept informal records throughout the decade. It cleverly captures the exact moment when the ball moves smoothly, without tackle or shoulder charge, from Bud Maxwell's foot as he races towards goal to Dad's foot as he changes the swerve of the ball; from the foot of a prolific goalscorer to the foot of a defender. This is the picture of a complete player in action. Underneath, handwritten in red ink, are Homer's notes:

'Eddie Hapgood (surely the peerless back of my generation? Ed.) takes the ball from Maxwell's toe in typical style. Note perfect balance and how he shields the ball which seems glued to his boot with his body.'

I have never seen Brazilian forward Neymar play either but a casual glimpse of him on television one night caught an extraordinary moment that might have been an illusion. Neymar wasn't collecting the ball; the ball was following him! I think that is what Homer meant when he chose the word 'glued' to capture the magnetic relationship between Dad's foot and the ball. Even more astonishing is an account by Henry Rose, the editor of the *Northern Sports*, who, rather than celebrating Liverpool's 2-0 defeat of Arsenal on 18 December as readers must have expected, headlined his article 'Hapgood Fills the Gap'. He vividly evokes what spectators and fans countrywide had come to expect and enjoy about Dad's game, 'This game will be remembered … as Eddie Hapgood's match. He played a captain's part in real schoolboy-thriller style. After saving a certain goal, which would have made it 3-0, by kicking off the line, he scrambled into goalkeeper Boulton's jersey to keep an heroic goal.'

As I read and make notes about a time before I was born, I become totally partisan, red in blood and brain, a complete Arsenal fan. The photographs, black and white and often shrouded in the gloom of bad weather or blurred by deterioration, show the faces of Dad's friends and team-mates that have grown familiar. I find myself delighting in journalists' praise, angered by their criticisms, despairing about defeats and elated by victories however 'undeserved' or 'boring'. I wait in suspense for the outcome of this tightly fought season as I turn the pages and read the yellowing cuttings. Although I know the ending, like the best of dramas, I am not convinced it will all turn out as I expect and hope. As I turn the final page and read the account of the last match, I hold my breath. Arsenal with 50 points must beat Bolton to win the title, but that is not all; Wolverhampton Wanderers with 51 points must lose. Yes, yes, I know that, but suddenly I have forgotten what happened. Deep in the museum where the spirit of Arsenal is kept alive, I go limp with relief and joy as I close the album and recorded cheers of the crowd from the museum penetrate the office wall. This was footballing history through total immersion. For a flash of time, I had watched the great Arsenal team of the 1930s play.

In fact, the 1937/38 season was not Eddie's last. 'Let us introduce another football season,' announced the *Illustrated Magazine* in August 1939, 'by paying homage to a king among players, Eddie Hapgood, Arsenal and England soccer captain.' 'Hapgood Starts His 12th Season with Arsenal' headlined another article covering every aspect of his career for Arsenal and England, describing yet again the uniqueness of his playing style, the old stories of his early frailty, his personal conduct on and off the pitch and the ordered domestic life that seemed to fascinate his fans in its contrast with the flamboyant presence on the pitch. A subheading 'The Hapgoods in Happy Mood' runs underneath a photograph, not of Eddie in action, but Eddie in a suit with Maggie and Tony, followed by the comment, 'To meet him off the field it would be a long time before one reached "professional footballer" in hazarding a guess at his occupation.' In those days, such a comment was intended as a compliment. A working-class footballer had not only defeated time, it seemed as if he had broken the hardest manacles of all, those of class, to become a 'gentleman'.

And there has to be one more, very particular photo 'to kick off the season'. It is necessary, essential. Before the stadium was flooded with fans and officials, with workmen and stewards who tidied, sorted and organised in readiness for the season, a few press photographers made yet another attempt to freeze in time the unique characteristics of Eddie's 'kick'. One journalist had already summed up what he often witnessed and what many journalists before him had tried to describe since 1930, 'Just as the referee lifts the whistle to his lips to blow for a goal a foot shoots out from nowhere, the ball is kicked away, a goal is saved. It is a hundred to one that foot belongs to Edris Albert Hapgood, captain of Arsenal and England known to thousands of soccer followers as "Good old Eddie". Those goal-line saves have become famous the world over where football language is talked … None of those little tricks which form part of some footballers' make-up find a place in Hapgood's play. He knows the game; he plays the game.'

Now Eddie, mounted on a specially constructed four-foot high dais, joins in the fun performing a series of kicks while photographers, crouched on the pitch, position their cameras upwards and attempt to reveal the secret of the 'polished technique' of the man whose 'kick goes around the world'. I have never read anything that claims they succeeded!

On 27 August, when Eddie led Arsenal out against Portsmouth to begin the 1938/1939 season, it really seemed as if Herbert Chapman's ambition had been realised. Strangely, the long roll call of great players from 1927–37 did seem to have metamorphosed into a single identity – Arsenal of the 1930s. There was that same shimmering mirage – that apparently time-defying Arsenal team. He was followed by revered veterans and great friends George Male, Jack Crayston, Wilf Copping, Ted Drake and Cliff Bastin. However, when Eddie led the Arsenal team out nine months later for the last match of the season, on 6 May 1939, he was the only player on the pitch who had played continuously throughout the decade. His permanence and the total merging of his identity with Arsenal's, was so astonishing that the *Daily Herald* joked that prising Hapgood from Arsenal was impossible despite the rumour, 'Newcastle had offered the Tyne Bridge for Eddie Hapgood.'

Bastin was still available but plagued again by loss of form, scoring only three goals in that season. Male was available too but had lost his place to Leslie Compton and unlike Eddie during his own unhappy period in late 1936, he had not regained it. Eddie and Compton had created a new partnership which gave 'just about the most impudent exhibition of an "attacking full-back" game I have ever seen' gushed one pundit about a convincing demolition of Stoke City in December. Compton himself had finally found himself a place in the Arsenal sunshine but for this historic match, the last of the last full professional season until 1946, he was injured. But Eddie was still there. Yet again, journalists did their best to sum up what was unique about him for the posterity they all knew was just around the corner, to define the personality that had somehow become more than a sum of successful football matches and architect of many thrilling moments of sumptuous football. Their match accounts read like attempts to encapsulate a total experience. It was, after all, the end of a decade.

By 15 April 1939, there was just a sliver of time before the final league fixtures to fit in a return match against Scotland. 'Eddie Hapgood ... to captain England – a noble and well-deserved tribute to the greatest full-back in the game,' wrote one newspaper. Three weeks before the end of the season, on a train to Glasgow, the England squad, spread out in friendly groups of twos and threes across the carriages, was given no peace. Eddie, charged with excitement and determination, patrolled the corridor and dropped in on them to discuss tactics, to share ideas, to swap opinions. He had no sooner left them to subside back into their seats and relax than he was there again, whipping them up into a frenzy of energy. 'It was obvious Eddie had made up his mind we weren't going to lose and when Eddie was in that sort of mood, it was infectious,' Stanley Matthews commented later.

It was in this hyper-charged state of mind that England met Scotland, the 'auld enemy', and defeated them for the first time in 12 years on Scottish soil. For Eddie it was a victory so sublime that the remainder of his season felt like walking on water. 'I have realised my last ambition,' he told reporters interviewing him after the match. For all the glamour of Eddie's international career, the tingling excitement of playing continental teams, the political and cultural intrigue, England always carried abroad with them an assumption of footballing superiority. Until after the war, the games against Wales and the Republic of Ireland, but more so the games against Scotland, were the truly significant dates in the English football calendar. It was a competition and England had to win.

By all accounts the noise at Hampden Park was 'terrific ; awe-inspiring', building to 'a shrieking crescendo' and dying in a 'weird wail'. Have you ever been part of a thunderous noise that surges unbidden and instantaneous until you are not you but part of everyone tossed in a vibrating clamorous force that crashes down into the bowl of the pitch striking concrete steps, barriers and turf before reverberating upwards to the sky? That was what Eddie heard, week in, week out for 12 years of playing football. From the torrid heat bowls of Rome and Yugoslavia, from the surging stands of Wembley, from the mud-bound, ice-bound glory of winter matches at Highbury where the crowd was within touching distance, he and his team-mates played every game inside the cacophony of an ear-splitting dissonance. But nothing equalled the Hampden roar, the roar that defies description, the roar from 150,000 (some say 175,000) throats. Hard as it is to believe, Dad always claimed that when he was on the pitch he heard nothing, not the roar, not the cheers, not the comments of fans hanging over the barriers to give instructions, to encourage, to criticise, not even the ecstasy of the crowd shouting 'Match over!' on the magical May day the previous summer when Arsenal won the First Division title. There was only one thing to do on the pitch –

play. Certainly, Matthews's comment in his account of the match, 'Here is Hapgood, unperturbable and a real captain,' confirms his point.

On the other hand, journalists – the radio, television, Sky pundits, YouTube, video artists of their time – vied with each other to escalate the drama of the occasion:

'The pitiless, driving rain from a dour sky soaked through the players' bedraggled kit and stabbed the turf like long, silver swords. A high wind blew the rain into the faces so they could hardly see. The Scots, exhausted by the fierce concentration of the Anglo-Saxons on the cut-up, mud-bound pitch, frustrated by Stanley Matthew's teasing super-brilliance and baffled by Joe Mercer's mastery, pulled a last desperate effort from their tired legs to try and prevent, in the final minute, Beasley's winning goal.'

The strikers had scored the goals but Tommy Lawton gave credit to the massive impact of the defence, 'Behind us, Eddie Hapgood and co. had broken the hearts of the Scots forwards with their relentless tackling.' And then as the journalists phoned their copy back to their offices, they had to find words to describe the England captain's uncharacteristic behaviour. He 'flung his arms in the air as the whistle blew', was 'exploding with delight', 'he danced a joy-jig in the mud', 'he embraced every English player within reach', and 'danced his way to the dressing room like a ballerina making a triumphant exit from a highly dramatic scene'! 'I mean it,' Eddie said to a journalist interviewing him through the train door window at Glasgow station as the train for London let off steam and prepared to depart, 'It's quite the biggest thing that has happened to me on the football field. Did I dance when we got that winner? What would you expect and what would you have done? I was tickled to death. That's been said before, but I was.' Another journalist was intrigued that Eddie's unrestrained expression of 'joy and satisfaction struck a new note in English football', inspiring 11 men, from eight different clubs, to become a team, throwing their arms around each other in triumph and delight. Looking back, Dad would smile and say, 'But, oh, we were so happy!'

As the long, anxiety-ridden 1930s lurched their way to the final crisis, and history-laden football matches ticked off the weeks towards inevitable hostilities, war fever seemed mysteriously to melt away; an 'Edwardian summer' as they said about the time before World War I. When Prime Minister Neville Chamberlain had flown into London from Munich a few months after the Germany v England match waving a piece of paper at the waiting crowds and declaring 'peace for our time', nobody had believed him but desperate hope alchemised doubt to certainty. There was not going to be war.

Extraordinarily, on 8 May 1939, the England team sailed again to Europe. Somehow released from political constraints, the best of football's talent watched by fans revelling in the fun of it all, reclaimed their sport and wove, for a fleeting three weeks, a magic spell over an unhappy continent. Somehow, impossibly, buoyed up by false belief, it turned out to be the most triumphant and joyous tour Eddie had ever participated in. He never forgot it. He knew that this tour was probably a personal last hurrah, a time above all else to be enjoyed, that the scheduled fixtures, even the first against Italy, were to be football matches and not political manoeuvres. There was no need for that now.

Interviewed by the press who were waiting when the squad arrived in Milan, he spoke with heartfelt sincerity, 'We are out to win – but not at all costs.' The Italians agreed. Like the British, they had convinced themselves that Mussolini would stay clear of Hitler and war would be avoided. In this delusory armistice football was even, oddly, allowed moments of nostalgia. Only two players remained of the Italian team England had played in 1934. One was Giuseppe Meazza, the striker whose last-minute effort on England's goal in the 'Battle of Highbury' had been cleared by Eddie, his nose heavily strapped with plasters all those years ago (or so it seemed). Now the two captains shook hands before facing each other for the toss on a pitch as sodden with recent thunderstorms as Highbury's had been in 1934. There is no record of the post-match banquet and Dad never gave us an account. I would love to know what they said to each other about their previous meeting, perhaps something as diplomatically dismissive as, 'That's football!' To most British journalists watching the match, remembering the 'Battle of Highbury' was less interesting than to comment that it is a 'source of wonder how Eddie keeps going on such a high note year in and year out'. Reporter Clifford Webb, sitting in the stands surrounded by thousands of Italian fans and in the heat of an international game was struck by a more personal memory, 'an odd thought' that united Eddie the player with Webb the journalist as fellow Bristolians:

'Above the din I hear the shout of Eddie Hapgood, England's skipper … Eddie, with an accent that pulls me back with a jolt to schooldays in Bristol, is urging his side on with the old Hapgood war-cry – "Come on; get up there; come on."'

The weather changed as they crossed the border into Yugoslavia where the heavy rain followed by intense heat had left the atmosphere swelteringly oppressive and swelled the pitch into a terrain of miniature mountains. Some players, still recovering from the long train journey to Italy and the demands of the following match, were 'languid and lackadaisical'. The opposition took full advantage, throwing themselves forward in the hope of a victory. The Yugoslavian centre-forward Aleksandar Petrović went in for a heavy tackle, bringing Eddie down and landing clumsily on his ankle. In considerable pain, Eddie somehow finished the game but he was not able to play against Romania in the last leg of the tour. For once, not even that could shake his serenity. He relaxed, happily watching his old friend George Male get his first game of the tour, Stan Cullis do an admirable job as captain and cheering as Don Welsh and Len Goulden buried two goals to win. Even so, according to Tommy Lawton, Eddie had given his signature team talk before the match, 'Our captain, and one of the best I assure you, got the boys together ... and we had a little pep talk,' while Joe Mercer, not surprisingly, commented that it couldn't have been easy for Cullis to follow Hapgood as captain but both 'were men on whom captaincy sat naturally'.

For the first 18 years of his life Eddie had rarely left Bristol's city boundaries. In 1933, after his first visit to Rome, he played in Milan, Belgrade, Holland, Zurich, Vienna, Venice, Berlin, Sweden, Norway, Finland and Paris. Now wherever they travel he and his team-mates are treated like royalty, or, more appropriately, as ambassadors of the greatest footballing nation on earth, of, indeed, the greatest nation of the Western world. Or that is what it feels like.

In Italy they are followed everywhere by flowers. In Milan they are mobbed for autographs. Incredibly, Eddie is asked to lay a wreath on the Cenotaph in a moving gesture of cultural reconciliation. In Rome he meets Benito Mussolini again, and accepted an invitation to an audience with Pope Pius XI, although with little enthusiasm, he told us later. ('How many people have kissed his ring before me?' he asked, rolling his eyes.) Although it is only dawn when their train arrives in Belgrade the station is decorated with flowers and hundreds of fans have gathered. The officials are so overcome by their arrival that Eddie has to make an impromptu speech telling the crowds how privileged they are to have been invited to play there before they will disperse. The crowd is so dense he becomes separated from the England party but is safely carried to his hotel by the happy swell which knows exactly where they are staying.

At Turnu-Severin in Romania they are again met at the station with crowds carrying flowers and flags and two bands for volume playing 'God Save the King', but not quite in time with each other. It was the Romanians, Eddie always claimed, who gave him the title of his autobiography, *Football Ambassador*, for it was the reception of the Romanian fans and their officials that had filled the English players with pride, surprise and delight and the Romanian press which hailed the England players as 'ambassadors from the land of the birth of the football game'. At Bucharest station the British anthem rings out again as the band plays 'God Save the King' several times without stopping. His hotel suite is again heaped with masses of flowers so he feels as he said himself 'like a monarch'.

Wherever and whenever they travelled they are received by the resident British ambassador and family over tea, over dinner. They are accompanied on tourist trips down the Danube, to Zurich's fairy palaces and Zoological Gardens, on gondola rides in Venice, to the vineyards on the slopes of Oplenae and even to the dramatic modern oil fields of Prahavo Valley. Nothing is too much trouble to please these heroes and everything is wonderful to the Bristol man who 'probably never would have seen these sights, had I not been able to kick a football'.

They can't resist going to the circus in Romania or daring each other to buy expensive lingerie for their wives in Budapest's sophisticated shops. Like thoughtless schoolboys, they stage a chariot race in Rome and they gaze in bewildered wonder at elegant monuments as if they have stumbled on the secret of time travel. The foreign press has always praised them unstintingly. In the Austria v England match programme in 1936, despite England's defeat, Eddie is singled out as a player who, in a fantastical translation, is 'exceedingly sympathetic, full of heart and fair'. The Switzerland v England match programme in 1938 congratulates Eddie and Cliff Bastin because they '*spielten schon vor fünf Jahren gegen Schweiz*' (played so beautifully for five years against the Swiss – beating them every time). For Eddie, touring with Arsenal and England over the years has been like touring with family. On this tour he is travelling with the team that had shared the victory over Scotland just a month before. Joe Mercer, Tommy Lawton, Stan Matthews, Stan Cullis, names that will be the great names of football's history, are all there with him, young, revelling and still silly with euphoria. And there were wonderful absurdities for him to recount and to laugh over.

According to Mercer there really was a film star moment when Eddie was persuaded to meet an agent of Metro-Goldwyn-Mayer to consider a role in films, a fact corroborated by George Male who many years later also remembered that Eddie was 'even considered a possible film star'. Perhaps he is a footballer; perhaps he is England's captain; perhaps he has glimpsed the true political power of football; perhaps he is just having fun. Time occasionally fingers the edge of their consciousness. Mussolini still in Rome; Hitler in Berlin; the troubled mid-European countries bounded by the might of Germany and Russia. When they begin the long journey home on 26 May, there are only three short months before Britain declares war on Germany.

Between 19 November 1927 and 2 September 1939, Eddie lived a time-bound, but timeless 12 years. He still 'tied his bootlaces with as much gusto as when fame first beckoned him', and was still as enthusiastic to win magnificently as he had ever been. He now knew how much Arsenal and England needed him. Although in his head there are dates, there is no chronology; there are record-breaking footballing events as highly coloured and fantastical as any *Roy of the Rovers* comic, but there are weeks, months and years of hard graft too.

Now he is back, no one wants to let him go again. He is lavished with gifts by the clubs and countries he visited; we children carry their history with us. We still have the tartan car rug, the silver cigarette box lined with delicious smelling sandalwood which perfumes the air when we open it, cut-glass water jug and tumblers, a set of ivory handle fish knives, an elegant canteen of cutlery. In my garden shed, there is still a set of garden tools with smooth ash handles and loops of leather for hanging up. They are isolated fragments which, like archaeological remains, serve to hint at past glories.

Children and their fathers wrote in for autographs. Fans wrote letters and posted them with just his name on, as if he was Father Christmas. One of his favourites was addressed to 'Herr Hapgood, Beroffussballspielfuhrer, England, London', which landed promptly at Arsenal. There were many poems of appreciation in 'Up and Play the Game' spirit. Newspapers wrote about him and invited him to write for them. He did, my mother told me wryly, receive many offers of marriage.

People hoping to bask in Arsenal's glory seek him out. Hangers-on proliferated. More than ever before, people clamour to meet him; places at home and abroad welcome him; journalists home and abroad celebrate him. Cigarette cards are tucked into the packs of major brands and numerous cartoons have fun with his thick wiry hair, slight body and skinny knees. He jokes with journalists about his age. 'Not bad for an old one,' he says.

Among all the noise and razzmatazz, he is bemused and troubled by meanness of spirit. He is taken aback to hear that the house in Hutton Grove had been burgled while the family was on holiday and his medals stolen. 'I'm afraid you won't get them back, Mr Hapgood,' said the policeman in charge of the inquiry. 'They'll be melted down by now.' 'Why steal medals you haven't won?' he wondered aloud. On the other hand, he remembers loyalty. He is moved to hear that over 200 supporters travelled from Bristol to watch Arsenal and 'Eddie Hapgood in particular' play against Birmingham in the chilly days of January 1939. 'You see,' said one of them, 'Eddie is Bristol bred and born and we consider him just the finest player the city has produced.' He is touched to read a tribute from Kettering, his first club, 'Rousing cheers from the Poppies!' He confides in a journalist, 'I somehow feel I am playing better than ever.' Perhaps he was, his sense of fulfilment creating a serene confidence, his maturity lending a new vitality and measured sophistication to his play. The young Len Shackleton, joining the Arsenal ground staff in 1938, names Eddie as his 'favourite … his confidence affected everything he did, and it spread through any team in which he played'. Certainly, the familiar compliments, written, read and repeated so often, seemed to suggest that there would be more to come.

Much of what was to be the last heady summer of peacetime was spent making a film. The experience seems to have been full of fun. This was one Arsenal story that Dad told again and again. The popular author Leonard Gribble had recently published *The Arsenal Stadium Mystery*. The rights were instantly obtained and filming began immediately after the end of the season, the first feature film where football is a central element in the plot. Of course, Gribble had selected Arsenal; conveniently located in London and the dominant team in English football, it was the perfect choice. The opening sequences were filmed at Highbury where the crime is discovered and so *The Arsenal Stadium Mystery* was created. It was not unusual for Highbury to be used as a location. In the summer of 1937 the BBC had used Arsenal to stage a practice match to test television outdoor filming techniques. Cliff and Eddie had already starred in a film as far back as 1932, at least their legs had. In the action sequences of a comedy about a professional footballer, much to their amusement, Cliff played the striker's legs and Eddie played the defender's. They had shared a few happy, idle weeks that summer, loafing around the set watching the filming and waiting to be called.

The Arsenal Stadium Mystery was a bigger project altogether and the players selected to appear earned £50 a week. They watched it later in a private showing but not until after war had been declared. It was a box office success and still pops up today in the listings of TCM or Sky Movies. Its popularity was such that a contemporary review suggested provocatively that it 'would increase Arsenal's unpopularity'! The football-playing sequences were filmed during an actual match which Arsenal won 2-0. Dad's great acting opportunity, staged later in studio conditions, involved running off the pitch into the dressing room and discovering the dead body. Well, I have no idea how many takes there were in reality before the director was happy, but Dad's accounts increased them steadily with every telling, with every performance. Apparently, instead of looking surprised, shocked or horrified on seeing the body as he had rehearsed, he burst out laughing, and then, of course, could not be serious for subsequent takes, laughter breaking through again before even reaching the dressing room. And on that hilarious note, the final game of football in the last full season played at Highbury before the war was captured on film.

That summer of 1939 was radiant for Mum and Dad with an almost painful happiness. Through those dramatically satisfying weeks and months when he was constantly in the searchlight of publicity, they had both held close the fact that Mum was pregnant. Hobbled by the injury he had got against Yugoslavia, Dad was unable to join the Arsenal club tour of Sweden. Once he was back from the international tour, he and Mum had the whole summer together. August 1939 would witness another football season begin, summer would drift into autumn and in September the baby was due.

> The falling leaves drift by my window
> The falling leaves of red and gold
> I see your lips, the summer kisses
> The sunburned hands I used to hold
>
> Since you went away the days grow long
> And soon I'll hear old winter's song
> But I miss you most of all, my darling
> When autumn leaves start to fall

It is not surprising that this song threaded its notes and words though our family memories. Our parents' happiness was written in its melody. Driving home to Bath from the occasional day out, the evening growing darker, Margot, Mike and I, free of seat belts, would be wound around one another in the back seat of the car, more asleep than awake drifting on the soft voices of our parents as they talked to one another so very far away in the front seats.

And then one or other would start singing, their voices would merge and we knew that absolutely everything was alright, and we could let go. Falling leaves ... days grow long ... start to fall ... autumn leaves ... my darling. Very few publicity photos I know capture the loving gaiety of the father I remember, the family man we children knew so well. Football enthusiasts were quicker to appreciate 'the grim-faced hard-kicking skipper' who rallied his team to score the equalising goal in front of 50,000 shrieking Italian football enthusiasts in Milan in early summer 1939.

* * *

On 3 September 1939 the nation, warned about an important announcement to be made by the Prime Minister, one they already knew the content of, obediently clustered around and switched their radios on. This was a war that no ordinary person wanted. Some men who had fought in World War I were still young enough for active duty. Everyone had family or friends who had suffered untold physical or psychological damage, their silence more potent than any words. Many who escaped death fighting in 'the war to end wars' faced unemployment and poverty, malnutrition and illness when they returned home.

Dad had grown up in a Bristol community torn apart by the aftermath of the war. The spirit of the country, if not its political energy, had resisted the encroaching horror as much as it could by denying it. The majority of the populace wanted peace; they were exhausted and yearned for the glorious ordinariness of a home, a job and football on a Saturday afternoon. From the national mood for pacifism gifting Stanley Baldwin a landslide victory in 1935 for declaring 'no rearmament' to Neville Chamberlain's hopeful but misguided declaration of peace in 1938, the inattentiveness and incompetence of consecutive governments had allowed a nation to crash into a brick wall and was now about to ask its people to fight and smile.

Mum, heavily pregnant with a daughter who would be born two weeks later, sat rigid with helplessness in front of the splendid radio that had so recently been displayed to a curious public in a popular magazine. Dad held her hand, blank with the impossibility of knowing anything. Mum's sister Liz, an hour's train journey away in Kettering, whose husband Mark had survived four years on the Western Front, sank to the floor. 'Not again!', her cries reverberating across the country.

A year later, Bristol was bombarded by six months of constant and heavy incendiary bomb attacks which thundered over the docks, the Dings and Barton Hill. For many, many individuals, for Dad and Mum, everything that had gone before was erased leaving charred and confused fragments that would be gathered up some six years later, peered at uncomprehendingly and labelled 'memories'. One of these was a yellowing page from the *Liverpool Echo* written the day before war was declared as if no one had got around to telling the writer not to bother and found crumpled years later at the bottom of a suitcase, 'And then there's Eddie Hapgood ... a quiet-spoken and gentlemanly-mannered player, but withal a leader who could encourage his team-mates to rise to their greatest heights.'

10

War-Torn Lives

After that, everything happened at once or perhaps afterwards; it was hard to remember exactly. It was a strange time of exhausting practical action and mental paralysis. After all, only a week before, on 26 August, Eddie had led the Arsenal team out at Wolverhampton Wanderers to start the 1939/40 season. On 30 August, they defeated the newly promoted Blackburn Rovers at home 1-0 and on Saturday, 2 September Sunderland were trounced in front of the Highbury crowd with a triumphant 5-2 scoreline. Everything was the same, wasn't it? And why wouldn't it always be?

Luxuriating in the heat of that glorious summer, Eddie and Maggie had already begun preparing to go to Kettering for the birth of their second child a month before war was formally announced. Their intention had been to travel before the season began so that Eddie would have time to help them settle and Maggie would have some time to rest. The lawn had been mown, more than once, the grass cuttings tidied, the house cleaned. Maggie's hospital bag had been packed sometime previously, her pre-pregnancy clothes washed and hanging in the wardrobe for later. During July and August the small bedroom at the back of the house had been made ready for its new occupant. Tony's clothes were packed in his own small case with his toys, cricket and football equipment. He was buzzing with excitement about missing the first two weeks of school, looking forward to a visit to his cousins and ever-indulgent aunts and uncles, full of anticipation about the arrival of his new sister or brother. As war rumours rushed backwards and forwards, they lingered, uncertain. Then Germany invaded Poland on 1 September. Knowing war might be only hours away, the car was hastily packed, the house at Hutton Grove locked up and the neighbours informed.

Was it on 5 September that Eddie drove Mum and Tony to Kettering to stay with her sister Alice before racing back to Highbury for training? He didn't want to leave them. He was suddenly unsettled by the brief glimpse he caught of them waving him off as he turned left out of the end of the street and was shocked to have to close his eyes for a moment against tears. It was getting dark. Had blackout for road travel been introduced so soon, he asked himself? Tired and emotional, he struggled through the thickening darkness towards High Barnet, driving slowly with dipped headlights. Somehow he had forgotten to buy slotted covers to darken the headlights but, he said to himself, 'I only have to make it to East Finchley.' And, as he had often joked, 'You can almost draw a ruler line from Kettering to home.' He made a mental note to confirm he could leave his car at the Arsenal ground for the duration of the war.

It is no surprise that he was completely disorientated. The day before, not knowing what else to do, Eddie had reported for work as usual, homing like a lost bird for a place of safety. He had driven in with the intention of storing the car in the large stadium garage and taking the overground home so he hardly heard the noise until he switched the engine off. Construction workers were already transforming Highbury at high speed from a football club into an Air Raid Precaution (ARP) base. The shock as he tried to absorb what he was seeing and to piece together its significance was swept away by a profound sense of injustice juddering through his body.

So much for 'peace for our time'. So much for years spent pandering to politicians. So much for the summers spent playing football matches against young men who, presumably, were now their declared enemies. So much for the English national team playing in support of international peace.

What sense could be made of all the happiness, the camaraderie, the fun and laughter as they had mingled with players and fans of so many nations? He looked around as some of his team-mates slowly gathered together, heads down, as shocked as he. While all the diplomatic games were being played, he and his team-mates had been deceived, praised for their 'patriotism' but left entirely unprepared for what was to come. Not so long before, he had been inspired, called to action, by the noise of the crowd reverberating around the stadium. Now the sounds of heavy machinery and the shouts of workmen seemed to assault him. Even as he watched, physically incapable of moving away, his home, his anchor was demolished in front of him, the pitch torn apart. It felt like a kind of savage surgery on his own body, his very identity being carelessly excavated and tossed aside.

The government had already ordered that all sports stadia be closed immediately and sports meetings suspended for public safety until further notice. More information was given out to them later that day. Players would be registered with their clubs until further notice but wages would be paid only until the following day, 6 September. They were being sacked! No warning and then, no money coming in, although most Arsenal players would be temporarily recruited into the ARP until their future postings were decided.

Everything Eddie heard seemed strangely irrelevant. What could he do other than play football? What *would* he do other than play football? George Male remembered it as a time of acute anxiety about the future, about money, about families, about careers abruptly ending. A few, while knowing as little, had been more pragmatic. Eddie suddenly remembered how dismissive he had been when Wilf Copping had decided to terminate his career at Arsenal several months previously and return north to his extended family in Leeds with his wife and children. That was way back in March, while Eddie was still absorbed in a late-season struggle and the anticipation of a summer international tour. But perhaps Wilf was unusual.

For a moment, before the players scattered to discuss what to do with their families, to look for work, most of them were disorientated by the personal tragedy of what was happening. Although no one could claim immunity against misfortune in those desperate, unhappy times, it is poignant to visualise Ted

Drake, who slammed home four goals in Arsenal's last three matches of the club's 'Golden Age', gathering his belongings and hastily arranging a job as a night watchman to make ends meet between the stoppage of wages and whatever he might earn when his call-up notice came. 'Who am I now?' was a question they all had to wrestle with.

For a brief time, the press carried their football obsessions into wartime, announcing Eddie's call-up to the Police Reserve Unit in October and noting the destinations of different famous players. But their concerns now lay elsewhere. 'The bonds of sport will survive,' thundered L.V. Manning in the *Daily Herald* on 4 September. 'An indestructible force Hitler never understood. The footballer hangs up his boots, and shoulders his rifle. He stands four square with every other sportsman in the nation with a single purpose.' The spirit of the article is patriotic and intended to inspire but its content was to be proved comprehensively wrong. The ban on public gatherings was quickly reversed and football's essential role as national entertainment important for troops and civilians alike was reasserted. New regional leagues were organised. The FA amended rules for the retention and loan of players to ensure an organised match could somehow, anyhow, somewhere field 22 men. In effect, footballers became home-front soldiers.

What was certain was that the footballer didn't, as far as was humanly possible, 'hang up his boots' but desperately struggled to maintain his skills, his fitness and his future wherever he was and whatever his war task, in the hope of retaining his contract at his former club or finding a new home elsewhere or simply retaining a connection with who he was. As public concerns shifted and paper supplies dwindled, press coverage was reduced to official announcements of the international programme, records of matches played and goals scored in the new regional leagues, the successes of charity matches in raising war funds. The glory days of colourful football match reports, interviews and footballers' photographs, of football gossip, drama and cartoons lighting up readers' breakfast tables were over. The immediacy of men so recently famous began to fade.

With great relief, Mum and Tony returned to London at the beginning of 1940 with Margot now just over three months old. Dad had been able to live at Hutton Grove for the short period he was on full-time ARP duties and waiting for his call-up but it had been difficult to get away for long enough to stay at Kettering with the car now in storage and travel by train increasingly unpredictable. Mum longed for Dad and for the security of her own home. She was also beginning to find living with her sister Alice difficult. It was nine years since she and Dad had arrived in Kettering for Tony's birth. Then she had been fretful waiting for the FA Cup Final to be over but now, looking back, she saw it differently. In 1930 she was young and newly married, secure in her mother's and sisters' support and full of excitement for her first baby. Then, the cheers of the Arsenal victory followed them as they travelled north.

Now things had changed. Her much loved mother and sister Annie were dead. At first Alice, older than Mum by several years, was happy to welcome her but friction had been growing. The noise and energy of a growing lad and the endless routines demanded by a tiny baby disturbed Alice and Dennis's usually peaceful and childless life. Mum, tied down by the long hours of breast feeding, found herself being criticised by silent reproofs for 'doing nothing'. Tony had begun to realise that this visit to Kettering was no holiday after all. Upset by the sudden changes, he missed his mother's attention and his father's presence. He did not even have school to help. As schools and local facilities struggled to cope with the number of children being evacuated from London to the country, most of them alternated morning and afternoon classes. Just nine years old, Tony would not attend a full school day for another three years.

At last Dad got leave to collect his growing family and together they travelled down from Kettering by train to London in total darkness, Mum clutching Margot and Dad holding Tony's hand even as they sat in the carriage. Although the blackout had been initiated before war officially broke out, Mum, witnessing its full impact for the first time, was terrified. Her familiar world had become first anonymous and then invisible as the country, its road, railways and streets, plunged into oblivion, signposts and station names removed.

The house was bitterly cold when they arrived. One of the most severe and unpredictable winters had swept over the country at the end of December bringing chaos to communications and transport, and misery to the men already in uniform waiting in growing tension for German attacks to begin. The weather had eased slightly over Christmas but in February 1940, not long after they returned to Hutton Grove, temperatures plummeted, snow fell in whirling storms and rain turned to ice as it hit frozen pavements.

Fear that Germany would mount a campaign of indiscriminate obliteration with the possible use of gas or chemical weapons had accelerated behind-the-scenes planning and galvanised public protection orders, especially in London which intelligence had suggested would be the first point of attack. Bomb shelters were distributed in IKEA-like flat packs to individual houses in areas thought to be most in danger and made available for everyone to buy. Dad had already begun constructing one in the garden of Hutton Grove, ready for Mum, Tony and Margot. Gas masks and chemical-proof 'baby helmets' were distributed to families. Despite all the information Dad had managed to give Mum, all the in and outs of preparing a safe home for them in London during her time at Kettering, all his attention to detail, nothing had prepared her for the reality of coming home to face life alone in the Blitz with two children.

'I swore I would never put Margot in one of the baby gas pods,' Mum told me she had decided when she first saw the one she had been issued lying on the kitchen table, grotesque and clumsy, with complicated instructions. The opening months of war in Kettering had been calm enough for her to believe this would be possible. Then in September 1940, with Margot nearly a year old, German aeroplanes poured over London for 56 consecutive days and 30 nights with systematic determination and a terrifying confidence they could not be stopped. How many nights Mum retreated into the shelter listening in terror to the sounds of engines barely above her head, feeling the vibrations of bombs falling too near and the dull roar of those falling on what she guessed was central London, she could not remember. She was stunned to the point of paralysis, going through the motions of parenting with no sense of what she was doing. At some point all nights seemed to concentrate into one night when she could no longer endure the terror, the horror of a robot-like baby whose oxygen mask prevented her from being cuddled and comforted, or the rash adventurousness of a young boy who pestered her to open the shelter door so he could watch the fireworks in the sky.

'I can't stay,' she told Dad in tears of desperation when he was able to get a pass out from RAF Cardington in October, 'I simply can't stay.' Mum found it difficult to forget the terror she had endured. She told me the story again and again. She frequently castigated herself for her stupidity. 'One morning,' she told me, 'after the all-clear siren went I was in the garden. My neighbour laughed when I told her what a terrible night it had been. "They were our planes," she told me. "We're beating them back." Everyone else seemed to know, but I couldn't tell one engine from another.'

In fact, Barnet, far out on the fringes of north-west London, was bombed, with 42 bombs dropped on Finchley Church End alone, no more than 20 minutes' walk away from her. By the time Dad was able to get home, Mum had endured the worst of the Blitz but how could they have known that? Responding to her anxieties and with the little time he had, Dad rented a house in Kettering in what he assumed would be a temporary measure. Mum's desperation to leave London and return to her family must have pushed any possible consequences from her head. She didn't look back as the taxi pulled away. Over the next couple of years, there were brief returns to check the house was safe but their longed-for paradise, 37 Hutton Grove, gradually became little more than a property. Mum and Tony never lived there again.

My picture of Mum's war is a scrapbook of fragments, words, phrases, the briefest of recollections. They remained with me over the years because of the intensity of the emotion that prompted them. 'It's not good to be old or poor in a war,' she said, telling me how the butcher greeted her with, 'Good morning Mrs Hapgood,' slicing her ration from the best cuts of meat while she was painfully aware that the gristle that fell under his knife would be ready for the last in the queue. 'They talk about "loss of tonnage",' she told me of merchant and naval disasters, 'so that you don't know the number of men who drowned.' She loathed Winston Churchill. She recognised his bellicose brilliance in conducting the war but that was no compliment. She felt he was brutal, his personality the kind that floated to the top at such times. 'He's nothing when he's not at war,' she said.

Her war was, like many women's, a lonely one. She had found a hermit crab refuge in Kettering but she no longer wanted to be there. She missed my father desperately but saw him as rarely as if he was posted overseas. Once he was called up, all his leave was taken up by playing football. His laughter and energy, his decisiveness had always buoyed her up and the silence of his absence was unbearable. There were times when she regretted leaving London even though she knew she could never make herself go back. Tony, growing up in an unstructured world where children could do pretty much as they pleased and school barely impinged on their freedom, was out and about with Rob, an evacuee from the East End he had made friends with and who was to remain his closest friend until Rob's death in 1985. Margot, 18 months old, who had begun her life with announcements of her birth to a famous father in the national papers was now walking, but the world was looking the other way.

Perhaps to a neutral observer Eddie's war was an easy one. There was some resentment that elite footballers appeared to be given preferential treatment and there's no doubt that top clubs moved quickly to protect their assets. On call-up, Eddie and several of his team-mates were nominated for training as physical training instructors and as far as possible were released to play when selected. It wasn't as easy an option as it appeared though. It only indirectly benefitted the players, although, of course, it spared them for a time from being posted abroad, much like a Reserved Occupation.

The forces made quite different physical demands from professional football training routines and doubled up the stress on their stamina and fitness. 'I wasn't Eddie Hapgood any more,' is what Eddie wrote about himself in these early days. He jokingly described his new identity as 'A.C.2 Hapgood (E.A.) RAF' after his first encounter with military discipline but, in truth, he was deeply bewildered by the separation of this outer Hapgood from the inner purpose that had always made his public and private identities indivisible. Outwardly his hands became a symbol of the problem. Any footballer will tell you that the skin of their hands is unusually delicate and vulnerable since it is so rarely exposed to the rough treatment endured by most working men. Reporting for RAF induction at Cardington on his first day in 1940, the corporal called his name from the list and then snapped, 'Any relation to the Arsenal player?' Exposed and identified, Eddie was subjected to a classic 'taking you down a peg or two'. This involved giving him the 'classy jobs', wiping down and polishing the barrack room floors and daily latrine duty. That particular endurance test was ended when strong chemicals broke his skin, causing multiple infections across his fingers and put him in the sick bay after a month.

Later, when requesting leave to play a match, Eddie was charged with disrespect for using his hands expressively instead of standing to attention. He was eventually released from camp accompanied by two guards (who, no doubt, enjoyed the opportunity to watch a football match). His reputation and his intrinsic leadership qualities were only an irritation to the men whose job it was to whip novices into military shape. It was an injustice that stuck in the memory of Stanley Matthews, the outrageously talented young winger and Eddie's old foe and friend, who was recruited to the same unit. 'Eddie Hapgood had tremendous qualities of leadership, motivation and courage,' he wrote almost 60 years later, 'yet they were never tapped into during his early service years.'

The result of this 'double' life, physical training instructor on military service and international footballer on public service, was that from 1940 to early 1943 Eddie played more football than ever before. During those years he played in over 100 league matches for Arsenal alone, continuing to captain England in the strange shadow world of 'internationals' while his ingrained sense of his public role urged him on to play in forces matches and charity games.

He drove his body to extreme efforts as if he was afraid to stop, as if only by playing could he defy the war, the price it was exacting from him and time itself. In the early years, despite everything, tumultuously exciting football could be delivered and cheered. Just occasionally, moments of personal happiness and pride broke through, as when his mother took 11-year-old Tony to watch Eddie play in an FA XI v RAF match at Bristol in 1941. It would be the last time Emily saw him play. During these three seasons, there were even times he could almost pretend that nothing had changed, that Chapman's 'key men' were indeed immortal.

Imagine the old-fashioned excitement of captaining in a cup final against Preston North End in 1941. No, he was not playing alongside the 'key men' of the early 1930s but even so he was playing alongside Will Scott, Jack Crayston, Bernard Joy, Alf Kirchen and Cliff Bastin. The match ended in a draw and in the replay Arsenal were defeated but the moment, as if from the past, was savoured. Once on the field it was perhaps almost possible to forget the service uniforms waiting in the dressing room, the distance from home and family, the tedious and unpredictable journeys back to base or the wearying haul up to Kettering if he could extend his leave.

Previously Eddie had always been happy to joke with journalists that age didn't matter as he had in 1939, heady with joy after the victory at Hampden Park over Scotland. Now at 32 he occasionally glimpsed the future as he travelled around the country witnessing a faded, jaded version of football, a negative photograph. Perhaps some matches even gave a sense of futility. Eddie's account of travelling to Scotland for a match in 1940 movingly conveys the contradictory feelings the players had to manage:

'While the B.E.F. [British Expeditionary Force] was battling its way back to the beaches and Dunkirk, we travelled north for a charity international with Scotland, for which the police had allowed only a 70,000 limit. Actually, there were only about 61,000 when we took the field, and Hampden Park was more or less deserted, with the barrage balloons over Clydebank looking like birds in the distance.'

Later he was to comment on other football grounds as when visiting 'bomb-scarred St Andrew's [Birmingham City], the most bomb-damaged ground of the Second World War'. Football was becoming a function of a sporting world motivated by fear and tense with foreboding rather than joyous with energy and beauty. The celebrities who crowded around them now were politicians and royalty, all anxious to use the national team to demonstrate their solidarity with civilians at home and their concern for those posted abroad. The Football Association was the most blatant offender. In its post-war account the governing body claimed that it 'played an active, and, indeed, an indispensable part in bringing us victory. It provided that relaxation so necessary over long periods and ... gave invaluable help in a nation-wide scheme promoting positive physical fitness.'

It is hard to tell from the FA's account whether any flesh-and-blood football players actually contributed at all to its great war-winning effort. If there was anger among players about how they had been used in diplomatic games before the war, there was now an undercurrent of resentment that they were being used as a social panacea, as a 'tonic' as Eddie said and that they were not being 'sufficiently protected', as Tom Finney claimed.

There is no doubt that Eddie was spurred on, as many of his colleagues were, by another kind of fear that chipped away at their dedication and optimism. The drive to professionalise football had been gaining ground for some 20 years. The lower leagues still employed many locally based part-time players, men who, with luck, could return to construction, painting and decorating, mining, useful wage-earning jobs. Very few First Division teams had amateurs in the squads any longer or players who had a second skill to fall back on. Arsenal were unusual in signing the amateur Bernard Joy in 1935 and a dual-sport player, Denis Compton, whose fame in cricket would be what he is best remembered for. Most of the team were dedicated to their sport and had never known anything else. They quite simply had no way to earn a living when their playing days were ended by age, injury or, as now, some social upheaval.

Eddie was more fortunate than many others. Players' wages were low, hardly secure or in keeping with their skill or status, but Eddie had played continuously for 12 seasons and there had been regular bonuses for winning. He had earned more for international duty and although sponsorship was nothing like it is today, from time to time his wages were augmented by advertising, films, educational visits and magazine articles. While his playing career continued, no doubt he appeared and felt a wealthy man, fit and healthy, admired and celebrated, regularly featured in the papers, travelling the world. Behind the scenes, however, he had always been vocal about the fact that players were trapped by the maximum wage and transfer structure. He argued as he had done all those years back for the apprentices at the cotton factory, that players deserved to earn according to their value to their clubs, their drawing power, and to receive some percentage of the transfer fees that were steadily increasing. 'Greybeard journalists' and 'football legislators' as he undiplomatically described them, had dismissively accused him of 'divine discontent'. They needn't have feared. That particular revolution was still well in the future with the maximum wage ceiling lifted as late as 1961.

In fact, despite living in what had so recently seemed a cornucopia of privileges, he was beginning to realise that he was playing with the fear of poverty at his back. During the war, a regional league match appearance earned £1.50 but players had to cover their own travelling expenses. Time away from base had to be organised as legitimate leave or, if released, as loss of earnings. Charity matches were organised similarly. International appearances, in many ways simply another version of a charity match, at least merited expenses. By 1943 crowds of 60,000 or more were able to congregate at the larger stadia again.

Eddie, once again cast as a national hero, found his financial position becoming stretched. The cost of travelling was increased by journeys to Kettering as often as possible and the cost of daily living by maintaining two houses. Whenever he could he found time to check on Hutton Grove. A burst pipe in the 1941 cold spell had done considerable damage to carpets and furniture. Maggie, in Kettering at the time, had been notified by her neighbour and, with Eddie unavailable, had rushed up with Tony as soon as she could get away. Of course it had been mended and things restored as much as possible to order but with no one living there and the months passing, it was looking increasingly abandoned. Once Maggie had settled into another house in Kettering in 1941 their furniture was being moved, first one item and then another. By 1943, the Hapgood family's presence at the house they had loved so much and been so proud of was leeched away. They were beginning to discuss cutting their losses and putting Hutton Grove up for sale.

Even so, when the 1942/43 season opened it seemed that the future held some promise for the first time since that terrible announcement, or that at the very least, there might be a future. Nothing was how they wanted it to be but at least Eddie was able to play regularly, which meant that his services pay was being subsidised – and he was still young, just 35. The number of games he was selected for on top of his services duties made it difficult for Maggie and he to see much of each other but at least he was sure she was safe and that his earnings for the time being could probably maintain the new family situation in Kettering. Margot was now a flourishing three-year-old with golden ringlets like an illustration in a Victorian children's book and chubby legs that stood their ground with disturbing determination. Tony was more settled. Mum had more time for him and his growing circle of friends and the Kettering family had gradually helped him get used to the unfamiliar absence of his father. Amid the chaos of war, they both hoped that in their own lives perhaps, they had found some breathing space.

But the turn of the year brought a terrible blow. During a January match for Arsenal against Portsmouth, Eddie was injured.

As he pulled up, he knew immediately from the depths of his muscle memory that this was serious, very possibly a torn thigh ligament, the result of making persistent and heavy demands on his body with no appropriate fitness regime to support it. Now there was no appropriate recovery treatment to rely on either. He had no choice but to return to camp and hope his self-diagnosis was wrong, that the pain would ease, that he could run it off, that a bit of time would heal it.

When Eddie finally managed to catch up with Tom Whittaker at White Hart Lane, where he was watching an Arsenal match, his worst fears were eased but Tom still suggested a six-week rest at the very least. Whether Eddie was sure he could conquer the problem by sheer willpower as he had done so often before, or whether a terrifying image of nothingness rose before him, he made a characteristically instant decision. There was, after all, no possibility of a six-week rest. Strapped up and full of analgesics, he played on. When the usual tried and tested routine of bringing an injured player back to match fitness seemed to begin in early February, he felt he had made the right decision and his anxieties subsided. Stationed in the Midlands at the time, he was loaned with Will Scott to West Bromwich Albion and apparently was a 'tower of strength'. The following month, his fitness was given another test run-out for Arsenal, as he thought, in an early cup match against Brighton when reporters delightedly picked up the story announcing 'Hapgood Reappears for Arsenal', a poignant echo of their celebration of him at the beginning of 1937. Towards the end of April he was selected for a friendly against Luton Town alongside three of his closest friends, Jack Crayston, Ted Drake and Cliff Bastin. Surely everything was back to normal?

Then, to his angry pain and chagrin, Eddie was loaned to Chelsea for a late-season match against Reading. This was very different. Chelsea were a First Division club and one of Arsenal's competitors. This 'loan' was not a guest appearance while posted out of London, but negotiated as an option for the following season. This *was* the signal he had feared, and he was right to be afraid. During the remainder of the war, he was never selected for Arsenal again. It was a devastating, life-changing moment of realisation. An invisible line had been drawn under his Arsenal career without any discussion. Whittaker was the only person to know the full extent of Eddie's injury. Had he passed the information on to the Arsenal manager, George Allison, with a more serious prognosis than he had shared with Eddie? In his own account after the war, Whittaker downplays the injury, stating that he had examined 'the sore place' and recommended Eddie 'rest for a while', yet their encounter that day effectively marked the end of Eddie's Arsenal career. Eddie immediately blamed Allison. All those years ago, at the peak of his career, Allison had been prepared to negotiate a deal with Leicester behind his back and now he was the victim of another humiliating betrayal, a sharp reminder that he was merely useful – or not.

Brought to heel by his injury, his grief turned inwards. He was an Arsenal player, still registered (as he thought) and available for selection. He was an Arsenal player, with every ounce of dedication and energy still driving for the club's success. In his 'enforced absence' as the papers saw it, he desperately tried to keep his career afloat guesting for Birmingham, Lovell's Athletic (a now extinct Welsh team) and playing representative games for an FA XI when the opportunity arose. But he was no fool. He knew he would never be able to rub out the line that had been stealthily but indelibly drawn.

Eddie's international career was concluded in a very different manner. During this uncertain time for him and despite being dropped from the Arsenal team, he was selected to play for his country on 27 February 1943. Once again he was appointed captain. He must have been proud, perhaps relieved and even reassured, that he was still acknowledged to be at the pinnacle of football achievement. The match between England and Wales was organised at Wembley to raise funds for prisoners of war and the Aid to Russia Fund. It was an important public event played out in front of an array of notable public figures – King George VI and Queen Elizabeth, Clementine Churchill, Clement Attlee and the King of Norway as well as 75,000 cheering supporters. By joining a huge crowd of football fans in London, the royal family and other dignitaries were signalling a lowering of risk and the easing of war tension. There was also a diplomatic gesture to Britain's allies with a large number of American soldiers posted in England given free seats for what was surely a mystifying experience – their first football match.

Eddie was surprised to hear that, before the match, the Football Association had arranged to honour his international role by ruling that his wartime games were to be included in his official record. Stanley Rous stepped up to the microphone to announce that the England v Wales match would mean the newly commissioned Pilot Officer Eddie Hapgood's record of 43 international appearances and 34 captaincies had therefore beaten Blackburn Rovers' Bob Crompton's pre-World War I record of 41 appearances and 22 captaincies. He also announced that the Football Association had agreed to honour Eddie with a cash award which would be presented at the Wartime Cup Final in May. After the match, King George VI congratulated Eddie on his record and agreed to present him with a signed photograph taken of their meeting in recognition of his achievement. It was a magnificent celebratory moment in a sea of uncertainty.

Perhaps with hindsight, Eddie's selection seems strange. Is it possible that the Football Association had heard nothing of his injury? That seems unlikely. The most generous interpretation is that it seized the moment in unpredictable times to recognise publicly his quite remarkable ten-year achievement as an England player and captain. The event was certainly organised as a fitting farewell to a great player. 'Hapgood's Honour' ran the *Morning News*' headline. 'Only an English victory is needed to put a crowning touch to the great record of Eddie Hapgood.' And that victory – a triumphant 5-3 vanquishing of Wales – was duly achieved.

Of course and inevitably, the event also had all the hallmarks of a diplomatic farewell that served several shades of patriotic purpose. Eddie's star quality, his history of national leadership, his role as national hero gave an important public occasion an extra stamp of glamour and significance. Either way, Eddie was not consulted and would never know what conversations, respectful or manipulative, had taken place behind his back. His award was widely praised in the press but his performance was barely mentioned ('he did not have a happy time' was one brief reference) while the glorious performances of the five rising star forwards, Stanley Matthews, Raich Carter, Ronnie Westcott, Jimmy Hagan and Denis Compton, were given the attention they deserved. It was Eddie's final match for his country and six weeks later, 'England's New Defence' was formally announced.

Cheered and congratulated at Wembley; dropped and redundant at Arsenal. A national tribute and a personal vacuum. But not quite. During the late autumn of 1942, just before the fateful January when he was injured, Mum wrote to Dad to tell him she was pregnant. Her letter unselfishly conveys her anxiety for the pressure a new baby will put on him and on their circumstances but while Mum always saw the whole picture with joy and fear mixed together, Dad always responded to the moment. His reply is full of happiness and optimism and reassuring words of love and support. Even so, her pregnancy meant there were decisions to be made. The birth of another child meant Mum had to stay in Kettering. Finally and with many regrets, Hutton Grove was sold. It had become little more than a drain on their finances and it was a relief to use the small amount of equity to pay off the costs keeping it had accrued. So I was born in Kettering on 22 April 1943, two months after the England v Wales match, Dad's last international.

According to Mum, I almost never made it to be a member of the Hapgood family. This is how Dad would tell me the story cuddled on his lap, 'You were born just outside Kettering in a beautiful nursing home in a tiny village called Finedon. Your mother was very tired afterwards so I went to visit her on my own until I was sure she was up to seeing us all together. But while Tony – after all he was 13 years old by then – understood immediately that Mummy needed to rest – you [looking at Margot] were still only little and kept pestering me. "I want to see my new sister. I want to see my new sister. I want to see my new sister. Yes. You!'" He would say that last part again teasingly to Margot, who wriggled with pleasure knowing full well the outcome of this particular story.

'As you know,' speaking to me, 'when your sister really wants something she makes sure she gets it. So,' leaning towards me and pretending to whisper, 'I thought of a clever idea.' Then sitting back and this time rolling his eyes at his own stupidity, he continued, 'In those days, the little girls' cradles were decorated in pink and the little boys' in blue and they were placed at the bottom of their mothers' beds.' A deep breath here. 'I told Margot that, if she was a good girl, when I took her and Tony to see Mummy and to meet their new sister, she could choose which baby she wanted to bring home! Well, I was quite pleased with myself. Margot stopped asking me about you and seemed to have forgotten all about it but when I told your mother how clever I'd been, she went pale. "Eddie," she gasped, sinking back on her pillows, "Say she picks the wrong baby! Oh no! I can see a tantrum coming."'

I knew this to be absolutely true as when I was little, Margot's tempers had the power to halt me in my tracks.

Dad said, 'You can imagine how worried I was when I heard that! Anyway, Tony and I cycled along together with Margot in a little seat on the back of my bike and I was worrying all the way. When we arrived, Margot burst through the door first full of excitement while your mother and I looked at each other anxiously. Margot looked at the four baby cradles – three were blue and one was pink. "This one!" she shouted as she leaned over the pink one to have a good look at you. So there you are – a very special baby, chosen by your own very special sister! Wasn't that wonderful?!'

That funny, affectionate story was handed down and frequently repeated as my birthdays came and went, yet at the time, the tears of joy for Maggie's safety and their new baby must have been mingled with a growing sense of grief and anxiety for their future.

11

The Ghost of Eddie Hapgood

As public awareness at the beginning of 1944 grew that Eddie's elite playing career was over, rumours abounded that he would join this club, that club, that he would disseminate the wisdom of Arsenal throughout professional football. Everyone saw management as his obvious route forward. His footballing knowledge, his famed leadership skills and his forces training as a physical training instructor made him a model for the new breed of managers who were needed to pull club football out of the dark ages of the war into a brave, new world.

Although everyone else seemed to be sure about what he should do, Eddie's famed decisiveness deserted him. Nothing he had ever known or learned fitted the circumstances he found himself in where every decision in his life seemed predetermined and irrevocable. He was confused and uncharacteristically brusque when he was questioned by a journalist. 'I am still a registered player for Arsenal,' he said in January 1944. 'I can say nothing about any plans for the future.' He had not played for Arsenal for a year but still no one at the club had spoken to him about his future.

Arsenal's silence left him floundering. Contradictions swirled in his head pulling this way and that. To become a manager also meant to stop being a player. That wasn't a possibility. He didn't know how to stop playing – he was still doing so every week while on loan to Luton Town. He also knew that if he chose to stop, his contract with Arsenal would stop simultaneously and his role in the forces would change.

The war did seem to be entering its final stages but no one actually knew when it would end or, when it did, whether life would simply fall back into normality. If he could play on until the war *did* end, surely the madness would go with it and he would have the time to work things out, get properly fit, and discuss the future with Maggie. Kettering seemed very far away. He felt sick with anxiety for Maggie and Tony, desolate without them and grieved that Margot and his new daughter were growing up without him. Then a rush of events forced his decision. The first was the launch of the Normandy landings on 6 June 1944 which marked the beginning of the end of the war. The second was a provisional offer from Blackburn Rovers for the post of manager. The third was a letter from George Allison, the first he had received in over a year. It contained no regret or praise or thanks, and no indication from him at all about Eddie's future. It simply informed Eddie that the board of directors at Arsenal were unable to award him the £750 benefit due to him because of the club's current financial position. So, on 24 July 1944, the press reported that Eddie had signed to be manager of Blackburn Rovers and that he would assume his role as soon as he was demobilised. It was an act of panic, of financial anxiety, an act of fierce anger against Arsenal's abandonment of him.

For a long time, nothing had seemed quite real to Eddie. From the moment when Eddie Hapgood, captain of Arsenal and England, was replaced by A.C.2 Hapgood (E.A.) RAF he felt he had become a ghost to himself, as if he could see land but never struggle through the opposing tide to reach it. For football fans, for journalists, for all those who had followed his career over the years it was quite different. He was still an urgent and necessary memory. During the war the ghost that he joked would haunt Arsenal's stadium after he died slowly morphed into a myth that sustained the spirits of fans and haunted the imaginations of thousands as football was driven to the recesses of people's minds and emotions. There seemed to be some kind of epic coincidence that war was declared as the apotheosis of his footballing career was internationally celebrated in such a generous and magnificent style. But now, it seemed, his ghost must carry his identity alone. Wherever he was posted, for training, for duty, to take up his commission, he found names and faces that were familiar and who recognised him among the squadrons of men, or thought they did. Away from the Arsenal strip and Highbury, in unfamiliar locations and in uniform, players from other clubs and fans from all clubs, were not quite sure at first. 'Eddie Hapgood? Is it Eddie Hapgood?' And he was as delighted as they were to chat football gossip and share memories, to find confidence in sharing evidence that they really had all existed in another world. For the first time perhaps he found solidarity with those outside the elite ranks he was familiar with, the coaches, the stewards, the kit man, the amateur players who occupied the grassroots of the footballing world. Sometimes he was lucky enough to encounter friendly enemies such as Bill Shankly at Cardington and Joe Mercer, as well as old friends Wilf Copping at Aldershot and Ted Drake at Uxbridge. They all reassured one another that when the war was over, football would come back.

As he faded further from the immediacy of professional football, his name became the holder of memories evoking a presence which lingered on, a reminder for many fans perhaps of some normal world that might be returned to or an emblem of better times. Pilot Officer Eddie Hapgood himself felt cast adrift from the football world but strangely, 'Eddie Hapgood' still evoked the possibility of his living presence. He was not sure which match was referred to but he was deeply moved to receive a letter from a group of POWs imprisoned in Stalag XXB in Germany who wrote, 'We all hope that by the time this arrives in England you have created a record. So here's wishing you the best of luck.' He 'reappears' in March 1943, a 'welcome surprise'. In May, a postcard from an Arsenal supporter registered shock that Arsenal had been beaten by Blackpool and a rampant Stanley Matthews, 'I am wondering whether the old head of Hapgood was missed at all in this vital match!' He is 'expected to be available' in August 1943. Ted Crawford of Clapton Orient is sure it was Eddie he deliberately kicked in a wartime match, suffering a guilty conscience for such spiteful behaviour just because Eddie's cleverness had made him look foolish.

Ghost though he was, he was seen playing in France late in 1943 for the RAF according to Stan Mortensen, 'Every now and again one could glimpse the skill and the knowledge that had made him such a famous back and such an outstanding captain.' On 5 November 1943 the *Daily Herald* mused on the futures of great players and Eddie in particular. On 20 November, in a game against Portsmouth, Eddie's star quality fleetingly glitters, 'One star does not make a team but it is surprising what a footballer of Hapgood's type can do in a side such as Luton.' As another Christmas loomed on the horizon and Crystal Palace trounced Luton 5-0, a local paper recorded with delight, 'But for Eddie Hapgood the Palace might have run up double figures.' Whether real or imagined, wherever fans or sports journalists were lucky enough to capture these moments, they were always recorded. Eddie's body vocabulary, that instinctive but knowledgeable relationship with the ball, never seemed to lose its astonishing power to make observers ask themselves, 'Did he really do that? That's got to be Eddie Hapgood!'

And so it went on. January 1944 witnessed 'the reappearance of evergreen Hapgood' whose perennial battle with Stanley Matthews was the 'prime feature' of an FA XI v RAF match. The fans knew they were watching history being made because, 'There have been no others since, so this Hapgood–Matthews duel is of exceptional interest.' On 20 March 1944, Eddie led out his Luton team, the lowliest in the Wartime League South and something of a joke, against Arsenal. The crowds had swelled from the usual 3,000 or so to 10,000 as north Londoners travelled to support Arsenal and perhaps to treasure a last glimpse, if it really was him, of their former captain. When the referee's whistle blew and the players scattered to take up their positions on the pitch,

Eddie faced Ted Drake and Cliff Bastin and further back George Male and Les Compton. He knew their individual strengths and weaknesses, the extent of their hunger to win but he also knew the team was patched together. The emotional power of his yearning to be with them was channelled into determination to beat them. 'Hapgood was the big man of the defence which can be no consolation to Arsenal,' began the next day's match account. Under the headline 'Hapgood Ruined Arsenal Chance', it continued, 'He never put a foot wrong and saved the game for Luton when, with Duke lying helpless on the ground, he kicked clear from the goal line a hot shot from Bastin.'

How often had the crowd seen that same last-minute goal clearance? Did Bastin really fall victim to a tactic he had seen baffle other strikers? Was it Eddie Hapgood of Arsenal? It surely was. Only he could kick like that. For a moment, the Arsenal fans saw double, as did the *Daily Mirror*'s commentator over a year later who watched young John Chenhall play for Arsenal but saw a young man who 'looked – and played – like a 1945 edition of immaculate Eddie Hapgood'.

The strangest of all his appearances, in November 1945, five months after VE Day, was in the best tradition of ghost stories. There were mysterious foreigners, a dark, impenetrable fog cloaking a newly liberated Europe in confusion – and a missing hero. As long ago as 1943, a letter had arrived addressed to Eddie. Struggling with his injury and its life-changing implications and used to letters of all kinds from all over the world, he had failed to register it at the time. It was a letter of historical and footballing importance. Alexander Divochkin of CSKA, honoured in 1941 as a Hero of the Soviet Union for extreme bravery, had written to Eddie to fill in the story behind negotiations that had been going on for some time with the FA to arrange a tour of Europe and particularly England for Moscow Dynamo of the Soviet Union, and to ask him to support it. He included stories about his life at the front, his admiration for Eddie and his fervent desire to play against Arsenal, concluding:

'I heartily shake your hand. Give my compliments to your club friends and tell them that our sportsmen are fighting in front lines with redoubled energy and in each of us burns the desire to wipe the fascist rascals from the face of the earth.'

A tour was finally organised and Moscow Dynamo arrived in England. But peace had brought temporary chaos to clubs. No one seemed to know where anybody was; players were hard to contact, demobilisation was gradual, club registrations were no longer enforceable, rules and regulations were dissolving. Even so, 'Hapgood Flying Home for Game with Dynamos' trumpeted the press. Yes, Eddie's name was on the team sheet but was he there? 'Yes,' claimed one fan. 'I swear I saw him – just about – in the game against Moscow Dynamo in 1945. This was played in dense fog … but I saw Eddie, the gentleman left-back, as well as seeing the first Russian of my life.' Such is the force of desire. Their resources stretched thin, Tom Whittaker had selected Eddie to play. His flight, delayed in fog-bound Brussels, prevented his travelling. Only his ghost swirled in and out of the fog. Somehow it seemed he had become part of the DNA of football, of his whole generation. Journalists and fans didn't want to let him go. What C.L.R. James wrote about the great cricketer W.G. Grace sums up the extraordinary influence of great sportsmen, 'He [Grace] seems to have been one of those men in whom the characteristics of life as lived by many generations seem to meet for the last in a completely and perfectly blended way.'

While treasured memories, real and imagined glimpses, reports, fears of loss and hopes of recovery drifted back and forth across and around his reputation in eddying mists, Dad was working on his autobiography. He had welcomed the opportunity suggested to him by the journalist Roy Peskett. He had a story to tell and he wanted to pass on the triumphant legacy of 1930s football and of Arsenal so it could never be forgotten. He also welcomed the chance to register his own angle on events and to try and convey to those he hoped would read it, the deep well of happiness and fulfilment he had experienced from being a man who was a footballer.

In 1944, soon after being appointed to Blackburn, Eddie handed over the manuscript of *Football Ambassador* to his publisher. Footballing fans might almost have been waiting for this chance to relive their own pre-war experiences, to say triumphantly, 'I remember that!' and with equal delight to say, 'I didn't know that!' but they could never have expected it because Dad's autobiography was the first of its kind. It sold rapidly and was reprinted five times. The recent 2010 reprint also produced lively responses, 'To have a book from an absolute legend is just fantastic,' and as always memories rushed vividly to the surface, 'I well remember an inter-services game when he was actually booed. The crowd had come to see the great Stanley Matthews perform and Eddie didn't allow him a kick! A great player and a gentleman on and off the pitch.' The *Daily Herald* took the opportunity to add to its review that he was more than a great footballer – that 'his singleness of purpose, loyalty and unselfishness have made him ... one of the greatest sportsmen'. The popularity of *Football Ambassador* proved a catalyst for a genre that today issues football players' autobiographies by the shelf load. At only 21 Wayne Rooney of Manchester United was contracted to write three life stories and wisely hedged his bets by giving his first autobiography, published in 2006, the title *My Story So Far*.

Yet again, the evidence of a single fan unexpectedly illuminates most sharply what Eddie meant to his admirers. In 1945, a young man, overwhelmed by reading Eddie's memoir, sent him a poem he had written. If I knew who he was I would have asked his permission to quote from it but the covering letter ended with, 'Forgive me for not giving my name etc. but I think I'd be rather embarrassed, but I've written just what I think.' In rhyming verse, the first lines sum up with disarming simplicity the complex combination of qualities and talents that won people's respect:

> To a modest, honest player I
> dedicate these words,
> He's a man with faith, ability,
> and iron-nerves,
> A temper curbed whene'er it's
> frayed,
> An example to his team-mates made.
> With soccer fame renown
> with countries, kings and lords
> is known.

What famous history his name
will make,
Of stainless character for his
son to take.
What faith, ability, sense to do,
What else could a team want
with a captain like you!

Dad had tucked the letter inside a copy of *Football Ambassador* and Tony had found it years later. In 2009, a friend, idly browsing in a second-hand bookshop in Leamington Spa, came across a battered copy. A yellowing newspaper picture of Dad was pasted on the title page and the cutting of an article by Don Welsh, a team-mate who had shared the great Scotland victory, tucked in the back. He bought the book and gave it to me. The thing about ghosts is that they never die.

VE Day brought no closure for Mum or Dad. She told me how she didn't want to be alone while the celebrations were going on or stuck indoors with her family. She desperately wanted to be out and about in the streets cheering and dancing with the crowds, knowing that at last Dad would be back and there would be time for laughter and singing. She had guiltily turned down a family gathering and rushed off to the town centre where the lights were shining. I didn't really understand the story. She was disappointed, she said. She hadn't felt celebratory at all. She had just felt lonely.

While the ghosts of football past lingered in fans' imaginations or reappeared in their imagined sightings, Dad was posted to western Europe on 5 July 1945 as part of the clearing-up operations following Germany's surrender. His VE Day was spent travelling to the continent, to countries, Belgium, France, Holland, he wasn't sure he wanted to see. Europe seemed as convulsed by the impact of peace as of war. It was a grim and dismal time and he was shocked by the devastation, the ugliness, the waste land created by wrecked buildings, the filth and stench of places left behind and best forgotten. It didn't seem possible that anything like towns and cities could ever rise again from such total destruction. Germany was the strangest experience of all. He tried to remember what Berlin had been like when he travelled there in 1938, but he couldn't. He couldn't even recognise the now heavily damaged Olympic stadium when, in October, he played there again for the Combined Services XI against a cobbled-together West Ham team. As his war stretched into its sixth year, he was living in a monstrous and haunted limbo-land, captured on near-tissue regulation paper in letters to Maggie.

August 1945. Berlin, Germany:

Dearest Mig,

You should see the Germans! There can be nothing like it. It must be seen to be believed. The people are living like rats in a sewer. Nothing is standing. Bands of people are still returning to these desolate areas with their pitiful belongings packed up in anything – old boxes, prams, push-carts only to find everything destroyed. The towns smell of the dead and nothing is being done. Trams, cars, other vehicles still left where they were blown up or burnt out. And this four months after the finish. Surely they must have known they were beaten?

Your Ever Loving Husband

August 1945, Miles from Anywhere, Holland:

Dearest Mig,

What a trip! It is a wonder the authorities allowed us to travel at all. You never saw anything like it. I slept by myself in a large Nissen hut. On enquiry as to sheets and blankets, I was informed – blankets but not sheets and anyway you won't sleep for the earwigs. I thought this an exaggeration, but no! Got into bed, had a little read, then looked around. The floor was crawling with small cockcroaches! Got out and finished them off with my boot then decided to drag the bed into the very centre of the hut. Finished this, got back into bed only to look up at the ceiling and behold, earwigs. They were dropping all over the place and you could distinctly hear them hitting the floor. So out again hitting them off with a newspaper. Couldn't get to sleep though without imaginary thoughts of these things crawling over me.

Your Ever Loving Husband

And always behind the incredulity, the impossibility of what Europe had done to itself, the daily horrors, the grinding discomforts was the longing to be home, the need to reassure Maggie that life could begin again.

September 1945. RAF Unit, Denmark

> As I strolled along with the crowds jostling me, I beheld the spectacle as if in a distance – my mind was on you. All day I have been thinking about you – how you walk and how you talk and how much I should like to have you with me – tonight, to walk slowly along without speaking. That's what I have missed, being alone with you. It has been a long time. I felt terribly alone tonight ... and so to bed. Me and my shadow ... Kiss the youngsters for me.

Eddie was finally demobilised on 21 December 1945. As soon as he arrived back in London, the Blackburn Rovers chairman was in touch, but so was Tom Whittaker. Would Eddie play for Arsenal in the final three games of 1945? All wartime club registrations technically ended with demobilisation but Tom had moved quickly to renew Eddie's. For the briefest moment of uncomplicated happiness and optimism, he allowed himself to believe the world really had at last returned to normal. Deluded by exhaustion and euphoria, he pushed away the image of Maggie waiting for him to arrive in Kettering and his own longing to be with her and agreed to play for Arsenal. He claimed his right to eight weeks' post-demobilisation leave and wrote to the Rovers chairman to inform him he would be playing for Arsenal until February.

As quickly as the fantasy of perpetual football had captivated him, it faded and vanished. Eddie knew perfectly well that George Allison would not sanction the terms of a new peacetime contract from 1 January 1946. He knew that Tom had only re-registered him to cover Arsenal's emergency. He thought he had found his way through personal grief and anger against the loss of youth, of fitness, of Arsenal's rejection and had accepted that his enduring fame was no longer in the present tense but in the past. But he hadn't. He had lost his way again without knowing it. He needed to find Maggie and his family. They all needed time. With regret and shame, he could hardly believe that he had stayed in London for a week rather than rushing immediately to see her after the long painful year they had been apart. What had possessed him? How would she ever forgive him? He wanted to tell her again how he had missed her, how he wanted to make a home for them all again, to have fun with Tony, to get to know his two daughters. To do that, he had to find a way to translate all his muddled thoughts and feelings into who he was again, his whole, unified self into the future with energy and optimism. As the fog in his mind cleared, the indistinct road to Blackburn became a clearly marked highway.

It was left to Harry Homer, who had abandoned his self-appointed role as Arsenal recorder in the autumn of 1940, to take up his pen again in 1946 as he surveyed what was left of the club he loved. In a sad personal note in his Arsenal scrapbook, death, separation and the loss of youthful hope merge to describe the grey, exhausted post-war mood and the irrevocable, unbridgeable break from the world that was. 'There are many changes and many of my old friends in football have died,' he wrote. 'Eddie Hapgood is now manager of Blackburn Rovers, the pacifist in me is long dead.'

12

Becoming a Football Manager

When Eddie first realised that his England and Arsenal careers were over, the offer from Blackburn Rovers had seemed an unexpected answer to his mounting problems, an excellent opportunity for a first stab at being a manager, a promise of financial security when the war ended. In the last full season before the war the Rovers had won the Second Division title and been promoted. Years before, they had given Arsenal a run for their money in a cup tie and Eddie, impressed by their performance, had written about their tenacity and their readiness to fight to the final whistle. It had the reputation of being a well run, stable club. He had met a couple of Rovers' players on international duty and knew they had an excellent squad which could hold its own in the First Division. However, the club had suffered badly during the war and was currently dropping steadily towards the bottom of Wartime League North. Now Eddie found himself welcoming the challenge ahead, to bring the club back from wartime mediocrity to the success their promotion promised. It was a characteristically upbeat response.

For Maggie it was quite a different matter. When the offer had first been made, it seemed so far ahead in the future as to be almost fantasy. June 1944 and the war still raging? She had long ago decided it would never happen, that they would find an alternative. Kettering had been her wartime haven but was now her home again. Their children had all been born there. Like many war wives, circumstances had forced her to organise a life for herself and her family. Tony was back in full-time school again and now, with London forgotten, Kettering was his home too. Margot would be starting school in a few months. Baby Lynne was flourishing.

Maggie's whole self recoiled from moving. As a vague future loomed into an ominous present, in her mind she refused to go. She had begun to worry about it all as soon as Eddie was posted abroad in 1945 after VE Day but while he was away they were never able to discuss things properly. Although she wanted to, she couldn't or wouldn't ask Eddie to give football up and get a job locally. What job? He would wither away. Early in 1945 she had written to him reminding him that he had no commitment to Blackburn until he was demobilised. Until that magic date was issued, they had time to change their minds. Sit tight was her advice to him. Circumstances may change. When you get home we can discuss the matter. But she hadn't seen him since then. It was now months after VE Day and they still had no idea when he would be home. As her anxiety increased she wondered whether the conflict with Arsenal Dad had mentioned might resolve itself when the war was over and whether a move so far away from London would make that less likely. No, to move was impractical, unimaginable in every way. It was crazy.

Caught up in her own unhappy confusion, Maggie had underestimated the interest the press still had in Eddie. As soon as his demobilisation date was announced, the press recorded Rovers' attempts to make contact with him, to clarify the date of his arrival in Blackburn, and, because of his silence, to query whether he had changed his mind. That was 22 December. Maggie hadn't known where he was either and couldn't answer the questions journalists asked when they phoned. She had had no word from him herself. When he did finally arrive home – it was a matter of days but felt like weeks – she was desperate and disorientated. There was suddenly no time for discussion and decision making had shrunk to a few days. Just bare facts remained. Eddie was committed to Blackburn Rovers. RAF pay had stopped. The benefit payment owed to him by Arsenal had been withdrawn a year earlier and that decision wasn't going to change soon, if ever, he told her. To ensure an income had to take first priority. 'And there is no way,' he said, his sense of honour reasserting itself and his head clear at last to the reality of their situation, 'war or no war, that I'll break my word to the Blackburn chairman, Mr John Caton. I just couldn't do that. I've said I'll go and I will.'

At some point in the emotional turmoil, Maggie's determination to find a way to stay in Kettering was lost. She found herself being uprooted with an abruptness that seemed almost brutal. There were no choices for her unless she opted for the ultimate one, to let Eddie go to Blackburn and for her and the children to stay in Kettering. On New Year's Day 1946, Eddie, his optimism checked, took the road north to Blackburn alone. Torn between anger and tears, Maggie struggled for calmness and understanding. Her longing to be with him became yet another acknowledgement, so familiar over the years, of his absence.

Appointed to bring Blackburn back to the 'promised land' like the ancient prophet Moses, Eddie was more like Daniel walking into a lion's den. On 1 January 1946 he took up what turned out to be a formidable managerial task. With hindsight it was acknowledged that of all the former players now trying out their managerial hand for the first time, his was the toughest job. Famous player and celebrated leader of men to take charge of a directionless football club might sound exciting but in fact there was not a vestige of logic in it. Despite the depression of the early 1930s and the fracture of towns and communities in the war, a passionate commitment to the local team had remained steadfast. Arsenal, for all their magnificence, were one of a cluster of London clubs, none of which claimed to be representative of the whole of London. On the other hand, the history of Rovers, like many northern clubs, was the history of the town or city in which it had evolved. The board of directors, Eddie's predecessor and most of the squad were Lancashire men. More than that, they were Blackburn men quite distinct from and competitive with other Lancashire clubs from Bolton, Preston, Burnley and Manchester.

Without a manager since Robert Crompton's death in 1941, 'luckless Blackburn Rovers' were desperate to get their post-war football back on track after their dismal wartime record had squandered their brief flirtation with glory and promotion in the 1938/39 season. If they looked outside their own district in search of a star player, Lancashire clubs tended to look to Scotland rather than to London for their transfers and business transactions. Manchester City appointed a veteran player as their manager. Liverpool appointed George Kay, a Preston player of some 16 years; Everton had a wartime manager, Theo Keepley, who was Liverpool born and bred. Manchester United recruited Matt Busby, a Scot who was already well known to the club's board. Burnley appointed Cliff Britton, like Eddie, Bristol-born, but who had spent his entire playing career in the north. Eddie was definitely an outsider.

Worse, Eddie had prevaricated just long enough to provoke mutterings among the Rovers directors that 'his heart wa't int'. Blackburn, impatient for their new manager to arrive, reported to the press that they had 'heard nothing from Hapgood' since his demobilisation. Having landed their trophy man 18 months previously, some board members found their enthusiasm for his arrival fading and their pride piqued by his apparent disinterest. It is possible that press reports had made them aware that Eddie, although not officially demobilised and therefore not yet their manager, was back in England and possibly playing for Arsenal. Resistance began to stir most strongly among the old guard, men who had benefited from the war to embed themselves in their club's identity. Verbally, way back in 1944, in their determination to get him, John Caton had promised Eddie an entirely free hand, a condition of his agreement to accept the post, but now the mood was shifting and some officials and directors began to balk at their loss of power to a young man with no experience and whom none of them knew except by reputation. Some began to question the wisdom of the decision to appoint someone so rooted in the London glitterati. Nobody, neither club nor new manager, had got quite what they wanted.

It was not a good beginning. Eddie later compared his arrival at the ground and his reception by the board to being directed to the Arctic regions. The chairman, four other directors and Eddie himself attended a meeting arranged on the evening of his second day. It was just as frosty. The chairman, formerly so enthusiastic, appeared hostile and inflexible and Eddie was made to feel like an interloper. He took the opportunity to apologise for his delayed arrival, admitted he was in the wrong and tried to explain what had happened – the turmoil involved in demobilisation, having no home in Blackburn to bring his family to and decisions about their home in Kettering. When he was met by an unsympathetic silence, Eddie offered to take the whole blame on himself, to shake hands and leave without acrimony. At this, Fred Wood, a long-standing director with Rovers and who was to become a good friend of Eddie's, poured oil on troubled waters and broke the silence, welcoming him and shaking hands all round. 'Eddie, start tomorrow!' he said. It was just what Eddie needed. He welcomed the open-heartedness of the invitation because, as he wrote later, 'Football is in my blood, there is nothing else for me, so then and there I waded in determined to get a good side together.' As far as he was concerned, the initial hitches were forgotten about.

A laugh and a handshake were never going to solve the many problems that Eddie encountered. The misery of war in Europe had ended but football's troubles had barely begun. In the grey transition season of 1945/46, the time of change from war games to football games, when hopes might have been flourishing, the damage that had been done to the sport became startlingly evident. Club buildings had not been fully maintained or facilities updated. Some had suffered bomb damage, been requisitioned as Highbury had been or used when necessary for war activities. Pitches had been grossly neglected and buildings only maintained when possible by local volunteers. If a club was to succeed, this first season was crucial. They could do without just about everything – safe stadia, old and in some cases no kit, non-regulation balls, kit man, medical staff, laundry system, even a decent pitch. Clubs could, after all, come up with coupon-raising schemes to help buy a full team kit. Players could be responsible for their own kit, certainly their own boots. Wives and volunteers helped when and where possible.

It was an entirely different matter when it came to putting a team together. The one thing that all clubs needed was good players, but they were in desperately short supply. Clubs had tried to recruit younger men to maintain their squads but war service had made their development spasmodic. Older players, like Eddie himself, had not been able to maintain proper training schedules or appropriate diets. Many had returned home unfit and exhausted from postings abroad, some injured. Many were living on borrowed economic time between the ending of service pay and the resumption (if they were lucky) of the still pitifully low but regular football wages. Those who had the power to state their terms not surprisingly did so. Housing, in short supply, became a vital bargaining tool. Much like the Great War, men returned to swell demand as they attempted to recover and set up family life again. This time bomb damage had added to neglect to make the problem much worse. Skilled players wanted a home, secure contracts and a club that could deliver regular bonuses. If these things could be agreed satisfactorily, they were ready to relocate.

As clubs struggled through 1946, preparing for the opening of the first formal league season in August and the realities of promotion and relegation, a covert negotiating currency began to perforate the strict lines of Football Association rules just as their rules of play had been bent, flouted or mocked to keep football going during the war. It was to become a battle for the survival of the fittest, of the canniest, the most ruthless, or the most corrupt. It was not a world that Eddie had expected. It was a world outside his experience and way outside his comfort zone. In a sudden insight, he realised that defending football values in the boardroom might be as necessary as defending them on the pitch. In one way, the war had ended but in purely personal ways he felt uneasily that a different war had just begun.

The squad presented him with other problems. Like most clubs, there was a mix of pre-war players, desperate to keep their jobs, to extend their playing days for as long as possible and younger players, recruited during the war and hungry for success. There were also some glaring positional gaps, particularly goalkeeping, which unbalanced the team structure. Inexperienced as he was, the manager in him rapidly decided that to avoid a boom-and-bust season, immediate results must be subordinate to a steady, long-term reconstruction of the playing structure. Looking to create his own spine of 'key men', he brought his old friend Horace Cope north with him as coach and signed George Marks from Arsenal to fill the vacant goalkeeper role. Delighted by the quality of Blackburn's younger professionals, he believed they could be the club's future. He set about identifying up-and-coming talent among local boys for youth development, a pragmatic policy that he hoped would also increase local match attendance. He was soon able to see where he was going, to maximise available resources and to anticipate the new season with renewed optimism.

Not all the players were inspired by his enthusiasm. His youth strategy brought him into open conflict with a number of the older players. Tony remembered a disagreement with the club secretary when Eddie wanted to drop Bob Pryde, a local hero and Scottish international who had begun playing for the Rovers as early as 1933. 'Eddie, he's a Rovers man, heart and soul!' the secretary had protested. Another dispute was about Walter Crook, a very talented and highly successful left-back. Another local hero, he had played throughout Blackburn's Second Division title-winning season in 1938/39, and once for England during the war when Eddie wasn't available – but he was formed in a different mould. He was a tough, aggressive defender, 'virtually indestructible'. He protested against Eddie's management methods, possibly feeling threatened as Eddie's training routines encouraged a playing style relying on positional sense, speed and energy. Perhaps tension between the two of them was inevitable. After 16 years playing for Blackburn, Crook asked to be put on the transfer list. Insult was added to injury apparently when Eddie selected himself to play instead.

Eddie was also slow to realise that relationships with officials and players were not simply football issues. His inexperience made it increasingly difficult to deal with rising undercurrents of resentment against him which he could sense but couldn't explain. One possible problem he thought might be the glowing reputation of the previous manager, Bob Crompton. Bob's entire life had been bound up in Blackburn Rovers as a player, manager and finally as an honorary director. He was 'the beating heart of the club'. It was Bob's international record that Eddie had beaten and which had been announced to 75,000 supporters at Wembley three years previously, prompting rumbles of resentment in the local northern press at London chicanery. But there were other odd, uncomfortable moments. On several occasions, some problem manufactured by one director had to be resolved by the jovial intervention of another. Would Eddie attend the board meeting to explain why he had ordered a bulldozer for the practice ground without authorisation? Apparently he had not. The board duly recorded, 'The manager had no knowledge concerning the order of the bulldozer for the practice ground.' Would Eddie explain why he taken transfer forms from the secretary's office without permission? Apparently he had not. 'Tha's making a mountain out of a molehill, Reg,' remarked one director as the board recorded that everything was settled happily. Was inter-board friction being played out via the manager? Did they simply want to show him who was in charge? Was there an informal strategy to belittle, undermine and finally remove him? He didn't know.

Even so, the 1946/47 season started well including a promising 3-1 defeat of Arsenal at Highbury and despite the fact that 'off the field it appeared there was something always happening' as directors' squabbles threatened to disturb the uneasy peace. However, a run of five defeats in September and October sent waves of panic through the boardroom. It was time, they thought, to buy in ready-made players, who could help them avoid relegation. Eddie tried to persuade them to hold their nerve, arguing for the talent of the young players, his conviction they would pull through this tough period and reminding them that three of their experienced players were carrying injuries and would soon return to action. He was resistant to gambling money he thought the club didn't have on new players. He argued strongly that if they were good enough to turn the team around in weeks, they would soon move on, but would also move on if Blackburn were relegated. The directors were not convinced.

And then the weather began to close in. Just as at the beginning of the war in 1940, when temperatures plummeted under freezing rain and unthawed snow and again at the end of the hostilities when the country was wrapped in impenetrable fog, now the country was hit by the bitterest winter in recorded history. As if things were not already challenging enough, Eddie was trying to protect players and to cover gaps when they were injured or ill. Matches that should have been cancelled were played and concerns for players overruled. Playing conditions were dangerous everywhere. 'We began to fear the referee saying, "The pitch is fit to play,"' wrote Tommy Lawton, Eddie's former international colleague, who played for Chelsea in the milder south during this terrible winter, 'when it was dangerous to every man to run, let alone slither along frozen-ridged, razor-edged ice.'

Over Christmas 1946, Eddie himself was laid low with a severe feverish chill, very possibly the flu. During his absence, the directors moved swiftly. Walter Crook was recalled but almost immediately, playing away against Charlton Athletic, he fell on the treacherous, ice-locked pitch. He wrenched a stomach muscle so severely that he never played again. Unknown to Eddie, word had gone out to a few Scottish professionals who had been covertly scouted. Negotiations were well under way by the time he returned to work at the beginning of January.

Unaware of backroom activities, Eddie's first concern was to get the team ready to play Hull in the FA Cup. A creditable draw at home led to a triumphant replay away a week later which was rapidly followed by another victory over Port Vale, and Blackburn were in the fifth round of the FA Cup. Then, in early February, shortly after Blackburn were finally knocked out by Charlton Athletic, John Caton came to Eddie's office to talk about new players in what Eddie assumed was a routine 'state of affairs' discussion. 'Eddie, if we had a first-class centre-forward we could win the championship,' Caton began. It was true that injury troubles had interfered with the consistency of the forward line but it was a temporary situation and conditions were difficult. Eddie replied he was happy with the players he had. But this was not a discussion, as Eddie later recounted. '"No," Caton said firmly. "We have already arranged to buy him and the figure is £10,000." I protested that it seemed an astronomical figure given that we were £25,110 in the red already. He cut me short. "That's not your affair. What I want you to do is this." Then he made the astounding suggestion that I pay the player £1,000 for himself. I refused point blank.'

This was Eddie's first encounter with the power wielded by directors. It was certainly his first encounter with the now widespread practice of 'under the counter' payments used partly to sidestep FA wage restrictions, partly to beat off competition and partly as disguised bribes. He had heard about them before the war, of course. There had been many jokes and some resentment at Arsenal about Alex James's 'subsidised' wages but Eddie had never taken much interest. This was real and he had no intention of getting involved. However, as instructed, he waited on the freezing cold, dank station platform for the train to arrive from Glasgow, hoping to enthuse the potential new recruit with Blackburn's chances as he drove him to meet the directors. Two other men whom at first he barely noticed arrived at the far end of the platform. The train pulled in, the doors opened and a fit young man stepped down. As Eddie hurried towards him, the new arrival looked right and left before striding purposefully to the far end where a wave had vigorously signalled him. Eddie stood for a moment in the cold draft of the retreating train, watching as the three men turned and made for the exit staircase. He knew who one of the men was. He knew him well from years of playing against Manchester City and Liverpool.

It was Matt Busby. The same age as Eddie, Scottish, a northern man, he had been appointed to Manchester United a few months before Eddie arrived in Blackburn. Eddie hesitated. They were clearly after the same player, a player who knew the Blackburn manager would be meeting him but had ignored him. Why had Matt been so decisively chosen? There was only one answer. Eddie didn't know how to play this game. He didn't want to. Football was surely better than this. His ideal of football was definitely better than this. He also knew he could not keep silent. The following day, he handed in his resignation to John Caton. He also wrote to Stanley Rous at the FA to inform him of the practice of illegal payments he had witnessed. He never received a reply from the man who had so thoroughly endorsed his moral probity a mere three years previously in his foreword to *Football Ambassador* as a 'model on which young players can mould their play and conduct'.

Perhaps fearing Eddie's version of events would be made public, the club moved into action to protect its reputation. An official press release was immediately issued, announcing his immediate departure and asserting incorrectly that he had demanded a three-year contract. Journalists smelled a rat and freely offered their opinions. One attributed it to Eddie's extravagance in attempting to rival big-spending Newcastle United's £44,000 transfer money. Several were nearer the truth when they guessed he had fallen out with the management now that he was no longer 'solely responsible for team selection'. Another interpreted the chairman's curious comment, 'A pity it had to come to this after such a short association,' as a charitable cover-up. But whatever anyone was saying or writing, Eddie refused to give journalists reasons for his resignation. He didn't even deny the simple untruth that he had walked away after a contract disagreement. He knew which directors had acted against him when he was ill. He knew who it was who had phoned the player in advance with an illegal offer and then instructed him to do the dirty work. He knew the identity of the manager at the other end of the platform who had shaken hands on a private deal, presumably a better one. He had had mud thrown at him. He would not let it stick. He would not throw it back.

Eddie's spirit reacted strongly against the squalid, grubby nature of back-door manoeuvring, whispers, phone calls, wallets of cash, dim station platforms or empty car parks like some spy movie. It was not so much the bending of rules that he objected to, although he did. It was the tilting of the playing field in the name of professionalism: unfair advantages, mercantile exchanges, club directors and skilled footballers as the givers and takers of bribes. If clubs paid players properly, if their talent was rewarded, if clubs worked imaginatively and with commitment to build up powerful squads, as players had been arguing for since the early 1930s, such underhand tactics would be unnecessary. Bernard Joy, Eddie's former colleague at Arsenal, put in writing in 1952 what Eddie had never guessed in 1946. 'It was not easy to preserve tradition in the disturbed, restless days after the war,' Joy wrote. 'League players were asking for a transfer on the slightest pretext and the game was beset with rumours of illegal payments as inducements to secure a transfer or to increase wages and bonuses beyond the permitted maximum.' He concluded that such a world was an assault on 'the moral fibre of men like Wilf Copping, Joe Mercer, and Eddie Hapgood'. But in immediate post-war football, moral fibre turned out to be a distinct disadvantage to creating a football team and earning a living.

Dad did not tell us children any stories about this time or about Blackburn Rovers. In other circumstances what might have been an adventure had turned into a horrible mistake and a bitter learning curve. To his relief and joy, Mum had agreed to join Dad in Blackburn. If she had stayed in Kettering then who knows what could have happened, but there would have been no way she would or could or wanted to destroy their life together. She now resigned herself to how life would be and would go on being. Dad had identified schools for us children, had organised a very pleasant club house waiting for the moment she was ready to move. In late January 1946, he went back to Kettering to help and accompany the family back up through bitterly inhospitable weather to Blackburn. She had caught this train once before, Mum remembered. It would go on from Blackburn to Blackpool where she and her friends had danced and laughed 20 years ago. Was it really 20 years?

The fragments that drifted my way over the years about life in Blackburn are so tiny they barely form a picture. There was something about boxes of fresh fish left each week on the doorstep from a local fishmonger, a fan of Eddie's. There was the warning given in a kindly way over the garden fence by Mum's new neighbour, 'Mrs Hapgood, best not to hang clothes out to dry in the winter up here,' as Mum stood disconsolately with an ice-rigid towel in her cold hands. There was the kindness of strangers as when Dad was told by a supportive Rovers director when he resigned, 'You're a good man, Mr Hapgood. Don't you worry. The house on Revidge Road is yours as long as you need it.' There was the yearning desire in both our parents to put the privations, the lingering ugliness and depression of war behind them, to colour the world afresh. 'No more green lino and brown paint,' seemed Mum's most passionate wish.

At last, I have glimpses of my own life in our story. I remember how, across the road from our house the big park plunged down a steep hill, leaving the horizon to unroll over tops of houses and chimneys in a misty grey to the distant hills. It was called Corporation Park, an ugly name now, but a triumphant signal in those days of a new public domain. I remember running through the kitchen door in terror from the local tramp, Itchy-Coo, and Mum laughing and saying, 'He won't hurt you!' I remember a local photographer taking a 'Welcome to Blackburn' snap, just Dad, Margot and me and Margot refusing to smile because she had lost a front tooth. I remember our house, number 313, so clearly because of this much-treasured family photo. I didn't know that Mum was unhappy, but I did know there wasn't much singing. I just remember one little song that had recently become popular which Dad sang to me when I was three shortly after we arrived in Blackburn. He would sit me on his knee and sing it every April until I was too grown-up to think it anything but silly:

April's a lovely lady
She wears a golden crown
She rides in a golden carriage
When she comes to town.

The tiniest fragments, too slight to make a story.

Tony talked the most about Blackburn, the only member of the family to remember it with great affection. For him it was a joyous reunion with both his parents for the first time since the sad and frightening flight from Hutton Grove in 1939 and a pleasure to help his little sisters become members of his family. Now 16, he attended the Queen Elizabeth Grammar School but he was always out and about, always laughing, enjoying his growing independence. He would help Mum by taking Margot to her new school sitting on a little saddle with stirrups fixed to the crossbar of his bike; he played tennis well enough to be selected for the Lancashire county junior side; declared he wanted to be a footballer but Mum had got very upset and said, 'No.'

When we were older and he came to visit he told us he used to be bored by school, rolling his eyes towards Mum and whispering with his finger over his lips. Many years later again, he told us that he had found the grammar school a struggle because he had lost so much time in education when he was younger, first through illness and then evacuation. He also told us that Mum finally gave up trying to persuade him away from football. Instead she went over to Burnley Football Club with him to make sure he got a fair contract as a junior with proper professional terms. When we all travelled south again in 1949, Tony stayed in Lancashire hoping to become a footballer in his own right.

I doubt whether Dad ever bothered to find out what had happened to Blackburn after he left, although he must have known because we continued to live at Revidge Road for another year. He would have been the first to say that the elements of a successful football club are finely balanced. With his departure, whatever happened, it was a different club. But 'What if?' is a seductive temptation. Blackburn did just survive the 1946/47 season, finishing 17th out of 22 teams with 36 points but, in a sad vindication of Eddie's prediction, they were relegated at the end of the following season. Of the controversial new transfers, Frank McGorrighan had gone in the blink of an eye, only managing to complete a few months before returning to Hull City. Two other new star signings, Jock Weir and John Oakes, were transferred out mid-season and Alex Venters left at the end of the season. Blackburn were to remain in the Second Division for the next ten years.

The bigger picture is the more interesting one. The frenzied search for players, the difficult social conditions, the meagre fixed wages and the cattle-market transfer system were a catalyst for two significant changes that now dominate the football landscape. Money, so necessary for security or, at worst, subsistence in those early post-war times, seems now the ultimate measure of footballing excellence. At the top of the game, great players at 27 or so might manoeuvre for a 'last big contract' with a top club and for top wages. Alexis Sánchez made sure he left Arsenal for a £330,000 weekly pay packet at Manchester United but his football suffered. Perhaps playing didn't matter so much any more? Team harmony suffered too as Manchester United's brilliant goalkeeper David de Gea refused to sign a new contract on a mere £170,000 a week. Years earlier, Michael Owen preferred to sit most matches out at Manchester United rather than take a salary cut with a lower club. Gareth Bale, the Welsh international becalmed at Real Madrid, felt the same. What he earned seemed to be more important than whether he played. There is some scepticism about Arsenal's own Mesut Özil. Did his manager, Mikel Arteta, choose not to play him or did he choose not to play himself? Throughout the leagues, a scaled-down version of the same hard-nosed bargaining exists.

Today, players have agents and lawyers to oversee their contracts and negotiate the most lucrative job. And who can blame players for jumping on the carousel or begrudge them victory in the battle for rights waged by their predecessors? Lionel Messi, in tears at leaving Barcelona when they could not afford to pay him even half of his salary, joined Paris Saint-Germain in 2021 where it is reported that 'every month he will bank more than twice what the average British worker will earn in a lifetime'.

The ruthless terms and conditions of contracts even as late as 1960 had treated players like possessions but on the positive side ensured a stability of team identity. The unintended consequence of the modern transfer system is the destabilising of teams as individual players move around the UK, Europe and, for their retirement gigs, the world. A team is built globally and is perpetually fluid. Fans still take to their heart players who, like Liverpool's Steven Gerrard and Southampton's Matt Le Tissier, are one-club men. Inevitably such localism grows steadily weaker and in the Premier League today is virtually extinct. Even the crowds are changing. Many supporters still live locally but more live nationwide, stoking their support with annual replica kits and televised matches. Others live worldwide. The crowds in the huge stadia at the top clubs are invariably filled with 'tourist' supporters who can buy seats on the club websites before they visit England. They support the club but come to watch their countrymen. In 2001 Arsenal signed Junichi Inamoto, a Japanese player, who never made a Premier League appearance but ensured Japanese television rights and increased merchandise sales. Sometimes the league looks like a player 'soup'. 'Doesn't James Milner play for

Manchester City?' I catch myself thinking, 'Oh no, Liverpool?' Frank Lampard was a three-club man, Michael Owen a five-club man, and Peter Crouch possibly a nine-club man. Keep up! Like a video game, or a game of Top Trumps, players are a basket of sponsored assets. Bad or good? Just different – but the drive towards this difference gathered impetus in the immediate post-war years.

The six months after Dad resigned from Blackburn Rovers were a kind of family convalescence, even a family honeymoon. Whatever the immediate financial difficulties were – and they were considerable – whatever the future was to hold, these next few months Mum and Dad agreed were for resting, recovering, remembering. There had been no time for this since the summer of 1939, eight long years ago. Now they both needed to stop, take stock, get to know each other again, forget sadness and remember joy, bring their children together into a family. It was, after all, safe not to worry anymore about what the outside world was up to.

In spring, when they did raise their heads above the parapet, they could see the severe weather conditions were beginning to retreat. People everywhere, even in cities still bomb-scarred and exhausted, had finally begun to try and live as if war was over. All footballers would have agreed with Tommy Lawton when he wrote, 'But let's forget these horrible days.' There was a sense of change in the air and one momentous difference had somehow happened within weeks of VE Day. As Dad was witnessing for the first time the devastation and misery of the impact of war in western Europe, back home a Labour government had been returned in July 1945 with a massive swing and a committed determination to provide pathways from war, ignorance and poverty into peace, education, health, secure wages and universal pensions. Dad, remembering his disillusionment with the Labour MP Walter Baker way back in 1923, was sceptical and refused to vote. Mum was excited and hopeful. The war had wrought irreparable damage but now at last, she thought, there was hope for a new world ahead. We even had our first family holiday in wild and windy Scarborough, so impossibly far away I have no idea how we got there or back. I learned later that a relative of one of Dad's supporters ran a guest house there and he encouraged Dad to accept the gift of a week's recuperation. Mum, Dad, Tony, Margot and me.

And in that briefly carefree time, Mum told Dad she was pregnant. Yes, a new baby was due in late October 1947, who would become my younger brother Mike, arriving eight months after Dad's resignation, the only one of us not to be born in Kettering. Discovering again what it meant to be happy even after sadness and separation, their imagination was caught by a song from the new London show *Bless the Bride*. They began to sing again.

> This is my perfect day
> This is the day I shall remember the day I'm dying.
> They can't take this away
> It will be always mine, the sun and the wine,
> The sea birds crying.
> All happiness must pay.

I was far too young to know what the words meant, but their voices echoed through the years, full of joy but aware of transience. 'All happiness must pay.'

There was a momentary flurry of speculation when George Allison announced he would be stepping down as Arsenal manager at the end of what turned out to be a disappointing 1946/47 season for the club. In a brief but curious note in May of that year, the press asked 'Who gets the job of Arsenal manager?' suggesting that David Jack, Frank Moss and Eddie were rivals to the current assistant manager, Tom Whittaker. Jack had been ensconced at Middlesbrough since 1944, and Moss never returned to football after the outbreak of war. Only Eddie was free to be considered. The journalist had either not done his research or was simply concocting a story. Had Eddie waited and hoped during that summer that his luck had turned? I don't think so. He had been regularly in touch with Tom and guessed that Tom would move swiftly and seamlessly into the manager's chair. What he did hope now that Allison was out of the way, was that Tom, his old friend and mentor, would call him back to the Arsenal 'family', would recognise that he was needed, would want him back at Highbury as he had hinted in 1945.

When Tom commiserated with him after he left Blackburn, Eddie raised the subject. According to Eddie, Tom had said, 'There's only the third team job Eddie, and you wouldn't take that,' and he had replied, 'I'd take anything at Arsenal, Tom,' but had heard nothing more. Perhaps Tom didn't realise that football was more important to Eddie than status, or knew Eddie better than he knew himself so that he was wary of inviting such an influential character back. Perhaps only newly appointed, he didn't have enough influence. Perhaps. Perhaps not. Perhaps.

Instead another old Arsenal voice came calling. When Leslie Knighton, who had preceded Herbert Chapman at Arsenal, heard that Eddie had left Rovers he invited him to join Midland League team Shrewsbury Town, where he was currently manager. On the condition he could leave whenever a suitable managerial position came up, Eddie signed for Shrewsbury. It was the right moment. He had played a couple of times for Blackburn and knew he was still just about match fit. He always worked hard at his fitness, breathing and muscle strength, drawing on what he had learned in the RAF to add to his familiar Arsenal routines. Playing for Shrewsbury he began to recapture the familiar joyous unity of mind, spirit and body, incredibly and wonderfully, to have fun on a football pitch. He was 39. Once again he gave journalists who were only too happy to enjoy a glimpse from the remembered past, something to write about. Shrewsbury swept into the spotlight at the beginning of this season by signing on players whose names were household words among football followers, particularly one who could double as a goalkeeper when necessary.

'Drawn to play against Arsenal in the [FA] Cup, he [Eddie Hapgood] stepped up to rescue Shrewsbury Town from defeat and to ensure a draw just as he had often done as Arsenal's reserve goalkeeper. Here, in pouring rain and on a sticky pitch, "Hapgood's safe hands gained the non-league club another chance".'

He played with energy and delight, helping his team to reach the final of the Welsh Cup and to win the 1947/48 Midland

1942 England v Scotland. Eddie introduces Mrs Clementine Churchill to his team-mates. She later wrote to congratulate him on England's victory.

1943 War Newly commissioned Pilot Officer Hapgood with his mother and younger sister Iris in Bristol

1946 Eddie now manager of Blackburn FC with his two daughters Margot (7) and Lynne (3)

In 1945 as war ended, Eddie published Football Ambassador and … found time for a game of golf with old friend Stanley Matthews

1948 Tony follows in his father's footsteps and signs for Burnley FC

1960 Beyond football. Eddie and Maggie move to Dorset

Sept 2011 Mike and Lynne join the Arsenal 125 anniversary celebrations in the Emirates hospitality suite

2011 Down the generations. Mike and Lynne celebrate their father on the Arsenal wall of legends

2012 Down the generations. Eddie's grandson Jacob flies the flag for Arsenal among other 'top fans'

2019 Down the generations. Eddie's grandson Sam brings great-grandson Benji to his first Arsenal match.

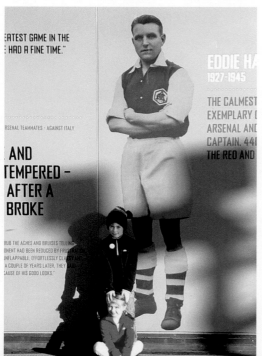

2021 Lockdown is over! Great granddaughter Abigail finally gets to watch her first match at Arsenal

A life-size Eddie Hapgood, red to the core, in the Arsenal Museum

England leader and captain from 1934-1943

League. Without pressure or expectation, he enjoyed again, if only for a few short months, the exultation of movement.

Then, around Christmas time, Eddie heard that Watford were looking for a manager. It fitted the bill. If he was appointed he could take the family back south, nearer to London and also nearer to Kettering. The football world was settling down. Yes, he had made mistakes and had taken too much for granted, but he now knew better what to expect and his faith in his ability to build and inspire a team was unshaken. Immediately after Christmas, Eddie, selected from nearly 200 applicants, was appointed manager. He had learned three important lessons at Blackburn: keep directors on your side, allow them to think they are right, and don't assume they'll be pleased if you're successful. There is a new-found caution in an interview with the local paper shortly after he arrived, with the journalist writing, perhaps disappointed by Eddie's response to his questions, 'Hapgood is not making prophecies. Neither is he discussing policy. He will rely on the team the directors pick until he has seen the boys play. After that we may see something of the Arsenal touch at Watford.'

Eddie was grateful to Shrewsbury but as Christmas loomed, he felt able for the first time to announce, 'I have wrapped up my football boots for the last time … and I am calling it a day.' He had always wanted to make that decision for himself – not the war, not journalists and certainly not George Allison. A new wave of optimism filled them. Mum and Dad moved Margot, me and baby Mike to 88 Raglan Gardens, Watford. He had finally accepted it was time to move forward and wholeheartedly join the rest of the 'Golden Line-up', his former team-mates David Jack, Bob John,

Ted Drake and Jack Crayston among others, in a manager's seat. He felt ready to take his passion and experience, his whole self, back into management. In a way, it felt like a beginning.

Eddie inherited the unhappy, struggling Third Division (South) club in January 1948. He desperately wanted to be given time and support to create a team. Pride in performance, individual effort, team cohesion and absolute commitment are the product of time. The changes he wanted, as he well knew, would not happen overnight. They needed belief and cooperative effort. Summoned by the board of directors soon after his arrival and asked whether he could build a successful team with £7,000, he had mentally crossed his fingers and confidently said he could, while wondering whether this was a trick to test him. His initial apprehension rapidly turned to glee as he tracked down five new players at bargain-basement prices who all did well, especially Geoff Morton, a goalkeeper, who Eddie regarded as a real capture, consistently turning in five-star performances. Gradually, as results went well and gates increased, he began to relax. Perhaps he had called it right. He began to enjoy himself.

The 1949/50 season saw positive signs of a change of mood, of football landscape, of supporter enthusiasm and results. As the new decade dawned, there was 'football fever' in Watford, the *Daily Mirror* trumpeted. 'People pat manager Eddie Hapgood ... on the back as he walks through the streets. They are proud of the way in which he has built up the team since he became manager in 1948.' The trigger for all this excitement was Watford's victory in a replay over the up-and-coming Second Division side Preston

North End in the FA Cup, a team recently catching headlines for their high spending on new players. None of these players apparently could 'break down the Watford defence', and Harper, the Watford left-back, came in for particular praise. Eddie's sense of team organisation was characteristically taking root from the defence outwards.

The thrilling victory over Preston earned the Watford team a fourth-round match against the favourites for the FA Cup, First Division side Manchester United, led by Matt Busby, the manager Eddie had encountered that demoralising night on the Blackburn station platform two years previously. 'UNITED, Beware these men from Watford' blazed the *Daily Mirror* headline. Watford were defeated, but only by a goal scored in the final minute. Watford got all the plaudits. 'Hapgood's boys' were 'magnificent throughout … the cheeky brilliance and enthusiasm of the Watford lads made them the equals of the Busby machine', according to the press. The final verdict was splashed in a headline: 'Oh, Mr Busby – What a Lucky Day!' Supporters were even stirred to write to the local paper, one of them full of admiration for how Eddie had turned 'an empty purse' into a 'team that can hold its own among the rest'. He had yet to discover how literal the phrase 'empty purse' was.

Eddie's two-year contract was due to expire just two weeks after the thrilling Preston victory on 11 January but, full of confidence and excitement, it was not at the forefront of his mind. To prepare for the match against Manchester United on 27 January, he took the team down to Brighton for training, declaring that this practice, unusual for Watford, was the best way to ensure physical and mental preparedness. Sadly, a lesson he had failed to learn was 'never turn your back'. While he and the players were away and the fans' attention was fixed excitedly on the upcoming match, some board members forced an incomprehensible move to undermine Eddie. The day before the match, the national press issued a formal statement from the club, 'The board have had under consideration the question of Mr Hapgood's contract and have offered him a further limited term of appointment.' Formal language yes, but in the circumstances, 'limited' sounded hostile and the concluding sentence barbed, 'The directors have not yet received Mr Hapgood's decision whether he wishes to continue on the board's terms.' It was not surprising that Eddie had not responded. He knew nothing about this 'offer'.

It isn't clear who originally authorised the press release but later the chairman acknowledged to Eddie in a private conversation that he was being badly treated and that the board's decision was by no means unanimous. In a one-to-one meeting, he tried to persuade Eddie to accept the 'limited term' contract to the end of the season, saying that during that time he would try to influence certain members of the board to agree to renew his contract until the end of the 1950/51 season or as promised in the original contract, until 1952. He kept his word but after an acrimonious meeting, the board confirmed they would only reconsider the situation at the end of the current season, and with no guarantee. Eddie was stunned. In his surprise he didn't know whether he was stung more by what seemed a complete lack of respect for him or an irresponsible disregard for the wellbeing of the club. He did not want to act hastily as he felt he probably had at Blackburn. He hesitated. He discussed what to do with Maggie. Should he challenge the board's decision this time, ask to hear and discuss their reasons? He re-read his original contract. Then the significance of an oddity about it dawned on him. He hadn't noticed it at the time. One sentence contained a word boldly underlined:

'At the end of this period [the initial two-year contract], the position will be reviewed, and if <u>both</u> sides are satisfied with the position as it stands at that time a further contract of three years will be granted.'

Eddie stared at it. He hadn't a leg to stand on. The three-year promise was fake; the club had reserved the right from the very beginning to make a unilateral decision on any issue of their choice. Upset and frustrated, once again Eddie felt bounced into action. His reputation was currently high. He could not risk working to the end of the season and going out of contract to face a summer with no wages and no job lined up. It was so illogical that he now felt sure they would dismiss him anyway. Despite what he had learned at Blackburn, he now discovered that there were many other ways directors could disagree and many other strategies for getting their own way.

The conflict in the Watford boardroom over strategy and finance from the moment he arrived cut his career short but he was not himself the focus of discontent. Every director had their own particular axe to grind. It was a nasty, self-harming mix of individual self-aggrandisement, resentment and considerable corporate incompetence. Directors are impatient, crowds fickle and players easily demoralised. It had taken Eddie longer to digest the knowledge that a manager was considered largely irrelevant, just someone a club had to have, to be employed or sacked as required and to take the blame when anything went wrong. He was puzzled by why their manager seemed to be the least of their concerns.

For the second time in his short managerial career, he felt he had no option. He decided to hand in his resignation. 'It was a bad moment,' he wrote later, and added, 'Never in my soccer career had I experienced a knockout blow such as this. I was really choked … All my ambition for the Blues [Watford's kit was blue and white at this time] was hit for six. I had organised Division 2 level football at Vicarage Road and now all my hopes and dreams were snuffed out and my castle was indeed tumbling down. As long as I live I shall never experience such a black moment of despair … I had always had enthusiasm for the game I loved, self-reliant and confident but I was fast finding out that these qualities are not enough if one cannot run with the board whether they want to keep you or get rid of you.'

His wretchedness can be heard in his conclusion, 'They are the people who call the tune.'

Rightly proud of his achievement, Eddie left Watford with little more than a bagful of congratulatory and commiseratory letters, the good wishes of puzzled supporters and two managerships behind him. 'What went wrong, I am still trying to find out,' he wrote later. Is it some kind of bad joke that Javi Gracia might have felt exactly the same nearly 50 years later? Appointed to Watford in 2018, he was the first manager in seven years to finish a season and still be there to start a new one with the club. He took Watford to the 2019 FA Cup Final against Manchester City in May but was sacked in September after the fifth game of the 2019/20 season. 'It's the Watford way of operating,' the BBC Radio 5 Live pundit chuckled the following day. No doubt they chuckled even more loudly when Watford's new manager, Quique Sánchez Flores, was sacked three months later.

To many directors, managers are, quite simply, irritants; owners can be just as bad. In good times, the press shower managers with praise; they appear to have all the power and glamour of team selection; they are assumed to have considerable football knowledge. They have their own footballing history. The public know them. It is the manager to whom the players turn for support, advice, encouragement and praise. It is the manager who is on show at every match. How can directors get their place in the sun? A director's most lethal weapon, according to Eddie, was to patronise his decisions by criticising team selection, questioning his transfers, suggesting their own preference in the transfer market or to pass information – wink, wink – to local reporters. In extreme cases, a director can openly override the manager, countermanding his instructions, limiting his funds, downgrading his tasks. It only takes one over-opinionated director to block a board decision or to convince others that perhaps he has a point.

Again, the apparent gap between the 1930s and today disappears. Despite the huge changes in money, management and football culture created chiefly by globalisation, little has changed. One example is Marcelino García Toral, who heard of his sacking as Valencia manager in September 2019 through the media several hours before the owner, Peter Lim, made a formal announcement. Marcelino had given Valencia stability, leading the team to a Champions League place and inspiring them to win their first trophy in 11 years, beating Barcelona to claim the Copa del Rey. Unfortunately, he had committed the cardinal sin for which few managers are forgiven. The general public, the press and the fans saw him, rather than the owner, as the architect of success – in spite of the owner, in fact. He had to go. Lim immediately installed his eighth manager in five years.

While boards squabble, managers have to cope. Eddie grew to learn that directors' provocative behaviour could swiftly narrow to cruel humiliation to prove a manager's incompetence or push him out of the door with minimum fuss. Watford were no different. In the summer of 1949, a new director joined the board and immediately set about establishing his position. Soon after his arrival, he dropped into Eddie's office, greeted him in an apparently friendly way, and then said, 'Hmmm … you'll never be a Herbert Chapman you know.' Before Eddie could reply, the director left the office, saying, 'You can't afford another Blackburn.' 'The wedge was in,' as Eddie wrote later. 'He meant harm to me.' More insidious and even harder to fight was humiliation rooted in class difference. In Watford's case, the chairman, Rigby Taylor, a wealthy businessman, often held board meetings in the evening at his large country residence. As various contractual disputes finally ran their course, Eddie was invited to attend one meeting to finalise the matter at the chairman's home. He was surprised but he had no reason to be unduly concerned given the chairman's declared support.

Eddie's account of what happened is painful to read:

'The outcome of all this was a request to attend the chairman's house and to be there at eight o'clock. I turned up on time and saw outside the house a fairly large car with a chauffeur in attendance. I asked him if he was waiting for anyone, thinking the board had other business to discuss before seeing me. I hung about for the biggest part of an hour until I saw the car drive off. I knocked and was admitted. I explained the reason why I seemed to be late, divested myself of my top-coat and sat down. The chairman, Mr Rigby Taylor, quite friendly, opened the meeting by saying, "Well Eddie, the board has discussed the renewal of your contract very thoroughly and has decided not to extend it any further." I stood up looking for my coat and said with great difficulty, "Thank you. Goodnight." "Do have a drink Eddie before you go." This from the chairman. I mumbled something about being a tea-drinker and left.'

As in the case of Blackburn, hindsight does not help and Eddie would not be interested. But the facts remain that Watford leapt 11 places in the Third Division (South) to finish a triumphant sixth in May 1950 only to plunge 17 places and require re-election the season after Eddie left. Watford's official club website records:

'The next 12 years [1948–1960] might be classed as the least remarkable in the club's history … the FA Cup offered the chance to escape the humdrum routine, but only one campaign delivered anything to recall fondly – a victory away to Division 2 Preston in 1950 followed by a narrow but controversial defeat to Manchester United.'

In 1956, Len Goulden, Eddie's international team-mate who had scored that blistering goal against Germany in 1938 and the sixth manager Watford had appointed since the war, resigned. Word was put around yet again that the club needed a new manager. It was a clear indictment of consistently poor financial judgement and incompetence, the frustration caused by short-termism, the failure of the board to agree a coherent policy and to co-operate in making it work. When Goulden stepped down, there was even a move among fans, nostalgic for success, to bring the long-gone but not forgotten Eddie Hapgood back. By then it was not surprising that Watford were in decline but rather than investing in tried and tested footballing values, the club continued to fight for their life by cutting wages, cancelling player contracts, advising them to go part-time and sacking managers before their summer wages became due. At the end of the 1957/58 season Rigby Taylor resigned, saying he was 'too old and tired, too disappointed and disillusioned'. He may well have regretted giving in to fractious board members in 1950 and releasing the man who created Watford's only starry moment in 12 years.

We children were learning that nowhere is for ever. My Watford world was only Raglan Gardens, a one-dimensional children's colouring book house where a few pages have bits coloured in. I can see it clearly but it was never alive to me. The house was set back from a wide road and seemed large with big bay windows to both floors. I remember the horse-pulled van crunching up the unadopted road to deliver milk. The milkman jumped off at each house taking bottles out of the crates at the back as the horse wandered slowly past, its head hanging heavily down. I would watch, half afraid and half excited at the idea he would run away, but it knew the whole round by heart and always stopped at the next house. I wonder whether it prompted memories for Dad.

It seemed odd to me that neighbours would keep their shovels at the ready in the hope of collecting some fresh manure for their rose beds but it did mean that the road was always clean. On the same day every week, the rag-and-bone man, long grown out of horse-power, would drive a dirty van up the road pulling a large trailer heaped higgledy-piggledy with petrol cans, old bikes, ovens and all kinds of unidentifiable objects. I would run to listen half fascinated, half afraid. Unlike the milkman who was accompanied only by the pleasant early morning ringing and pinging of bottles, the waste collector added to the dissonant bangs of metal by shouting loudly to announce his presence. There was a definite growl to his voice.

I don't know what Mum remembered. I don't think she ever mentioned Watford after we left. She had barely reconciled herself to the move and now she was having to adapt again to more changes, of place, of neighbours and friends, of domestic circumstances, at the same time supporting Dad through the different stresses and strains, pleasures and triumphs of his new job. Far from returning to London, Watford seemed as cut off as Blackburn. With a young toddler and two schoolchildren, she was unable to jump on the nearby Watford overground train and enjoy a day in London or even revisit Hutton Grove. The war and its aftermath had taken Dad's youth but it had taken hers too. She had had four homes in nine years and, during those uncertain times, she had had three children. I think she was drifting, dreaming in a kind of self-defence that communicated itself to us. She temporarily lost her light-heartedness and her pleasure in everything we did or said.

I think it was at this point that Margot began to take responsibility for me. Not that either of us noticed it but it just became how it was. When we left the house in the morning in our brown school uniforms, we turned left to walk down the road to catch the bus. Holding my hand, she took me to our new school and brought me safely home. On Saturday mornings when we left the house we turned right and then left on our way to elocution lessons. I would wait for her to finish her drama lesson, sitting at the back of the room, my attention partly drawn by her voice as she recited the words she had learned. Acting had already become her passion. Then she would sit and wait for me but what I did in my lessons I cannot remember at all. The best thing was that we would talk to each other all the way there and all the way back.

Among several offers Dad had received when news of his departure from Watford became known, one I only learned about many years later was from a Dutch club, but I never discovered which one. Apparently Dad was tempted. He had visited Amsterdam in 1935 and thought it a wonderful city but Mum wasn't sure it would be a good idea for us children. She had never been abroad and may well have felt daunted by such a big change.

Another option was as a freelance sports journalist with a national paper, no doubt prompted by the success of *Football Ambassador* and Eddie's friendships with some sports journalists. Yet another was from Bath City, an established Southern League club. After much heart-searching they chose Bath, despite their non-league status, because he was offered a five-year contract and a house. Five years, Dad thought, would take us all just a bit further down the line to security. Mum was sceptical but Dad still hadn't learned or wanted to learn that people don't keep their word. He would ask what kind of a world would it be if you assume bad faith whenever you strike a deal? He would give Bath the commitment and skill he had given Arsenal, Blackburn and Watford and trust to the future.

And so we moved to Bath, a glorious honey-coloured city, where the buildings roll up the hills in symmetrically curved terraces of 18th-century urban elegance and look down on the deep Avon Valley with its long Roman history fostered by the hot springs that flow into the town centre. But football was located in Twerton on the fringes of the city, on the fringes of Bath life, consciousness and politics. We learned soon enough that it was where many people thought we belonged.

13

Dreaming of Bath

Now I have caught up with where I began our story: Bath, 1950. Memories of family times, of Dad's stories, of this house where we felt so loved and secure was where I began because that is where, at about seven years old, I first became conscious of them. Each of us had a different take on our move to Bath. Tony, now 19, would have been well aware of the significance of Dad's resignation from Watford but he was doing National Service (and hating it) so we only saw him occasionally. Perhaps Margot, who was 11 when we left Watford and moved to Bath, was more aware of the change in our lives than I, and perhaps even had some sense of our parents' anxieties. I had not quite forgotten a place called Watford although probably only as a reflection of Margot's memories. Mike remembers nothing about Watford. For him life began in Bath.

Whatever our different pasts, we all felt and lived as if the house we moved to in March 1950 was ours, the beginning and forever. A large detached 1930s house set in generous gardens, backing on to farmland and towards the end of a road that turned into countryside, this time-limited, club-tied home was the crucible of our happiest memories. Even when you find out later that what you remember was only a tiny part of the picture, it doesn't change anything. The clarity still remains. Pull those memories up for a moment and, if anything, they become clearer, more substantial. To us children, it always seemed that our family walked on air. All we knew was a fluid, easy-going security in which we played and talked and tumbled towards a distant maturity we never thought about. We didn't realise that we *were* walking on air, that we floated unaware buoyed only by a closely woven raft of love. We had no home of our own, no security, and yet somehow, as in a fairy tale, we were able to imagine we did. This was the gift our parents gave us even as their own world darkened around them.

The back garden was the place of dreams. Unsurprisingly, since he was barely three when we arrived, Mike's earliest memory is the back lawn, where playing through that first summer, he witnessed our father's quest for a perfect lawn. Dad would mow it, weed it, examine it for flaws and mow it again. Then, with a sharp cutter, selected from a set of garden tools given to him years before for a *Weekly Illustrated* photo shoot, he would slice the edges into dark, horizontal lines. Mum would sigh in frustration as the flower beds grew bigger and the lawn smaller. Many years later, I watched my brother stoop and pluck a small daisy head from his own lawn with a careful, instantly recognisable gesture internalised from our father. The garden was large and made larger by the field that ran beyond the garden wall and on which we would sit and talk. Sometimes, we'd drop boldly to the other side but mostly we'd just sit and swing our legs. Mike was, after all, not big enough to jump down or scramble back up. He did once fall into the field and into the nettle bed just below so we were very careful after that. The wall couldn't be seen from the house, shut off by a trellis that divided the flower garden from the vegetable patch.

We were different ages but one person – rather like toddler triplets, who put their spoons into the mouth beside them thinking it is their own. There were odd moments when we realised we were separate such as when Margot and I watched Mike sitting on the grass with his best friend John. They were four and their heads were bent towards each other. They were talking very seriously and intently. 'What could they possibly have to talk about?' Margot wondered. Or when I was playing the corpse of Edward IV while Margot practised a speech for her forthcoming drama exam. Although she was cross with me for opening my eyes and making her giggle, in that glimpse, I had seen her flashing eyes and proud shoulders looming above me.

In that garden, Margot (marvellous Margot) would play tennis against Lynne (luscious Lynne) keeping up a Wimbledon-like commentary ('and marvellous Margot has established a good lead') on every ball until the garden next door or twilight swallowed the ball. When I was alone, I'd play tennis against the wall, banging the ball triumphantly over a chalk-line tennis net. In that garden, Dad would interrupt play, catching the ball and juggling it from head to shoulders to knee to foot, challenging us to try and retrieve it. We never could because we laughed so much, and he laughed too but the ball never fell. In that garden, Mum successfully rode a bicycle for the first time but forgot to turn, sailing triumphantly into the hollyhocks. She would laugh as vigorously and totally as Dad when she missed every ball he threw to her. 'No ball sense,' he would inform us children, shaking his head in mock tragedy. In that garden, she spotted the raspberry canes moving gently in the still air and rushed down the path to pluck Mike, his fist and his mouth full of fruit, from his own cornucopia. But it is the silence, or a sort of silence, which I hear most clearly. Deckchairs ('don't move them up or down, in case you get your fingers pinched') only came out during the cricket season. Dad, apparently asleep but alert to the cricket commentary whispering through the French door into the sunshine, would hold the mood of the garden in stillness.

The house itself was large, full of rooms with uncertain usage which made it seem larger as we drifted from space to space as the mood took us. The front room was shadowed by a large morello cherry tree that leaned over from the garden next door, cutting out the light and deepening the heaviness of the solid dark oak furniture. We rarely used it because it was too cold for even the gas fire to warm it in winter, but it was good to be quiet in and it was, after all, our parents' library. The number of books never seemed to increase. This was a collection that predated the war and the births of their three younger children. There was the *Beauty Blue Book* (my mother's – an American publication; where did she come across it?) full of pictures of women doing the oddest exercises with cushions and chairs. Mum knew the exercises by heart, carrying them out with scrupulous care, her hand on the bedstead swinging her legs and arms backwards and forwards until she burst out laughing at my expression. It also offered gnomic wisdom, advising me to make sure I always looked my best to welcome my husband home from work and, mysteriously, to be sure to tuck a tissue under my pillow when I went to bed. There was the Harold Fink book, *Relief from Nervous Tension* (my father's book full of breathing exercises – a legacy of his air force days). He would amuse us by doing relaxation sessions. We would lie on the floor with our eyes closed while he coaxed us to draw in our breath and then expel it slowly through our bodies and out through our big toes. Another favourite was learning to clench and unclench one muscle at a time until we could achieve complete limpness. 'You have to feel the tightness of a muscle to know when it is fully relaxed,' we learned. The best times were when we did 'relaxation' and he would conjure up pictures of sunny beaches and warm air while our minds wandered.

When I was on my own, I read my way through *Bulldog Drummond*, *The Scarlet Pimpernel* and, although Mum forbade me, Mary Webb's *Precious Bane*. Pleasingly disturbing was a book of freaks, photographs of Siamese twins, hairy ladies, giants and dwarfs. Sometimes I would do my homework in that room, my books spread out on the large refectory table facing the unlit fire. Then, I could enter the world of the painting hung over the fire on the opposite wall. It was an oil painting in orange and brown hues of an old woman (three blobs of paint) about to cross a small rustic bridge (two blobs) and nearly invisible in the darkness of the woods and the lowering sky just glimpsed inside the frame.

If the front room had any specific identity, it was as the arena of important events. We ate Christmas meals there and we ate every meal there when Tony was home. We would hang about longing for breakfast and nagging Mum to serve it up, but she was adamant that there was no breakfast until Tony appeared, even though he often didn't come down until nearing mid-morning and by then even Mum began to show signs of irritation. Meals had other irritations. When he turned sidewards, Mike could see his face in the sideboard mirror and took every opportunity to pull faces and admire himself until Margot thwarted him by hanging a towel over the mirror. The single most significant event that happened in that room for me was the day I was summoned by my father, who was standing with his back to the painting. He handed me an envelope. I knew my FA Cup Final tickets had arrived. As an FA Cup Final bride, I needed a special dress. During the weeks that followed, the big table was covered with the pattern, material, cotton and pins for what Mum would turn into my Wembley dress. I still have a fragment of the sky blue cotton decorated with the tracery of white cow parsley and dotted with folded yellow rose buds. Nothing, absolutely nothing in this room survived the fire.

The 'sitting' room was a more boisterous arena. Although our father regularly chanted the 1950s mantra, 'Children should be seen but not heard,' and solemnly assured us that his dearest ambition was to live alone without any children around, his words and actions whipped up an ecstasy of laughter while his evident pleasure in our company, our conversations and our achievements made us bold. In winter, he would set up trays of objects for memory games. Margot would partner Mum and I would partner Dad for whist games before bedtime. Dad always won, and Mum would smile wryly and say, 'He always gets the good cards.' When Mike and I were on our own, the large sofa became an embankment with a tow path. Mike would steer his boat vigorously, reaching unprecedented speeds while I galloped alongside, the dressing gown cord reins expertly controlling the back of the sofa as I dug my heels into its side. But often it was just radio times, with *Journey into Space, Take It From Here, Round the Horne, Paul Temple* shared or ignored as we did homework (Margot and I), read the paper (Dad), knitted (Mum) or thrummed dinky toys around the carpet (Mike).

Going to sleep and waking up were the only activities that took place in the five big, unheated bedrooms. There was the pink room, the blue room, Margot's and Mike's rooms and the spare room, the fascinating L-shaped one on the second floor. The pink room, which had an eiderdown covered in pink, was our parents' bedroom. We didn't go in there much unless we were frightened in the night or we wandered in because Mum was there, exercising or making the beds or making up and therefore a captive audience. I used to be fascinated by watching the ritual of making up. Mum was beautiful but not in a Hollywood kind of way. She was unusual in a way that would not draw an observer's immediate attention. Her face was extraordinarily symmetrical. I would sit on the bed watching her actions in the mirror. She would draw her lipstick firmly and surely on her lips, blotting the excess by kissing a tissue. Her dressing table had two wing mirrors and I would watch the multitude of identical mothers until she burst out laughing. And that was her true beauty. Her laughter would bubble up, her head would be thrown back and her face would brighten with delight.

The blue room, which had a double bed with an eiderdown covered in blue, was my room. If I opened the door as wide as possible and pushed my book into the pool of light cast by the landing light, I could just about read at long distance. I wasn't supposed to. It also had a light switch hanging down over the mid-way point of the pillow which summoned up images of the poisonous snake in Conan Doyle's Sherlock Holmes story, *The Speckled Band*, as soon as the light went out, driving me into my parents' bed on more than one occasion. In a way, I shared it with Margot. She had a sort of *pied-a-terre* in the house, a room filled with her precious collection of china horses and horsey souvenirs, and walls covered with posters of horses, but she wouldn't sleep there because one day she spotted a spider running under the bed. I suppose it became a kind of spare room because I slept there when I suffered some unspecified illness when I was 12 that was never given a name but which promoted me for several weeks to a bed on my own in Margot's room.

During one of those boring days without energy, a new song was introduced to the family repertoire. Mum and Dad had recently gone to the Bristol Hippodrome to a Frank Sinatra concert, part of his 1953 British tour, and couldn't stop singing 'I've Got You Under My Skin'. There was a dark, pulsing undertone to it that I found troubling. A child's anxiety when drawn in to adult feelings perhaps, or the presence of a grief I didn't understand? 'Don't you know little fool, you never can win.' 'All happiness must pay.' Mike's room was the smallest, looking out over the front garden and next to our parents' room. One happy autumn, I helped my mother put fresh wallpaper up there, silver grey with white sprigs. I was always considered the practical one.

School was the ultimate structuring force for us children in this fluid, easy-going life. For Margot and I, primary school and secondary school were the same, the Bath Convent Grammar School, La Sainte Union, which she attended from 1951 for six years and I attended for ten. It was located in the centre of Bath and somehow it was routine for us to nearly miss the bus from our out-of-city home near Weston village. Margot, four years older than me and physically strong, would seize my hand and shout 'Run!' as we raced to the bus stop. If I faltered, she ran on ahead, planting her foot firmly on the platform until she could heave me to safety. Oddly, even when we caught the bus, we were still nearly late and would run, chests heaving, from Kingsmead, across the Parade, over Pulteney Bridge, through the back gate, across the tennis courts and into the dark, musty-smelling cloakrooms. During school, we led separate lives but after school, after netball or tennis practice, after elocution and drama classes, we would meet up as if by accident and make our way home together. Sometimes we would get off at the stop before home, at what was called a fare stage in those days, and spend our saved bus fare on aniseed balls, liquorice root or cherry lips to cheer the final lap of our journey home. There was still sweet rationing in the early 1950s but those sweets we could afford slipped under the net. I never understood why going home was such a leisurely affair compared with the hectic start of the day.

Coming and going changed with the years, largely, as I now realise, to accommodate Margot. She refused to eat school dinners, her resistance so total she coloured some mashed potato with green ink and brought it home in her satchel to prove her claims that it was mouldy. For a time, we were given lunch money and had milk shakes and ham sandwiches at Hans Milk Bar in Bath, where we could stare out at the statues of Roman leaders whose heads topped the walls of the Roman Baths. We also learned to perfect the art of sucking up all the raspberry-flavoured bubbles while leaving the glass still full of untouched pink milk. That must have become too expensive for the family budget because for a time, our father picked us up on the Parade in the centre of Bath outside the newsagents and took us home for lunch. On Fridays he would share a Cadbury's chocolate bar with us, 'bought with my last sixpence' he would say, and we both believed and did not believe him. We knew he might be prepared to be extravagant because Mum often told us in a teasing voice mixed with exasperation about his eating a whole pack of three walnut whips on their first date without offering her one, but our minds skipped away from believing him totally because the phrase 'last sixpence' had a frightening ring.

When Margot left school, I submitted to the rigours of school dinners again. Eating what was offered was preferable to being spotted scraping it into the waste bowl, having it retrieved by a nun saying, 'You gave thanks to God for your food and then threw it away,' as she slopped the muddled mass back on to my plate. Sometimes I went to the library after school. The City Library in those days shared the massive Victorian building overlooking the River Avon with the art gallery. I would often wander up the stairs and gaze at the paintings of ships and of Admiral Lord Nelson, a fitting backdrop to Bath's naval connections. I remember deciding that Nelson was beautiful and, of course, in

Abbott's idealised portrait, he is. His serene gaze, the suggestion of a smile on his delicate features transcended the gaudiness of his medalled uniform. Oh, to be so sublime.

School and happiness were inseparable for me during my day-pupil years. It was a comfortable world where I was always approved and could always fit in. I enjoyed my lessons and notched up a happiness level if I was unable to close my satchel because of the bulging demands of the evening's homework. For Margot, school was a trial. She was irritated by its restrictions and irreverent in her attitudes. She longed to be out and away, free to follow the acting career she had set her heart on. She could do anything she put her mind to, but she mostly chose not to. A real talent for tennis, fostered and encouraged by our father, was squandered by lack of concentration. It just didn't matter that much to her, and whatever she was dreaming about would seize her at a crucial moment, and the point would be lost. She left school too early, after one year of sixth form study, to work in the imposing Admiralty building overlooking the Parade Gardens while she applied for theatre school and prepared her auditions. I stayed long enough to garner a clutch of exams and leave with overwhelming relief.

My mother's choice of schools for her children reflects the strange paradox of working-class aspirations in those days, burgeoning opportunities but sluggish social change in the immediate post-war years. At some point, Mum became a warrior for her children. She and Dad shared the same social values but in the early years of their marriage they came to understand them in different ways. Sitting in the back row of the footballing theatre our mother saw the bigger picture, the insecurity behind the glamour, not immediately, not clearly, not entirely, but with an instinctive political acuity. Our mother grew to see Dad's successful football career as a way of keeping her eye on another ball. Perceptively and unselfishly, her vision made it possible for her three youngest children to enjoy all the social and educational largesse that began to flow from 1945 over a drab and under-achieving country. Dad's desire for his children was quite simply for their happiness, the joy of the moment, the fulfilment of themselves in whatever they chose to do. Coaching us at tennis, cricket, football was never about sporting achievement, but was the means through which he shared his deepest values with us, sons and daughters alike. For her daughters, Mum's choice of Catholic schools (we also attended an Ursuline convent school in Watford) was nothing to do with religion. It was a determination to give us an education as far away as possible from the world my father's job now occupied. It was the nearest she could get to ensuring, as she saw it, our future safety.

Today perhaps, the obsession with social mobility in someone who wished she had faith but had none and who was always a passionate and angry socialist, may be open to criticism. My mother inherited her own mother's darkest fears of us all slipping out of reach below society's Plimsoll line. She could never quite shake off the terror of the workhouse and of the 'abyss' of poverty. The word summoned up the vision of an earthly hell.

Mike went to the local primary school, a short walk from where we lived, so he left after us in the morning and got home before we did. He briefly brought scandal on the family when he wrote for a school exercise that his mother always got up late and drank gin juice. Concerned teachers and our bewildered, embarrassed mother finally agreed to acknowledge his vivid imagination although our mother remained baffled about how he had learned the word gin. Our house was strictly teetotal, and, while we were growing up, Mum was never able to enjoy the sherry or damson wine with a slice of fruit cake she would nostalgically mention at Christmas as a country custom.

I think it is very likely that she found it hard to cope with three children, a large house and the uncertainty of my father's job. Mum had not been well during her most recent pregnancy and Mike was a delicate child. He would wake in the night with painful legs which my mother would massage to relieve the pain. Four years younger than me, he developed his own idiosyncratic life. He collected Dinky Toys, information about dinosaurs and, much to Margot's and my fascination, admirers among the elderly ladies living in nearby houses who invited him to tea. One gave him her collection of *London Illustrated News*. Another, who can't have been elderly despite our perceptions, stayed in touch with him all her life. At the tail end of the family, he was adored and ignored by his sisters in turns. He was too young to understand the nature of his parents' looming crisis in Bath, but for the same reason, he was unfortunate to be young enough to be closest to its aftermath.

Our parents were our best fans and greatest supporters. Mum showed me how to cook, to sew and to knit and packed me off to piano lessons on Saturday mornings and horse riding in the afternoon. She would test my irregular French verbs and Latin conjugations. She would suggest ideas for my English essays and listen when I read out the final version on Sunday afternoons as she ironed. When Margot failed the 11-plus, Mum decided that money must be found for her to stay at the convent. By a strange anomaly, Catholics had to pass to get a place but non-Catholics could pay. She encouraged her to act, enjoyed her flamboyance and sense of drama, accompanied her to local amateur dramatics whenever she could and occasionally even bought tickets to performances at the Bristol Old Vic. Margot's flamboyance and talent was a household fact. Although it was Mum who did the encouraging, and I suspect nursed fantasies of her own about acting, surely Margot's art must have come from our father. He enjoyed nothing more than an audience for a good story. The Bath house was his own theatre. When we prompted him, he would gladly rise to the bait, alive with energy and mischief. The suitcases would be retrieved from the L-shaped bedroom and even as he opened them he would begin talking. I don't remember ever hearing a story for the first time or the last. They were forever different and forever the same as he embellished the details and exaggerated the scenarios he created.

The various versions of momentous events made us laugh until we clutched our tummies and struggled for breath. A favourite was his account of his crucial role in leading the Allies on D-Day, which apparently he did single-handedly. Having warned his men to step in his exact footprints through a mined area, he would demonstrate across the sitting room carpet with absolute care and concentration how he had done it. Unimpressed, none of his cohort had followed.

Dad gave us all the spare time he had. When I attended a school reunion in 2006, I was greeted by the exclamation, 'You're the one whose father used to watch you play tennis over the school wall.' And yes I was. When I played for the school, Dad would watch and then melt away to discuss with me later how I had played. He would play on one side of the net with Margot and me on the other, coaching and playing and larking around. He had coached Tony in football and tennis, and now he coached Mike in cricket as well, always turning up to watch his matches when he could. He had the knack of filling us with pride in our achievements whatever they were and investing sport with a very special value. I remember how choosing my first proper tennis racquet with him was an extraordinary event. Each racquet was systematically tested for weight and string resilience, each one prompting a discussion with the shop assistant. Nothing was too good.

Our lives appeared to flow in an uncomplicated and inevitable continuum that bypassed the years, but there were family routines that marked down the hours and days. At least they seem like routines now. Even single events can assume the status of routine, and loved but occasional patterns be inflated into family rituals. There wasn't much room for anyone else in our tightly knit family life. Our group mentality, increasingly fostered by both our parents, although we didn't know why, was of 'one for all and all for one' and our father enjoyed it as much as we did. I think he revelled in the family companionship and his naturally extrovert personality found an ever-admiring audience in his children. Meals were a keynote of our family life. We would sit for hours – when there were hours to spare – talking about anything and everything and eating up what had been left until we all grew hungry again. They were punctuated by mini-rituals, Margot finding a caterpillar or fly in her salad; Mum buying four cakes the same and one different 'just to try it' and provoking the inevitable quarrel; the pale dullness of poached fish, mashed potato and parsley sauce on Fridays, the glory of rissoles and crisp, slender chips on Mondays and the agony of suspense as to who would be allowed the skin on the custard on any day. We talked and talked. The spirit of conversation was never vanquished and we were all encouraged to share our day with each other in a mixed flurry of seriousness and banter.

Christmas was short – squeezed between football fixtures, it lasted only from Christmas Eve to Boxing Day – and was gloriously intense. We knew the routines as if hard-wired from birth to make paper chains, to twist long green and red crepe ribbons for the dining room ceiling and pink and pale green crepe ribbons for the sitting room. When Dad had finishing struggling with the tree lights which somehow always forgot how to work while hibernating the year away in their box, he would hang the coloured ribbons from central light to each corner, while Margot passed up the drawing pins. Then he would set up the Christmas tree, anchoring it into the tub with broken bricks. Mum would take over organising its position to find the most symmetrical angle while Mike and I would unwrap the baubles kept lovingly from year to year and festoon the branches with sparkling lametta.

Then, as order finally asserted itself, the fire was lit, warming the fragrance of the pine needles and when the flames flared

red and blue, Mum would place the angel on the top of the tree. Each year she dressed a little plastic doll with long, curly blond hair with a new outfit made up of fragments of lawn, net and lace collected during the year. Then came the moment of magic. The harsh central light was switched off; the tree lights switched on, and all the world (it seemed) fell silent. The last angel outfit Mum made was entirely of lace. That was in 1956 when Mike was nine, Margot 17 and I was 13. Mum withdrew from Christmas after that, but after she died I kept the box of decorations. In the early 1990s I finally found the courage to dispose of the angel and her now tatty grey lace outfit, although a few of the original baubles still survive. Our simple ritual was the same for families the country over but at that time it always seemed unique to us. I have never lost the sense that Christmas Eve evening is the very best part of Christmas, the very still point of wonder.

We couldn't afford holidays but we did have treats. Two day trips stand out, framed by the unusualness of the event and the journeys back sleeping against one another while our parents' voices flowed warmly but undifferentiated from the front seats. On the way back from one – from Weston-super-Mare, I think – we crashed into the side of another car which pulled out suddenly from a side turning into our path. 'Hold on,' my father said fiercely, and Mum, who was sitting in the back cuddling Mike and me on each side of her, protected us from the impact but she got a deep cut on her scalp which left a permanent scar. When Dad realised the offending driver was a deeply upset elderly man, we had to wait until he had been reassured that he shouldn't worry and that we were all safe. When he felt calm enough, he waved goodbye and drove away.

On the way back from Lyme Regis on another occasion, fog closed in on us as if the air had changed its nature. Ahead of us, the registration plate GRR 770 was just visible. 'He's a good driver,' Dad said, so we children crossed our fingers, huddled together and watched that dim registration plate all the way back to Bath before turning off towards home. 'Thank you GRR 770,' we all chanted, only we rolled the rs and growled like baby tigers. And there was one memorable 'day' trip which Margot and I bullied Mum into allowing. We were going out for a whole day on our own. We set out full of dreams of camping and brave resourcefulness to the grounds of a nearby deserted orchard surrounded by high crumbling walls heated by the sun of that sunny summer. We dutifully explored, picking withered apples from the neglected trees and hunting for wild flowers in the dry grass. Then it was lunchtime. We built a very small fire on one of the paths (try doing that today!), and put two eggs on to boil. We were unsure about how to time them so we took it in turns to run the length of the path and back again – about one minute we estimated for each distance. Unperturbed by our calculations, the eggs spilled out their watery contents on to our plastic plates. But, after all, it would soon be time for tea, that is, for orange squash and rock cakes. Tired out and very satisfied with ourselves, we arrived home. 'I didn't expect you home so soon,' Mum smiled. Our day trip had lasted for all of two hours!

How then, surrounded by such carefree and close-knit happiness, did we get to know of the existence of another, less loving world? Somehow unfamiliar emotions and unknown threats began to seep into our emotional landscape and eat away at our security although we didn't understand their source. Margot and I would often accompany our father to home matches on a Saturday, sitting quietly and obediently in the directors' box. At half-time Dad's head would emerge at the top of the stairs to talk to the chairman and whichever of the directors was present. Although I wanted to see him, I always looked away when he arrived to avoid seeing his face drawn in strain, the rawness across his knuckles and the cracked skin between his fingers as he grasped the stair ledge.

We usually made our own way down to the football ground. Once, I was spoken to by a boy who was hanging around the players' entrance waiting for autographs. 'Can you go in there?' he asked as I went to step through the cubby hole door cut in the barrier. 'Yes,' I said, 'I'm the manager's daughter.' I was probably 12 years old. The yearning in his face went far beyond envy into wonder that such persons could exist. Dad would drive us home, stopping at the newspaper stand to buy a *Pink 'Un*, chatting to the men in the queue as they all waited for the near-miraculous arrival of paper bundles within an hour of the final whistle. If we couldn't go to the match for some reason, we listened to *Sports Report* on the radio at five o'clock. When the trumpeting signature tune faded the room fell silent as we waited to hear whether we had won or lost.

The players were the unseen presence in our house and on whom our domestic happiness depended – men who shared the highs and lows of victory and defeat. It never occurred to me that anything would matter more to them than winning or that they wouldn't suffer as I suffered for them when we lost. Although Mike was too young to go to matches, as a boy, he was allowed to see places Margot and I barely knew existed. He sometimes went with Dad to work where he played in his office with the Bath City mascot teddy bear. He became so attached to it that Dad finally gave it to him to take home where Teddy gradually succumbed to various teddy illnesses – lost eyes, broken arm and mange. Mike was allowed to go to the dressing room after training and, a little boy among men, meet the players, just as his elder brother Tony had at Arsenal.

Margot and I knew all the players' names and caught fragments of information about them as Dad told Mum about the latest developments but we never met any of them. Before important matches I would lie in the dark in bed and give them a talking-to to inspire them to win. Some names still linger in my memory: Jimmy Newman, who came with Dad to Bath in 1950 and made some 248 appearances, scoring a near record 83 goals; Selwyn Watkins, who moved up from the reserves in March 1952 to play 149 games and score 41 goals. One of my most grief-stricken memories was for Harry Liley, a regular player in goal signed by Dad in 1951 and later culled in the 1956 clear-out by Arthur Mortimer, the chairman. In the second round proper of the FA Cup in the 1953/54 season, we played Grimsby in deep December and lost by one goal on a night when fog rolled in from the North Sea over the pitch. When the result came through on the radio, I burst into tears for Harry and the misery I was sure he must be experiencing.

And there were the interrupted walks. Wherever we went, men would stop us with an exclamation, a question, a retold memory. 'Is it Eddie Hapgood? How are you?' A vigorous shaking of hands would follow, then, 'I remember when ...' and then they would talk. We learned of another life, that every ball kicked, every decision made, every player encountered, every match on every day of the season and beyond, was intrinsically memorable. I learned that my father had the power to make grown men's faces glow with unashamed delight, to bring tears to their eyes. He seemed like a Wizard of Oz. As total strangers grasped his hand again and said their goodbyes, they seemed to take with them some kind of confirmation.

There were other random glimpses of that mysterious life which were both extraordinary and disturbing. When my parents went to the FA Cup Final dinner in 1952, the year Arsenal lost by one goal to Newcastle United, we children knew it was a great event. It was the first time they had left Margot to look after Mike and me. My mother dressed up for us the day before and we sat on her bed in wonder at the glamour and grandeur of the vision she created. When they returned, full of gossip and memories, she showed us the evening bag the wives had been presented with. Made of a cracked cream glaze with a gold clasp and gold braid handle, it opened up on two sides, a mirror and powder compact on one side and a cigarette case on the other. It remained my standard of female luxury for a very long time. Young as I was, I recognised that my mother had, if only briefly, returned to her element, but that my father for once left all the anecdotes to her. Returning to Arsenal and briefly to the company of so many old friends must have been bitter-sweet.

Then we were unexpectedly given our second proper holiday, although it felt like the first one since we had forgotten the so-long-ago trip to Scarborough. It was a week in a caravan at Bude in Cornwall. Mr Walters was not an Arsenal fan or even particularly interested in football. He was our milkman who ran a successful dairy business and enjoyed football conversations with Dad when their paths crossed. In 1957, he suggested to Dad that they had a break as a gift from him in a caravan on his brother's campsite. 'Your father's a good man,' he told us. We weren't quite sure why he said it but we knew we needed to hear it. I think our parents must have realised that we all needed to get away from Bath. It was more than a holiday, or they would never have accepted the gift.

Bude was to become a kind of sanctuary, a haven for us all over the years, but that first summer was lifted out of time. For my parents, Cornwall was already special from before the war. As we drove down the A30, cheerfully negotiating the bottleneck at Honiton by picnicking on the roadside, they must have been full of memories and saddened by the unbridgeable divide between that time and this time. They must have been frightened too, at least my mother must have been, for this was a time when there was no money coming in, and no secure home. We would never have guessed. Our parents had a gift for being happy. The caravan, high above the beach, was called Pandora, a fitting name for a family still holding on to hope even as a disaster we knew nothing about, stalked us. Margot, Mike and I played out a book-reading life based on Enid Blyton adventures, Malcolm Saville mysteries and Arthur Ransome's *Swallows and Amazons*, but we began to realise that Margot was changing. The lifeguards on Bude beach, a bunch of young Australians holidaying in England on the back of their life-saving skills, were mesmerised by her mixture of mischievousness and hauteur. They made friends with the whole family but Mike and I looked on darkly as they swept Margot off to learn to surf.

When did seaside habits change? When did eating out become eating in? When did foreign sun and pre-packaged novelty make England tedious? If I look back over holiday photographs that start with the Pandora week, they all look exactly the same, and it was the sameness that was the heart of our happiness. Mum and Dad sitting on a rock, children sitting on a rock, Mike with a cricket bat, Dad in his swimming trunks, children eating ice creams. Every day – and every day of subsequent years – was happily the same. We would pack a picnic hamper (presented to Arsenal players from Glasgow Rangers), organising the food in neat packages around the familiar green plastic cups and plates and the flask of tea. At the beach, we would spread out the car rug (another present from Rangers in Campbell's hunting tartan in rich navy and green with yellow splashes), unearth our swimming gear and change with wriggly but expert movements under our towels. Most of the family were good swimmers, but I was nervous and Mike still young enough to be watched in north Cornwall's treacherous waters. Even so we learned to surf in the shallower waters. Mum would leave Dad playing cricket with Tony and Mike, and stride out across the beach, her face turned towards the wind while her slug-like daughters remained wrapped in towels. Mum never lost her love of walking and my father, who had no great enthusiasm for walking, would comment admiringly, 'She always walks as if she's going somewhere.' Then it was beach cricket, or rock pool hunts or shell and pebble collecting before the lunch ritual, officiated by our father, began. Sandwich packs were opened, hard-boiled eggs with paper screws of salt, large, sweet tomatoes and crunchy lettuce were spread out. It is a cliché that eating in the open when you're hungry is a special experience, but clichés are clichés because they're true. Hot tea, partially dried bodies, wind and sand, and a place on the car rug.

In the afternoon, we'd do the whole pattern again before heading back to the caravan, perhaps if we were very lucky, picking up fish and chips on the way. In the evening we played tennis, Dad, Margot, Mike and I. Mum would always come too and sit watching us until the sun went down or we grew tired. Even then, I used to wonder what she thought about, whether she got bored or felt left out. She always assured me she loved watching us, and I think I believe her. While we were together, playing, laughing, honing our skills, and while Dad could forget what awaited him and enjoy again the pleasure of movement and, not to mince words, of winning, her own worries subsided and she could relax.

Without realising, we absorbed a world view from what mattered most to our parents. Mum's words were spoken aloud, necessary knowledge for shaping us into responsible adults, words to do with good manners, education, speaking and dressing appropriately, dizzying flurries of conversation and examples to illustrate an important political point. Dad's words were not spoken. Football was never a word, the name of a game; it was always a state of being, an absolute of existence, a daily context – the hamper you take on holiday, the rug you smuggle into when you sleep on the back seat of the car, the funny story told when you go to bed, a stranger's smile when he grasps your father's hand.

We all intuitively knew that the bedrock of our lives was something that surely had a vocabulary if we could have grasped it, a philosophy as we came to understand later. My father embodied it, hardly knowing that he did. Protected between them both, we learned that we were special but different, special but embattled, special but vulnerable. And like clouds across a sunny field in summer, Bath City's results, as Saturday followed Saturday, had the power to block out the sun for a cold moment. The sound of the crowd, far away but just audible in our garden, could as easily be intimations of distant thunder as cheers of glorious triumph. *Sports Report* at five o'clock might bring grief or glory as James Alexander Gordon's voice filtered down through the leagues, past the magical Scottish names like Hamilton Academical and Heart of Midlothian until he reached the Southern League, when our stomachs tightened and we didn't look at one another. The *Pink 'Un*, spread out over the table, judged our latest performance. And there were other obscure hints of changes, numerous, complex and intertwined, that passed by almost unnoticed but which made our magic carpet dip and shudder for a bewildering moment. The full meaning of this daily paradox began to unfold on 14 February 1956 when our father received a letter telling him he was sacked from Bath City with immediate effect, and on 16 February when the *Daily Mirror* told the nation, under the headline 'Bath Sack 30-cap Hapgood', 'One of football's all-time greats, Eddie Hapgood, 30 times capped when Arsenal's left-back, was sacked yesterday with four and a bit years of his contract as manager of Bath City still to run. "We just couldn't go on any longer," Councillor Arthur Mortimer, the Southern League club's chairman, told me yesterday.

'"During the past five years, the club has done absolutely nothing. Little wonder our gates have dropped as low as 1,200. Our new board is dedicated to putting Bath back in the limelight, and that means no Hapgood."'

It hardly helped that the reporter, Ross Hall, had plucked a random number of international caps from his memory. Eddie was diminished in both his past and present achievements.

14

A Case of Libel and Slander

It was defamation. It was also ludicrous; the stupid, inaccurate venting of a man flattered to be phoned by the national press and encouraged by an experienced journalist to allow his ego and his tongue to run away with him into a mire of despicable dishonesty. When Eddie challenged him face to face, chairman Arthur Mortimer preferred to stay with his story, to trash a man's reputation and endanger his livelihood rather than say, quite simply, 'I am sorry. I was wrong.' At the beginning, that was all Eddie wanted but Mortimer then dodged and ducked for over a year. He refused to make a personal apology, refused to give an explanatory statement to the *Daily Mirror* and refused to offer a public apology in the local Bath paper. When Eddie consulted solicitors, Mortimer failed to reply to their letters.

To bully Eddie into giving up and disappearing from the scene, he stoked up animosity in the town towards him and our family. Mike, only nine, was taunted by children who had been told by their parents that Eddie was scum and a liar, and came home crying. My best friend, Jenny, suddenly stopped sitting by me in class, walking to the town swimming baths and going with me to the cinema afterwards. 'I'm not allowed to,' she told me without understanding or personal malice. Like many others, her father, a successful nursery man, was not going to risk losing contracts from one of Bath's best-known businessmen, particularly one who in May 1957 was to become mayor-elect. As the Hapgood family was to learn, challenging Arthur Mortimer did not just involve director v manager conflicts. It meant taking on a significant section of the Bath business community, allied interests in local government and the stigma of social ostracism.

There was, of course, a long back story in which Eddie was a late arrival. As Eddie went about his daily work at the club, he was unaware that his popularity with the directors and his success on the pitch were creating a formidable enemy out of the man at the heart of Bath City's story. When Eddie arrived in Bath in 1950, he had been appointed by Mortimer, who was then the club's chairman. He was an affluent businessman, a city councillor and a well-known personality who enjoyed publicity, was a frequent visitor to Bath events, always ready to present prizes, cut fete ribbons and take to the stage to support local charities. He was equally ready to keep the local paper acquainted with his every move.

Bath City Football Club was his personal hobby, his distinctive contribution to a city famed for its rugby and a personal fiefdom where his desire for a public face could be indulged. Mortimer's story with the club began as far back as 1932. When Eddie was first making his mark with Arsenal, Mortimer was planning a move for Bath from the waterlogged ground at Lambridge to a new stadium in Twerton Park just outside the city. It would be an expensive business but if the club was ever to find its way into the Football League, investment was necessary. It was an exciting time of possibility and community effort. It was also a profitable time for Mortimer Ltd, the construction firm founded by his father, as the Twerton site was gradually transformed, the pitch laid and stadium and facilities built. His employees were backed up by players doing overtime as builders and locals with the appropriate knowhow offering their services. It was a mutually profitable arrangement. The club was able to bolster his business and to create a network of local businessmen, local contacts and local dependencies. For some years Bath City's business was conducted at the offices of Mortimer's Weston (Bath) firm of builders.

The changes in wartime regulations initiated by the Football Association were a boon for him. Mortimer learned the value of the one-off big occasion to boost finances. An occasional friendly match against a professional team, for example, would always attract the punters but FA Cup ties were crowd certainties. Their promise of giant-killing and a home match against a famous team stirred up excitement and filled the coffers. These hoped-for successes became Mortimer's economic and public relations lodestar. He was able to build guest teams with good footballers stationed nearby and hungry for a game. He had an astute eye for a familiar name or an interesting reputation. He approached players near retirement or those whose injuries had ended their top flight football but could still be a star presence in a one-off match for a Southern League team. It became a feature of the club. Mortimer had powers of persuasion and was able to buy the services of a sparkling name with a good deal and much bonhomie.

He had another considerable advantage. At a time when jobs were difficult to find, Mortimer could offer, and often did, part-time or even causal work in his business, boosting his recruitment with fit young men while minimising professional wages and summer retainers. Big occasions, big names and short-term contracts became his footballing philosophy and his financial strategy. In 1950, 'Eddie Hapgood', recently resigned from Watford, was a name that caught his eye. He offered Eddie an improved salary and a long contract to catch his man. Mortimer didn't want a manager – he probably felt he could do that himself – he wanted stardust. 'I wanted "a prestige name", to create "something of a precedent",' he was to say later. Mortimer trumpeted Eddie's introduction to Bath in the local paper under a headline of 'The Man Who Brings Top-Line Knowledge', praising Eddie's realism, his 'acute business brain', his 'comprehension of life' and (rather oddly) with ambition 'as dispassionate as any farmer before the harvest'. The return to FA rules in 1946/47, however, soon made consistency more necessary for survival than football 'events'. Unfortunately for Mortimer, the bombastic phrases, designed to bring him reflected glory, were swiftly reassigned to the man he had employed whose presence and steady success began to claim the spotlight.

Two years after Eddie's appointment, at the end of the successful 1952/53 season, the board, of which Mortimer was still a member but no longer chairman, voted to give Eddie a £200 bonus. Always delighted to have an opportunity to boast, in December, before an FA Cup second round tie against Grimsby, Mortimer stepped into the limelight to tell journalists, 'I think we will surprise many people. We could easily be the "giant-killers" this time. I have never known such optimism here in all my many years' association with the club.' At the end of the 1954/55 season, pleased with the club's direction and its consistent achievements, members voted to offer Eddie a contract extension until June 1960, another five years. Bath had finished fourth in the Southern League and won the League Cup, in both cases for the second consecutive season. Twice they had reached the FA Cup rounds proper, including the second round in 1952/53. It looked as if the club was making real progress. Even so, two directors voted against the contract extension and resigned in protest. One, Ronald Brighton, said his resignation was entirely a personal matter. The other was Arthur Mortimer, who also said his resignation was due to the demands of his business commitments. Events rapidly proved this claim to be absolutely false.

1 December 1955–13 February 1956

Increasingly irritated by his lack of influence over team affairs and the waning of his personal glory, Mortimer had voted against the extension of Eddie's contract and decided to free himself from the board's collective decisions. He resigned and set about removing the board, and Eddie. To that end, he stirred up unrest through the supporters' club, now swelled by the entryism of many of Mortimer's business colleagues, contacts and employees, calling for change. The regular financial support it contributed, along with shareholder investment was put on hold, which hit Eddie hard in a difficult opening to the 1955/56 season. Then, in the fallow, post-Christmas days, when no one was paying attention, in an illegitimate boardroom coup Mortimer called an Extraordinary Meeting for shareholders. On 29 December they voted to dismiss all members of the incumbent board, elect an entirely new board and restore Mortimer himself as chairman. Vic Reynolds, who as a shareholder had attended the meeting but was a strong supporter of Eddie, informed him that his character had been heavily criticised at the meeting. Another shareholder, a Mr Cook, had apparently claimed that Eddie was disliked by the players who thought him 'pig-headed'. 'That's just a lie, Eddie,' Vic had told him later, 'because it was only at the back end of last season on this same spot that Mr Cook made reference to the high regard you were held in by the players!' The shareholders' meeting had been little more than a staged Mortimer-fest.

On 2 January 1956, immediately after the new year festivities, Eddie, summoned by the board, was asked to describe his policy for the benefit of the new directors. It was a tense moment. He knew the decision to extend his contract had infuriated Mortimer. He knew this request was an invitation to expose him to the criticisms of the newly constituted board since Mortimer was already well aware of his football policies. Was it possible, he thought, that against all the odds, he was confronted again by a director who preferred his own self-importance to the success of the team and the harmony of the club?

Choosing his words carefully, Eddie explained that he believed success would come with a stable professional team, youth development and proper training strategies. In the early days of

Eddie's appointment Mortimer had appeared to agree with him, but more recently he was arguing that professional players, who required regular wages and summer retainers, were a financial drain, in short, troublesome. The systematic development of a youth side as advocated by Eddie required uncertain long-term investment. He had no time for that kind of continuity. He preferred older part-time players attracted by the promise of part-time work at his construction sites, and the convenience of easy hiring and firing. However short-term it might turn out to be, he wanted 'entertainment', 'performance', stand-out 'events'.

Sensitive to the shift in power, and faced with a group of new directors none of whom he knew, Eddie acknowledged the need for change and that when the new board had developed its policy, he would do his best to carry out its decisions. Under Any Other Business, Eddie then asked the board to clarify his position since he had heard that criticisms of his management style were being circulated and he would appreciate their support. Mortimer dodged the issue and closed the meeting saying that for the time being he remained the manager but then, returning to bullying mode and familiar humiliation tactics, he added that Eddie should remember that he was supposed to be at the chairman's call at any moment and time of day. 'You weren't here on Saturday morning. Where were you?' he demanded. There was a moment's silence and then Eddie replied, 'At that time I was at the station picking up the strip to bring to the ground.' There was another silence. Eddie then turned to the board and asked through the chairman whether any of the directors would like to offer suggestions about future football policy. There was no reply.

Eddie knew his time at Bath City was up but there was absolutely no way he was going to walk away. He couldn't. That was no longer a possibility as it might have seemed at Blackburn and Watford. He had to do everything he could to avoid being sacked and attempt to negotiate a redundancy payment. Two days later he wrote to Mortimer. In exchange for compensation for breach of contract and to avoid any animosity, he was prepared to offer his resignation if that was what the new board wanted. Turning up to work the same day, he discovered he was already excluded from the administration of all club activities and team affairs. For a worrying and humiliating month, he went to work as usual so he could not be sacked for deserting his responsibilities. Over the next few board meetings, Mortimer further attempted to humiliate and bully Eddie into resigning. He was instructed not to travel with the players to the first team matches, but to arrange the transport. He was told the club couldn't afford a manager and he was to respond to that information by the end of the week. When Eddie agreed to do so, he then asked, 'What will you do in the meantime?' Without any specific acknowledgment that his contract would not be honoured, he was repeatedly asked to name a compensation figure and then told any payment would put the club into liquidation. 'So,' Mortimer added, 'if you try to sue through the courts you'd get nothing anyway.'

On 28 January, Eddie attended what would be his last (although he didn't know it at the time) board meeting at Bath. As the uncertainty and fudging continued he asked to speak on the subject of compensation, 'Last season I reduced my salary by £4 a week to help the club through a difficult time. Up to the present time I have given the club roughly £1,000.' Mortimer interrupted him, 'Not exactly, you had terms of security for another five years.' 'And where is that security now?' Eddie retorted. 'Gone!'

Security for his family had always been Eddie's motive for taking on a Southern League club. It was what he had told the *Bath Chronicle* on his arrival in 1950. Knowing there really was nothing more to say, he stood up and asked, 'Am I dismissed?' Mortimer, thinking he was referring to being sacked, panicked. He certainly did not want to sack him. That would be too public and he could be faced with the possibility of a big pay-out. 'Wait a minute,' he blustered. 'I don't like that word dismissed.' As Eddie left that last painful meeting, he noted that with only one exception, a director who formally endorsed Mortimer's role as chairman on 2 January, not one of the nine new members of the board spoke a word for the duration of four meetings. They had nothing to say. They knew nothing about football. They had no idea what the conflicts were about. This was Mortimer's stage, but Eddie's determination not to be bullied finally forced Mortimer's hand. On 13 February, Eddie was sacked by the decision of a shareholders' meeting. A letter the following day informed him 'they had to dispense with his services'.

Mortimer immediately posted his version of events in the local paper but he did not expect and was taken aback by the instant reaction the news provoked across the country. Ross Hall, a sports journalist working for the *Daily Mirror*, rang him for details as soon as the news was out. During their conversation Mortimer was emphatic and voluble about Eddie's long-standing incompetence and continuous record of failure that was destroying the club. Once he had put the phone down to Mortimer, Hall phoned Eddie for his response. He also wanted to be careful. It was clear that he was on to a good story but perhaps a questionable one. Eddie, taken completely by surprise and angry with shock, replied that he had nothing to say.

Mortimer's statement was published on 16 February. It took Eddie just 24 hours to change his mind. He phoned Hall and said he was ready to tell his side of the story. It was a difficult and uncharacteristic decision for a man who always preferred his actions rather than his words to speak for him in the public realm. Under the headline '"I was success at Bath" says Hapgood', the article read, 'Eddie Hapgood, former Arsenal and England back, yesterday hit back at Bath City, the Southern League club who sacked him on Tuesday. He told me, "So far as I am concerned my stay with Bath as manager was a success story.

'"Four out of the five years I was with Bath, we finished in the top half of the Southern League. Twice we were fourth.

'"The first year I had charge of the reserves they gained promotion to the First Division of the Western League. Twice we reached the first round proper of the FA Cup." Hapgood leaves these figures to speak for themselves.

'One of Hapgood's backers is Mr Eric [Alex] Brown, former Bath chairman. He said, "In my 40 years of football Eddie is one of the straightest and best fellows I have met."'

15 February–17 February 1956

I was too young to know what my parents discussed as they struggled to decide on their way forward. All I knew then was that there had been two newspaper statements, that Mr Mortimer's had been printed first and that Mum and Dad were deeply distressed about what had been written. Nothing of their terrible dilemma was ever shared at that time with any of us children.

Much later, I learned from my father's written notes and my mother's accounts that they had talked through the night of 15 February and long into the two days that followed once we were all safely at school. The conversation they had that was to change their lives would have gone something like this:

– 'So, what now?'

They looked at each other, for a moment caught up in helplessness.

'Are the children asleep?'

Mum nodded.

'This time I've got to fight back, Mig.'

'Fight back?'

'You know I always thought I didn't need to. You know I always believed that what I'd done was right and would be enough evidence. Perhaps that's what I wanted to believe. I just resigned from Blackburn. I let everyone think and write whatever they wanted.'

'Eddie, don't think about Blackburn. You were ill! We were still reeling from the war, the move, all the changes. You and I had so much to sort out. Everything, everywhere was still a mess.'

'I know. I know. But, Mig, there were people in Blackburn, players, who believed in me. Despite all the problems, the team was beginning to come together. Some of the directors were trying to help. And I said nothing … Do you remember when I took Mike to that Bristol Rovers game last season and bumped into three Blackburn directors? They were really pleased to see me. Laughed about all the in-fighting. "Oh there were some nasty ones there," they said. I didn't know what to say. Perhaps I acted too hastily, took it all too seriously. I just walked away. Looking back, I wonder if I was just too concerned with my own dignity. Funny, Alex always teased me about that you know.'

'Eddie, at the time it would have been your word against theirs. What good would it have done?'

'Perhaps none … I felt tired. I felt belittled by it. I couldn't face what football was becoming, Mig. I couldn't face becoming mired in lies and bribery instead of standing up and telling the world what was going on. I let Blackburn down. When all's said and done, I let football down. I did write to Rous … but I should have spoken up. I can see now I was proud enough to think that if I resigned everyone would know that something was up; that I was protesting about something. I think I thought my reputation would prompt questions. Journalists following it up. I hadn't realised some directors just wouldn't care when I walked out the door. "Good players don't necessarily make good managers!" I realise now why that old cliché is endlessly repeated. It's really useful for directors. They just use it as an excuse to get rid of you however well-known you were, to humiliate you without anyone asking questions.

'And anyway. It wasn't just Blackburn. Look at Watford. What happened there? What club would choose not to enjoy success, to want to build on it? What club would choose not to retain a successful manager? We were really on our way. How could I see that coming when our next match was a big cup tie?

'The truth is Mig, I wasn't going to wait to be sacked. I resigned from both those clubs to defend my own reputation. I saw resigning as taking a stand. Now the only things mentioned are my supposed failures, and the press writes what people tell them and people believe what the press writes.'

'Eddie, that isn't fair. You know that journalists, the press, have been great friends of ours. You could have been one yourself when we left Watford if you'd wanted to. You had the chance. Ross Hall wanted you to tell your side of the story before printing Mortimer's words. He knows who you are. I think he wanted to balance the scales for you.'

'Perhaps ... But Mig, who knows what could happen if I do speak out now? What would I be letting loose to stand up now, an ageing manager of a minor Southern League team, and say of the chairman of the club, of "Mr Bath City" himself, "He's lying. And he's kept on lying. He did everything he could to put me in a bad light"?

'But if I don't. What then? If I sit back and do nothing, I'll never get a job in football again, however good my record. And you know, Mig, it is about more than just me, isn't it? It's about football. Ted [Drake] is doing well at Chelsea now and David [Jack] at Middlesbrough but it seems to be just a matter of luck how things go. I hear that Jack [Crayston] is having a tough time at Arsenal. How's that possible? All round the country, directors treat managers as disposable, to be pushed around, to be blamed, to like them or loathe them as they please. There's no protection.

'There's more than just my fight to be had, Mig, isn't there? What's the alternative?'

In fact, it is possible that Dad had made his decision the moment he had read the board's letter dismissing him. Every gesture of reconciliation he had made had been ignored. The last option was to take Mortimer to court – and risk getting 'nothing' as one director had mocked. The hours of discussion with Mum, that we knew nothing about, helped them to try and understand exactly what taking that path meant for them and to ready themselves for the consequences.

The law wasn't cheap. They knew that if their case was lost, they would be bankrupt and homeless. Would pursuing that course be an act of courage and self-belief, a fight for football's integrity, or an act of madness, and what's more, an act of madness that would bring the children down with them? Wouldn't it be better simply to fade out? To resign not just from a club but from football? They both thought about that line of action; they both rejected it. However, it wasn't easy to find anyone to act for him. One after another, Bath solicitors were mysteriously too busy to give them advice, certainly too busy to take on Dad's case, or, they said, they were not specialists in libel and slander. One he approached was honest enough to warn him. 'You've got a sound case Mr Hapgood but I can't take you on. Believe me, you won't get a fair deal with any law practice here in Bath. Not a chance. I suggest you explore further afield.' He had hesitated but then pushed a card across his desk. 'Try Devizes,' he said.

Eddie knew the truth of the old adage, 'Law and justice are not necessarily the same,' but he had made up his mind and there was to be no more hesitation. He firmly believed that if he was to have a chance of working in football again he must defend his reputation and, in doing so, defend the right of men like himself to be treated fairly and with respect across the footballing world. He picked up the card, thanked him and said goodbye.

March 1956–8 October 1957

Towards the end of August 1956, and with Dad having been without a job for nearly seven months, Bath City finally agreed compensation with him for breach of contract at £1,500. It should have been £4,000 but Mortimer declared, 'If we had not reached this settlement, the club would have had to close down.' Bath City didn't close down, but results had plummeted as the club staggered to the end of a badly disrupted season. Bath finished 22nd in the Southern League, were knocked out in the first round of the League Cup and failed to reach the first round proper of the FA Cup.

It really didn't matter. Bath City Football Club wasn't our world anymore. It was a strange time, a kind of limbo. Other worlds were about to change anyway. Tony and his girlfriend

Irene were now married and their first son was born in 1954. Margot, still working at the Admiralty, had won a place at the Bristol Old Vic Theatre School and she would soon be moving to Bristol. I was working hard at my O-level examinations at school. It was Mike, still only ten, who became our father's great companion during this stressful time. There was cricket and tennis coaching during the summer months and visits to Bristol Rovers matches during the winter of 1956/57. Rare and valuable times when Eddie could relax, laugh and share time with his youngest child.

It was also a time made bearable by a considerable act of kindness that secured for us children and our parents a kind of stability. The house that was our home and that we loved so much was owned by one of the directors who had been voted off the board in Mortimer's coup. Burt Guest had always been one of Dad's firm supporters. 'Don't worry, Eddie', he said. 'The house is yours, as long as you need it.' So we children weren't homeless, although in a way Dad was. The opening of 1956/57 was the first season since he had signed for Kettering in 1927 when Dad was a mere onlooker. Over the summer he had applied for various jobs, not only in football. Margot, now 17, recorded in her diary, 'Dad went away'; 'Dad home today', 'Don't want Dad to go away again', 'So glad Dad home' in a dull litany that traced his attempts to find work and his failures.

Dad followed up various advertised coaching opportunities abroad. He wrote to officials he knew at the Football Association, including Stanley Rous, to say he was available. In the close season, he systematically wrote to all Football League and non-league clubs to offer his services. Some never replied, some were brusque and formal, some wrote in tones of conventional regret saying there was nothing at the moment and wishing him good luck for the future. It seemed a cruel conspiracy, a squeezing down of his life to nothing. 'When the case is over,' he said to himself. He kept all the replies.

And then, in October 1957, after being unemployed for 18 months and still waiting for his case to come to court, Eddie was contacted by a young man who had heard him give a talk in Bath to young footballing hopefuls. He was from the YMCA, a national organisation dedicated to the education and care of young men, which the government had contracted to run a new hostel they were opening in Weymouth for apprentices at Winfrith UKAEA. In the nick of time, Eddie was appointed to be trained as warden. We children were told nothing about any possible future; we were locked in a frightening present we shared but barely understood.

18 November 1957–22 November 1957

Hapgood v Mortimer opened at Bristol Assizes in the city of Eddie's birth on 18 November 1957. Mortimer was finally dragged against his will to defend himself in court against an action for libel and slander nearly two years after his outburst. In a last delaying tactic, when the case opened the first words of his counsel were a request to the court for an adjournment. Justice Cyril Salmon, the sitting judge, refused, pointing out with some acerbity, 'This is a serious matter for the plaintiff which has been hanging over his head for a year.'

The 'serious matter' as far as Mortimer was concerned was that his own reputation and status in the city would be damaged; Eddie's reputation and livelihood were hardly 'serious matters'. Now the stage was finally set to test Eddie, his integrity, his resilience, his composure, not on a green pitch with trusted team-mates encircled by the ringing terraces of Highbury under driving rain or brilliant sun. There, and places like it, had led to this point but they were no longer the arena of action. The stage was now a cool, imposing, impersonal court of law, the green was the leather of the court benches and he was alone.

Despite all Eddie's early efforts to resolve the dispute with Mortimer face to face, and his solicitor's efforts to reach an out-of-court agreement, Mortimer was unable to accept that the alternative was to stand in a court as a defendant against a charge of libel and slander. When the court rose for the judge, the public spaces were packed – some of Eddie's family were there – but the cast of dignitaries was small. Defending Mortimer was a legal team instructed by Kingsford, Dorman and Co. of London, led by Edgar Fay QC, a distinguished barrister. Acting for Eddie was Mr L. Herrick-Collins, instructed by Wansborough and Co. of Devizes. Justice Salmon had been appointed to the High Court earlier in the year and assigned to the Queen's Bench Division.

And then there were Mortimer and Eddie. Eddie did not look around him but he was not intimidated. His purpose was to restore his reputation; to do that Mortimer had to be shown to have lied. He needed to be focused and composed. He had no idea where this would all end but Maggie and he had staked everything on this moment. He would be vindicated. To contemplate failure would create failure.

During the first day, Mortimer inspired immediate contempt for his blustering, his self-importance, and his blatantly contradictory answers. He seemed ill-prepared and unable to keep focused or logical. During his first questioning by his own counsel about the reasons for sacking Eddie, he betrayed his questionable attitude towards truth and corporate responsibility. He had suggested to members, he said, that they record Eddie's sacking in the minutes of the meeting as 'dispensing with his services because the club could no longer afford a secretary-manager because of its poor financial position'. The club was on the edge of 'financial disaster', he explained. He then volunteered that the reason recorded was actually a 'white lie ... To soften the blow for Eddie', and the reason for this 'camouflage' was 'kindness'.

In a follow-up intervention from Justice Salmon, Mortimer was asked with some asperity why, if his intention was 'kindness', he told a journalist from a national newspaper whose words would be read by anyone interested in football, a completely different story – that Eddie was 'incompetent' and had been 'a continuous failure' since he was appointed five years previously, and that they just wanted rid of him. Was that what he meant by 'kindness'? After Thomas Hale, chair of Bath City Supporters' Club from 1951–53 and board member from 1954–57, was questioned on the same point, Justice Salmon intervened again. He asked a confused Mr Hale to clarify whether he had knowingly supported the false minute as legitimate and whether he agreed that it was not the actual reason for the dismissal. 'Was the court to understand that the reason for the dismissal was because Mr Hapgood was not accommodating himself to the new board? Is that right, Mr Hale?' Mr Hale replied, 'Quite, sir.'

The question of whether Bath City was indeed threatened by 'financial disaster' grew in importance as the case progressed. When asked by Mortimer's counsel, Mr Fay, if the club was on the edge of a 'financial disaster' during the first half of the 1955/56 season, before he was dismissed, Eddie replied that money was short but that to call it a 'crisis' was an 'unnecessary storm'. He claimed that the drop in attendances was affected by the fact that all of Bath's full-time players had been released by the decision of the new board at the start of that season, so supporters had been unable to follow familiar players or watch good-quality football at Bath. To make matters worse, he explained that the neighbouring Football League club, Bristol Rovers, had been promoted at the end of the previous campaign and burst into the new season by clocking up four wins and one draw out of their first five matches. There was always a worry that good football in Bristol would entice Bath supporters to take the short trip to the city to watch it. However, Eddie felt, 'It had only needed for the board to pull together for the crisis to be averted.'

Pressing him harder, Mr Fay asked Eddie why he thought attendances under Mortimer went up during this time and the club made a profit. He replied simply, 'I don't know.' This turned out to be an important moment. Bath City was a limited business under Mortimer's chairmanship. How aware was Eddie that Mortimer had the power to stall investment in club amenities, divert donations, and take action such as cutting players' wages, removing bonuses and pulling the reserves out of the Western League if he wanted to build up evidence that under Eddie's management the club was getting poorer? Eddie had been prepared to take a cut in his wages when his new contract was offered, presumably accepting what he was told about the current financial position even while disagreeing about how it could be dealt with. He could have had no idea about changes in Bath's financial position after he was sacked.

Mr Fay's questioning of Eddie continued into the second day. During the interrogation, Eddie was clear and articulate, consistently making a distinction between fact and opinion. No, he did not object to the newspaper's headline about being sacked. That was fair enough; it was true. Yes, Mortimer and he had disagreed on how a team should be built but he had no resentment about difference of opinion. He did, however, firmly object to some of Mortimer's language: 'Clear the lot out,' Mortimer had said about dismissing the current professionals, lacking all respect for men with careers and families to support.

At one point Eddie challenged Mr Fay's assumption about the nature of the payment that Bath City had made to him in August 1956 of £1,500. 'I did not receive £1,500 for being sacked,' he corrected Mr Fay. 'I received it for breach of contract.' Eddie also dismissed Mortimer's comment in his interview with Ross Hall, that there was, 'Little wonder our gates have slipped as low as 1,200,' a figure Hall later confirmed when questioned was the one Mortimer had given him. Such a number had never been mentioned, Eddie claimed. It might have been a dramatic throwaway number in a good story but it was not a fact and could never be offered as evidence. In conclusion, Eddie declared that he was not interested in Mortimer's 'mind', that is, his reasons for making up facts and figures and lying. He simply wanted the statement Mortimer had made altered or withdrawn.

The third day opened with Eddie's counsel, Mr Herrick-Collins, taking centre stage. He questioned Ronald Brighton, who had resigned with Mortimer from the board in July 1955 and was giving evidence on behalf of the defendant. Mr Brighton had apparently had nothing to do with Bath City since that time. He appeared uncomfortable but he had learned his lines well, repeating the opinions Mortimer had voiced earlier in the same words and phrases and drawing a suppressed murmur of laughter from the public gallery.

Mr Herrick-Collins, 'What do you think was the reason for the decline in attendances?'

Mr Brighton, 'The extremely uninteresting and unenterprising type of football played.' That comment sparked laughter from the gallery.

Mr Herrick-Collins, 'Was this the reason would you say for the sacking of Mr Hapgood?'

Mr Brighton, 'The teams were not doing very much.'

Mr Herrick-Collins, 'Did the first team enter the second round of the FA Cup?'

Mr Brighton, 'Yes.'

Justice Salmon intervened, 'That was pretty good, wasn't it?'

Mr Brighton, 'Yes.' Again, laughter came from the gallery.

Justice Salmon's interventions were to get more frequent, his irritation visibly deepening as the hearing went on. After an unintentionally absurdist exchange between Mortimer and Mr Herrick-Collins, Justice Salmon interrupted again.

Justice Salmon, 'Mr Mortimer, we would like to know *what* your opinion is.'

Mortimer, 'That I have a right to make statements to the press.'

Justice Salmon, 'I think you mean that you thought you were entitled to make *any* statement as long as you believed it to be true?'

Mortimer, 'Exactly, sir.'

Towards the end of the third day, Mr Fay went on the attack. He blamed the *Daily Mirror* for publishing comments from what was an informal telephone conversation as 'unfair and unsporting' since Mortimer had not thought the journalist, Ross Hall, would report his words at all. But then he turned his attack on Eddie's claim that his reputation would be ruined by these words and that he would no longer be able to get a job in football. Mr Fay concluded with a summary of inaccurate facts that, even so, struck painfully at what Eddie knew could seem incriminating in public opinion.

'It is hard-headed businessmen who employ him. They would say that he started at the top with Blackburn Rovers in Division One and lasted one season. Then he went on to Watford, who decided not to renew his contract at the end of three years. They will learn he has been dismissed by Bath City. That is what is making it difficult to get a job.'

Addressing the jury for his summing-up, Mr Herrick-Collins took issue with Mortimer's flawed and feckless character which had been so brutally exposed:

'Mr Mortimer blames nobody nor anything but Mr Hapgood. He is made the scapegoat for everything.

'And what has Councillor Mortimer done to reduce the libel in this case? Has he raised a little finger to reduce the sting of this thing? Or is it Mr Hapgood himself who did what he could to get this matter put right?

'I ask you, members of the jury, to award a substantial sum to make it abundantly clear to everyone that there is no substance in these allegations: that Councillor Mortimer uttered words he had no business to and that he was a thoroughly foolish and obstinate fellow not to have withdrawn when he had the opportunity. Mortimer may be one of those men who cannot climb down.'

It was time for Justice Salmon to sum up. He duly set out again the purpose of the case, the meaning of libel and slander, rehearsed the arguments around what is an 'honest opinion' and what is speaking with 'malice'; asked the jury to consider what 'success' meant in relation to a football team; summed up the arguments on both sides and emphasised the points most relevant for them to consider. Then he unexpectedly drew the session to an early close, announcing an adjournment with the words, 'I have more matters to touch on.'

Justice Salmon was a scrupulous and conscientious judge. As we learned later, he had called in all relevant club records and spent the rest of the day double-checking the figures for gates, results, income and expenditure against Mortimer's claims. Although figures had been frequently referred to in the defendant's answers, no formal records had been submitted as evidence by the defence or even under questioning by his own counsel. That was not surprising, as it turned out. Mr Fay, well-known for his 'radar-like intellect' and his firm belief that 'it is inbred in every Englishman to act fairly' had either uncharacteristically prepared his case lazily or realised early that it would be better to let Mortimer offer obfuscation rather than evidence.

But Justice Salmon needed to know for himself. He saw clearly that there were further questions to be asked about the relationship between gate numbers, profit margins, supporters' club donations and shareholder investment. Why, as Mortimer claimed, would attendances in 1956 rise from a total of 51,000 from September to December at which point Eddie was effectively dismissed, to 81,000 in 1957 from January to May during which Bath Football Club achieved their worst results in five years – six places from the bottom and knocked out of the FA Cup at home by a Western League team? And how was the club in profit that season when apparently there had been a 'financial disaster' looming?

The following morning he spelled out what he had learned with unequivocal firmness.

'In the first complete year after Mr Hapgood left [season 1956/57], the gate amounted in all to 81,000 which is *worse* than Mr Hapgood's *worst* complete year [1954/55] when it was 88,000. What is more, Mr Mortimer claimed that, "This year we are doing magnificently." In fact since the gate is *less* than Mr Hapgood's *worst* year, Mr Hapgood's achievement was *more* magnificent.

'The season during which Mr Hapgood left [1955/56] shows a similar pattern. There were poorer gates than usual for which a number of different reasons were given. The gate for the season was recorded as 53,000. The first 19 matches when Mr Hapgood was in charge and when newly promoted Bristol Rovers was attracting large crowds, was 31,000. The 20 matches in the second half of the season after Mr Hapgood was dismissed was 22,000.'

He then concluded his summing up in a resounding endorsement not only of Eddie's case but of Eddie himself and concluded with his recommendations to the jury.

'Mr Hapgood had spent his whole life in football. He had played for England 43 times and captained England 34 times and enjoyed the highest reputation in professional football. Now this statement has gone out to the world and has caused his reputation to suffer. His reputation as a footballer was one which he was entitled to have vindicated by the jury. The only way we could vindicate that reputation was to award him such damages as would show the world that there was no truth in the imputations.

'No evidence had been given to show that Eddie Hapgood was incompetent when he managed Bath City. If he was incompetent you would have thought they would have brought evidence to show how he was incompetent. Not a shred of evidence had been produced to prove that Mr Hapgood was lazy or did not attend matches, or upset players or failed to encourage youngsters or anything of that sort of which he has been accused. Not a spark of such evidence had been brought by the defence.'

Journalists, football fans, friends, family and well-wishers gathered outside the courtroom but all Eddie could find to say as he clasped their hands and, as if from a great distance, saw their smiles and heard their congratulations was to repeat with heartfelt relief, 'My reputation has been restored.'

Mortimer made a swift exit from the courtroom. Incredibly, it was not long before he was triumphantly back in the public eye. Two days after the case closed, he attended a dinner, held by the Bath City Supporters' Club at Fortt's, a smart restaurant in Milson Street, Bath, to celebrate the club's achievements. It was also attended by the mayor of Bath, Tom Jones, who thanked Mortimer and raised a toast to Bath City, expressing his belief that before long the club would achieve Football League status.

It was an evening of many congratulations and frequent toasts. A particular achievement being celebrated was Bath's defeat of Football League side Exeter City in the FA Cup the Saturday before the case had begun. Apparently Mortimer had changed his mind again about team policy. From the moment Eddie had been dismissed, Mortimer had returned to the very strategy he had vilified.

Having ended the contracts of the professional players Eddie had signed, Mortimer declared to the local paper, 'Three, if not four, new professionals were being scouted and the reserve team was being reformed with an emphasis on recruiting promising local players.' Apparently the 'financial disaster' had been averted and the mayor congratulated the supporters' club on the amount of money and voluntary effort they brought to the club and the happy relationship they had with the board of directors which had brought the club this success. Money had been diverted back into the club to improve amenities. Players were treated as the professionals they were. Preparation for the match against Exeter included 'juicy steaks' prepared in a splendid meal funded by a member of the board, a director of a catering company, and a two-day holiday for special training.

Mortimer's response to the case was printed with an account of that evening in the local paper. His words were boxed in the centre of an article under the headline 'Overwhelming Appreciation', and he said, 'I had thought, quite frankly, within recent days of probably making a break with all my many public activities and fading, shall I say, into oblivion to an easier way of life but because of the wonderful, in fact, overwhelming appreciation of what I have attempted to do I am prepared to go on making whatever contribution I can for the betterment of soccer and soccer followers in the city of Bath.'

A week later, the supporters' club announced, without irony, that it had launched a public appeal to raise the £1,500 damages awarded against Mortimer. If Mortimer was left to pay the court costs himself, he would not have cared. A troublesome manager had finally been dispensed with and would rapidly be forgotten. Meanwhile, another, Paddy Sloane, appointed as player-manager to Mortimer's new intake, had come and gone. Bob Hewison, suspended before the war for making illegal payments to amateurs at Bristol City, and nearly 70 when he had arrived at the end of May 1958, would be gone two years later. Mortimer had obviously decided against any more 'stardust' managers.

After the hearing, stunned but relieved, Eddie continued to repeat to journalists that the only thing that mattered was that the verdict meant 'his reputation had been restored so that he could now return to football'. It had been his only ambition. As it turned out, the verdict counted for nothing in the world outside his family, friends and those colleagues who always knew his value; it even seemed to have created a vacuum. He discovered to his heartbroken bewilderment that if a manager resigns and says nothing, he is labelled a failure. If he is sacked and then proves he is unjustly judged, he becomes invisible, as if he no longer exists.

It is hardly surprising that not only was he the first but also, as far as I know, the last football manager to take legal action against an individual director for an unjustified attack on his achievement and his integrity. He fought for acknowledgement, respect, fair treatment and fair wages. He fought to achieve the very best for his family, his club and the players in his charge. It was not until 1957 that he realised that he had won the battle but been completely defeated in the war. 'He deserved better of the game than his experience of management after he had finished playing and he left league football with such bitter feelings,' his friend and colleague Bernard Joy wrote regretfully.

Perhaps we children wouldn't have understood what football being over would mean or even that we were leaving Bath – but it was and we were. The family began packing up the house, preparing to leave and to readjust our lives again. Next stop, Weymouth.

Two images of those days of high hope and deep disillusionment, of justice ignored and injustice celebrated, have remained indelibly in my memory. The first is hurrying to school alone – Margot had left the previous summer – on Monday, Tuesday, Wednesday, Thursday past the sandwich boards in Westgate Street with their thick black headlines dragging our name through the city day by day.

DAY 1: 'EDDIE HAPGOOD SUES BATH
CITY F.C. CHIEF'
DAY 2: 'HAPGOOD LIBEL-SLANDER ACTION'
DAY 3: 'HAPGOOD-MORTIMER CASE IN
ITS THIRD DAY'
DAY 4: 'EDDIE HAPGOOD …'.

On I went past the Roman Baths, Bath Abbey, following the gentle curve of Orange Grove, over the River Avon, all that beauty blurred by tears. I was sick with fright although I didn't know why.

The second image comes a week or so later. I arrived home from school to hear sobbing. Sitting on the stairs in the hall by the telephone was Mum, her eyes and face blotched with tears, too distressed even to pretend. I sat beside her but she couldn't talk at first to tell me why she was crying. She finally told me she had written a letter to the *Bath Chronicle* thanking all those who had supported us for their letters and cards, their good wishes, their apologies for not being able to help more, their hopes for us, their thanks, as always, for what Eddie had done for football as a player and as a man. When it didn't appear, she had phoned the editor to prompt him. She was told in no uncertain terms that her letter was not appropriate for publication.

15

'The Arsenal Was My Heritage'

Like a child startled by a loved father's unexpected blow, Dad's struggle to understand Arsenal's rejection of him set in motion a wasting away of his vitality as he felt pulled back even as he felt pushed away. He had walked into the grandeur of Highbury, inexperienced and unsophisticated, and knew instantly that he belonged. In a cocksure, uncomprehending, idealistic way he knew that this was his world and he had the power to shape it. He self-adopted into the Arsenal genealogy when he was 19 and, as luck would have it, at the beginning of it all. From that moment, his history and Arsenal's history were an inseparable process, a way of being and thinking. He never questioned it.

Over the years, of course, he had sometimes felt let down; there were disagreements, quarrels and questions; he was angry about what he saw as unfairness. He was upset when some kind of hierarchy showed itself and he and his team-mates were not consulted or their opinions listened to. But that was just family stuff, the Arsenal world to which he had given his absolute trust. The phrase 'the Arsenal family' was never a metaphor, much less a marketing tag; for him it was a lived truth. Arsenal was always the present, written by the moment in his emotions and lived daily through his actions. It is hard to understand. The meaning of it all is his alone and Arsenal's break with him a shattering of meaning, the pieces scattering and embedding themselves like shards in everything he did, thought, felt and said for the whole of his life. The crumbling away of trust, the dawning realisation, although heroically resisted, that the Arsenal he believed in was an illusion, a delusion, was a slow but unstoppable process.

The requisition of Arsenal's stadium to the war effort at the end of 1939 began the process of separation or at least an awareness that separation was possible. It was not just a practical inconvenience but an emotional blow. Highbury had been a place of work but also his spiritual sanctuary where he could return at any time for relaxation, for laughter and conversation, for games and extra training, for advice, for healing. Where better on a cold, snowy winter's day, a few days before Christmas and everything in its place at home, than Highbury, exuberantly running round the track with Ted Drake and warming up afterwards with big mugs of tea? Where better on a hot summer's day before a new season begins than to be larking around with Alex James, Frank Moss and little Tony in his made-to-measure leather boots on the bouncingly green pitch? What is more unforgettable than the crash of sound as he crosses the magic line from tunnel to pitch? What more joyous than the gales of laughter ringing round the coach as they head home from a victorious away game? An unexpected feeling of homelessness, exacerbated by the sudden move of the family from their home in Hutton Grove not long after, left him bereft. While posted around the country and abroad, his longing to be home had no permanent resting place for his imagination and emotions to return to.

And where had the familiar faces of the Arsenal family gone? During their decade of success, the players had subscribed to the notion, 'Once an Arsenal man, always an Arsenal man,' a publicity phrase intended to promote to the public the eternal nature of the bond that held players, fans and management together. The players never questioned it. At least Dad didn't and he assumed all his colleagues felt the same. In fact, for the players a sense of unity, powerful in the moment, was always fragile. Amid the ebb and flow of individual talent from youth to age, and the exits and entrances of players from season to season, friendships are difficult to form and even more difficult to sustain. When a player retired, for instance, he faced a void between playing and not playing that his former team-mates could scarcely imagine. When a player was badly injured, he waged a lonely, psychological battle to repair his ebbing confidence as well as his damaged body. Personal circumstances, illnesses, divorce or a family death could dissipate a player's concentration and dull his form. Competition was always lurking behind outward camaraderie and misfortune to one player offered a rare opportunity to another player. The crude vocabulary of buying and selling prised open any fissures even more widely. Players sold against their will, as Ray Bowden was to Newcastle in 1937 when a minor injury temporarily lowered his goal tally, would be physically separated from his team-mates by geography but also emotionally by a new set of loyalties. War, with its arbitrary disregard of personal connections, would inevitably prove the toughest test of all.

Dad never forgot any of the players he had played with or played against but he saw little of them during the war. Closest to his heart and his memory was the group of younger players he grew up with who had joined Arsenal at roughly the same time: George Male, his partner on the pitch and a loyal friend over the years; Cliff Bastin, who played in front of him throughout the 1930s and shared many international campaigns; Leslie Compton, a calm supporter of his more brilliant colleagues. Together they were the four shining hopes of the new Arsenal team that Herbert Chapman was building, three defenders and one a winger of unbelievable speed and goalscoring acuity. As they played together, won or lost together, they were bonded in an extraordinary intimacy which was dependent almost entirely on circumstances.

Occasionally Dad came across former team-mates at different RAF camps and for a few years in the Wartime League South there were usually enough of them available for a match to look something like the Arsenal team. It might not have seemed very much but it was important to him, ensuring precious moments when he could reconnect and exchange news. As the war dragged on, there were fewer of these encounters. Players were scattered across the country or abroad and the squad from week to week was uncertain and changeable. In 1943, when he was injured and no longer granted official leave to play, Dad felt stranded. Training routines and health checks had become patchy, which explains why his injury was not immediately diagnosed and his discussion with Tom Whittaker delayed. It is also one possible reason why Arsenal did not appear to notice that he was no longer around. Bastin, unable to join the armed forces because of his deafness, was the best placed to see most clearly the drifting away, not just of his team-mates, but of the Arsenal they had shared. 'The end of the 1942/43 season witnessed the break-up of the Arsenal team,' he wrote later. Matches went on being played. Players criss-crossed one another on the football circuit, but the sense of community, of being 'family' could no longer survive.

War is always extraordinary, affecting every man, woman and child in a different way as a tornado of change whips round them. Trying to understand the depth of Dad's personal unhappiness at this time, I asked friends how their parents had coped with the war only to be astonished by how many had not only *coped* with the war but *enjoyed* the excitement, the relaxing of social rules, the opportunities for interesting, skilful jobs. Dad's experience was utterly different. War was an executioner slicing a savage, clear-cut line across his career and severing his life from Arsenal's life with surgical precision. And, like a doomful god, the war watched him grow older. He always played with an undimmed desire and delight and yet, at the same time, he knew he was playing in a kind of shadow land where nothing was the same. When he felt low, he couldn't stop his thoughts drifting back to how George Allison had considered selling him all the way back in 1935 when he was only 27 and other clubs came knocking on the door. There was the failure to support him when both his mother and his son were seriously ill that dreadful summer of 1936. Now he also began to see how Allison had surely relied on him as acting captain while kowtowing to Alex James's ego, his dodgy fitness and increasingly erratic behaviour. But why hadn't Allison ever discussed anything with him? When King George signed a photograph of himself with Dad in recognition of his international record, Allison was immediately on the sports pages of the newspapers announcing that he would have it framed and formally presented at the end of the season. He didn't congratulate him. He never spoke about it, about anything. The reasons for loans to Chelsea and the following season to Luton were surrounded by silence. Allison just ignored him. It had to add up to more than rejection, he thought, more like the obliteration of his very existence.

And there were other moments, trivial perhaps, but which niggled in his memory. Dad found it hard to forget when blackout was finally lifted in April 1945 and he organised his first visit to Highbury in six years to collect the car he had been given permission to store there in 1939. I don't know whether he expected to put the key in the ignition and drive off but if he did he got a shock. Despite knowing that Arsenal had not been in charge of the stadium during the war, the skeleton of the car, dumped by the barricades and stripped of everything of value months, perhaps years before, felt like a living statement of his own irrelevance.

Somehow, all of Dad's negative thoughts led back to George Allison. It seemed the obvious explanation. Writing to Mum from Brussels, where he was posted, Dad commented in a discussion of their future and his hopes of returning to Arsenal, 'I could not see Allison in any way entertaining the idea even, of playing me.' It was Whittaker who selected him for his final three games in the first half of the 1945/46 season. Wherever Allison was he was not dealing with Arsenal players directly and he was not present at any of the matches Dad played in. As far as Allison was concerned, from January 1943 'Eddie Hapgood' was simply a useful name, a feather in Arsenal's cap, a golden anecdote in its history.

And then there really was an unmistakeable falling out. In fact, it was not George Allison, who as secretary was the messenger, but the board of directors who in June 1944 delivered the killer punch, Arsenal's brutally unambiguous dismissal. The board decided not to pay the benefits for which Eddie, Ted Drake and Jack Crayston had all become eligible. Eddie had played for Arsenal for 16 years and made 393 appearances, Drake for 11 years and 238 appearances with a record 171 goals. Crayston, his career ended by injury during the war, played for nine years with 168 appearances. In the usual run of events they would all have been honoured with a cash benefit of £750 for longevity of service, an important act of recognition and at that particular time a significant contribution – equal to around £30,000 today – towards helping their transition out of footballing life.

During his career at Arsenal, Dad had already been awarded two benefits and now qualified for a third. It wasn't a right but it was certainly a long-respected tradition. However, on this occasion, pleading extraordinary wartime circumstances, the board claimed that the club's financial position was too weak to honour the benefit payments. Allison wrote individual letters to Dad, Ted and Jack informing them that the Football League could not award anything for wartime appearances as it was contrary to the organisation's rules, but a 'grant' could be made based only on pre-war services. The amount had been calculated at £100. Unfortunately, Allison added, £50 would be deducted for tax so, 'Please find enclosed cheque for £50. In the meantime, the board will do their best to get the fullest possible concession from the Inland Revenue.'

Dad was shocked, insulted, upset, belittled, but also sceptical. The Football Association had publicly announced that his wartime matches would be included in his record and this statement from Arsenal was a flat contradiction. Even in the case of Ted and Jack, he was sure the money was insignificant and Arsenal could have got round the FA's ruling by paying the benefit to them all in the form of a retirement gift. The withholding of the benefits was a clear signal to him of the players' lack of value in the eyes of the club and a fundamental lack of care for their futures. He could hardly believe that Arsenal would treat them in such a way. It was his first, but not his last, experience of the power of directors to say 'Yay' or 'Nay' like Roman emperors of the past.

Did Arsenal regard their responsibility to players as a choice not a duty? Dad wrote later, 'The dead-end system whereby a man goes out of football without a trade when his playing days were over is pernicious, and that, I contend, is one of the things the Post-War Planning Committee must tackle first.' He wasn't talking directly about himself or Arsenal but, characteristically, about a system, an arbitrary and unjust system he now realised, that affected all professional football players. His comment was only one of a rising tide of protest at the contractual position of footballers. 'I've been sold like a slave for a bag of "gold",' said Hughie Gallacher in dramatic terms of his transfer from Newcastle to Chelsea as early as 1933. Tommy Lawton (Everton and Chelsea) and Tom Finney (Preston North End) were two former international colleagues who wrote after the war specifically linking poor terms and conditions to the growing scandal of bribes and bungs.

Although Eddie would have found it hard to believe, Arsenal were not entirely innocent. They never had been. Alex James's position was an early example, transferred from Preston North End in 1929 with much brouhaha about his salary which was temporarily resolved by having it doubled by a bespoke PR role at Selfridges, the London department store. In 1954 Tom Whittaker offered a similar post-in-name-only to Stanley Matthews in an attempt to coax him away from Blackpool. It would double his salary and in addition Arsenal would buy him the house of his choice which would be his until he decided to leave. Matthews didn't take the offer up and kept Arsenal's secret until he wrote his autobiography in 2000. The arbitrary power clubs wielded over their players stoked the burning anger that led to the successful campaign for the abolition of the maximum wage in 1961. Dad, Ted and Jack were not lucky enough to benefit, stranded on the edge of peacetime poverty by the whim of Arsenal's directors.

Despite the rift with Arsenal in 1943, Dad's anger and pain were temporarily sidelined by the general emotional messiness of war. He was delighted to play for Arsenal after demobilisation and even during his hectic and unhappy start at Blackburn, he made a consistent effort to keep in contact with his former colleagues. In his conscious mind Blackburn were his first concern, their success important, the challenge welcome, but the subterranean threads that held Eddie to Arsenal and his Highbury colleagues were infinitely stronger, always pulling him back to the source of his being. When Arsenal played in the north or Rovers in the south, Dad would try and find time to catch up with former team-mates George Male and Leslie Compton, and Cliff Bastin too, on the rare occasions when he was still playing, as well as those he had got to know better during the wartime games, Dave Nelson, Bernard Joy and Jimmy Logie. In London, there was always Joe Shaw and Jack Crayston who worked with the youth teams ready to share tales of the past. However rushed the conversations were, and how little of the match he was able to watch, whatever opposition stadium they were playing in, these encounters still felt like coming home, richly rewarding and reassuring.

Being nearer to Arsenal was a significant if subconscious factor in his taking the Watford role. What a relief it was for him to be easily in touch with former team-mates and to play occasionally during the early 1950s for The Ancient Lights, a wittily named veterans team conjured up by Alex James. He loved larking about with the likes of Joe Hulme, Bernard Joy and even Wilf Copping when he came back south to join Southend United as a coach. When George Allison finally retired at the end of the 1946/47 season, Highbury even began to feel like Dad's own territory again. It was an easy journey from Watford and Tom Whittaker, now the manager, a pivotal contact. He travelled the short journey whenever he could and relaxed with Tom over a cup of tea, talking football, tactics, swapping stories about former colleagues, musing on the past and the future. Outside the family, Tom was probably the only person he felt he could trust to share some of the difficulties he was facing. After his unexpected break with

Watford in 1950, it was Tom he went to for support. Tom's frank astonishment was a comfort. 'What happened, Eddie? Watford seemed on top of the world!' and he could share his bewilderment about boardroom conflicts with a sympathetic listener. It was a sort of belonging again.

Perhaps matters might have rested there and time would have quietly healed the immediate pain of what he felt was Arsenal's abandonment of him in a period of war, personal distress and financial need. However, on a later visit to Highbury in 1956, he found a very different Tom, a man whose health was beginning to fail. As they shared their different problems, Tom confided in Dad that Arsenal were looking for an assistant to take some of the weight of club administration from him. It seemed a moment of extraordinary luck. Dad knew his position at Bath was insecure. He knew he could do a great job at Arsenal. He would be working with an old friend. Perhaps at last the gods were on his side again.

He asked Tom to put in a word for him and wrote immediately to the Arsenal chairman, Sir Bracewell Smith, applying for the post. He did not even receive an acknowledgement. Provoked by such uncalled-for rudeness ('now and again a little sentiment doesn't come amiss', he was to write later) his memory of the unpaid benefit, buried by Arsenal and buried by Dad below the level of remembering, was triggered again almost 12 years after it happened. As 1957 dawned and Dad's savings shrank – he had now been unemployed for nearly a year – he determined to re-open the benefit question with Arsenal. A sense of fairness drove him, but the urgency of necessity too. The Arsenal 'family' had long been shown to be a façade but his own family was a living reality. Arsenal owed him that money and he needed it. Dad wrote to Sir Bracewell Smith requesting that his benefit payment be reconsidered, somewhat ironically suggesting that sufficient time had passed for a decision. In reply the board, clearly intending to stall his request, asked to see the relevant correspondence. Members were surprised when Dad was able to forward the letters from Allison. The correspondence was to drag on for 14 months as, so he was told, no response could be made between board meetings which, apparently, tended to be few and far apart. Arsenal refused to accept liability but when Eddie persisted eventually stated that they were now prepared to pay him an 'ex-gratia' payment of £50. He wrote again asking the board to reconsider their decision and award the full benefit amount. This request was turned down. Although he would never have criticised Arsenal publicly, he did comment privately, 'As I see it, they are simply making good the £50 Inland Revenue deducted from the £100. What a way to treat an old player!' He refused the offer and the benefit payment was never honoured.

It turned out that this unsavoury episode trailed on because the board had dodged the truth to justify their original statement in 1944 and were determined to cover their tracks. None of the 'facts' in Allison's original letters to Dad, Ted and Jack were true – except perhaps the fact of tax deduction, although a 50 per cent reduction seems unlikely. The Football League *had* authorised the full payment of £750 to all three players for pre-war service in 1944. Arsenal, reluctant to pay, had prevaricated and regardless of the players' wellbeing had come up with a patronising gesture and a letter carefully worded to offer hope, but not too much hope, that they might revisit their decision later. As time passed and other players built up similar records in post-war football, Arsenal were happy to allow the wartime past and the achievements of three men whose careers were over to sink out of memory. As far as they were concerned, the matter was finished.

The key to the truth didn't emerge until Bob Wall's autobiography was published in 1969. Wall had been appointed to Arsenal as office clerk just after Dad arrived, moving gradually upwards almost by default until he was appointed secretary in 1956. Presumably wanting to embellish his own life story with anecdotes about famous names, he wrote his account of the benefit issue and concluded with this claim, 'Eddie's reaction was to tell us he wasn't interested any longer in the money.' Negative gossip that Dad would never have known about had apparently been circulating behind closed doors for many years which claimed that while Ted and Jack had agreed to wait for their benefit payment, Dad had refused point blank and immediately appealed over Arsenal's head to the Football League. Whether Wall himself knew that what he wrote was untrue or whether he was just repeating gossip is hard to judge.

When Brian Glanville, a lifelong admirer of our father and an established sports journalist, read Wall's book, he set about checking out Wall's version. Access to Arsenal board minutes for the period was refused (the minutes were later destroyed when Arsenal moved from Highbury to the Emirates Stadium in 2006), but the Football League minutes for the period confirmed that the FA had authorised full payment in 1944 and that Eddie had never made an appeal against Arsenal's decision. Nor, for the record, had Ted Drake or Jack Crayston. When Glanville visited Dad to hear his side of the story, Dad immediately told him that it was all a 'complete fabrication' and produced the carefully conserved correspondence with Arsenal for him to read. This correspondence included letters from Wall, one in particular written in 1957 which acknowledged Dad's benefit appeal but stated that Arsenal had no liability in the matter. Dad concludes his letter to Bob with the words, 'My thanks to you for any personal effort you have brought to bear on my behalf.'

It would never have occurred to Dad that Wall, who had been alongside him at Arsenal throughout his playing career, would not be supportive of his claim. To Glanville, the whole episode was mean-minded beyond belief. Why, he was to ask later, did Arsenal never look after Eddie, their most distinguished player? It was incomprehensible. Whichever way you look at it, Arsenal's response, maintained over 12 years, was absolutely out of proportion to the paying of a legitimate reward to three outstanding players.

Because Dad was incapable of questioning his Arsenal identity, he could never come up with a satisfactory reason to explain what had divided the club from him. How could he find an explanation for the inexplicable? The benefit issue was only one of the sorrows that Dad carried. In a way, it was one of the easiest with its clear-cut rights and wrongs, its clear-cut offenders and victims. Harder for him to deal with were the nudges and hints of treacherous relationships that haunted him. After leaving Arsenal, his experiences as a manager had also been poisoned over the years by so many small treacheries, hidden malice, subtle patronising and injustices at Blackburn, Watford and Bath that he couldn't understand or explain but that seemed to have woven a net around him. Drained and unsettled by their influence, Dad found himself wondering if anyone could be trusted. Even Tom Whittaker.

Between Dad's application for the post of assistant manager and his revival of the benefit issue, Tom had died after a long and difficult year with heart trouble. With Tom's death, Dad's close personal links with Arsenal finally snapped. As far as I know, his last visit to Highbury was in 1956 to gather together with David Jack, Joe Hulme, Jackie Lambert and Cliff Bastin as pallbearer at Tom's funeral. The last reference to him in the Arsenal records note that he had not replied to an invitation to attend the 1970/71 FA Cup Final. It had arrived at the Weymouth address when he was in hospital and too ill to know or to attend. As had happened over the years, no one bothered to check any further. For Dad, it was the end of a long and trusted friendship that had survived his earliest days at Arsenal, the six years of war and the muddled days at Blackburn and Watford. It was also a physical blow. With Tom went the last sense of Highbury as his territory. He would no longer be able to drop in, expecting a warm welcome. From Allison's retirement in 1947 Tom had always been there for him.

And yet, Dad found himself wondering how much of a friend Tom had really been. He remembered talking to Tom about returning to Arsenal shortly after leaving Blackburn. They hadn't seen much of each other during that time but had always been in touch. Something Dad had very nearly forgotten drifted back into his consciousness. He had never sorted out the chain of information from his injury in 1943 to his loan to Chelsea the following year. He had sought Tom out and told him he thought his injury might be serious. In fact, it wasn't. Tom was right. It only needed time. It wasn't career-ending. Then how come Allison dropped him for everything but two run-out matches? Even so, why would Allison have dropped him at all unless (was it possible?) Tom had contacted him and passed on Dad's fears? When Tom took over at Arsenal, Dad had been happy to consider the only job Tom said was available – third team coach – but Tom had been clear it wasn't good enough for him. Where Dad had seen the potential of working with youngsters, had Tom seen a threat to his own new managership?

Sometimes the past rose up again with such force that he would find himself yet again distressed by unresolved questions. If Tom had wanted to get Dad back into the coaching staff as he said he did, he could have used the third team job as a lever. He wondered whether his experiences at Blackburn had made Tom wary, or whether he had been too critical of Allison in casual conversations. Had Tom put forward Dad's name for the post of assistant manager as he said he would? He claimed to have mentioned several names to the board including Ted Drake, but he finally supported the board's choice of Leyton Orient's Alec Stock, which seemed quite a move away from the old Arsenal 'family'.

Much more recently, a few months before Tom's death, there was that very odd business about Bedford Town. Tom had asked Dad for a favour, one he didn't feel entirely comfortable with. He asked him to write a report on Bedford, a non-league team who Arsenal had been drawn to play in the FA Cup and who Dad was familiar with. Tom had been very impressed by his report but surprised Dad by submitting it to the Arsenal board under his own name, as he told Dad. Later, Tom asked Dad for another favour. Would he give the pre-match team talk to the Arsenal players? This was an even odder request which Dad immediately explained was impossible. Not only did it come at the very time of Mortimer's takeover when Dad was unexpectedly fighting to save his own career but it would hardly be legitimate given he was still employed by another club.

Unhappy thoughts kept circulating. If Tom admired and respected his opinions so much why had he not made greater efforts to bring Dad back to Arsenal when the opportunities arose? Had he just been used? Or was Tom simply relying on an old and trusted friend when he was too ill to face the task himself? Unsettled, Dad's thoughts would wander. Had Tom really put in a word for him when he was trying to negotiate the overdue benefit payment as he said he would? Dad had written a long, unusually personal letter to him in July 1956, part of which explained the difficult financial circumstances his sudden dismissal from Bath City had created for him and the family, asking for Tom's support. Tom had replied telling him when the benefit issue would next be on the board's agenda but that he had been in hospital and lost touch with the progress of his appeal. Then Dad would vigorously push such thoughts aside as unworthy, reminding himself how the players thought the world of Tom and how much he himself owed him. Like everyone else, Tom had to look to his own life and career, he reassured himself. 'All for one and one for all.' But Dad was struggling to believe that such loyalty existed any more.

The questions, the doubts, would circulate, be pushed away only to seep back unbidden.

And so it was with George Allison whom fate had decreed would face Dad across the pitch at the beginning of the 1946/47 season, the first when Dad was not an Arsenal man but the manager of the opposition. Dad kept very few match programmes, but the dozen or so he did keep all tell an important story. One of them, the last, is from the Arsenal v Blackburn match that September, and Rovers' first away game with Dad as manager. For Arsenal it was a triumphant and emotional occasion as they were playing at Highbury again for the first time since war had broken out seven years previously. Full of glorious memories laced with anticipation for the future, fans flocked noisily into the restored stadium to make it theirs again. The last time they had been there they had watched their hero and captain lead Arsenal out to a resounding victory over Sunderland.

Had his history been written differently, it might have been a restorative, healing occasion for Dad, an exuberant delight at being back at last in the old, loved stadium. As it was he was thrust into the joyous celebrations as an outsider, a spectator from the opposition dug-out. Was it Allison who wrote the conventional 'welcome to the opposition manager' paragraph in the programme? Of course not. But whoever had that responsibility must have had a very stern word in his ear, 'First match back at Highbury. Big moment for looking to the future. Very nostalgic moment. Eddie very popular player. Captained the last match here. Play it light. He's the opposition now.' It is easy to second guess this conversation because the relevant paragraph in the programme is strongly coded, under an article headed 'Saloon Bar Story', 'When a great player leaves a club after a long, renowned career, the names often remain associated in the public mind. Blenkinsop of Sheffield Wednesday, Hibbs of Birmingham, and Hapgood of Arsenal. But the day of retirement must come to us all. E.A. Hapgood, Manager. Yes, our Eddie has his own desk now. But it is told in the bars that on his arrival in Blackburn, a local recognised him in the street and looked horrified. "Ba' goom but it's Eddie 'Apgood! As bluidy Arsenal taken over Ewood Park now?" "No lad," said Eddie, "It's all right. I've taken over Blackburn Rovers."'

The message is amusing but clear. 'Hapgood' is only a name from history, no different from other great players. He is listed third behind the player whose England place he claimed for his own and never lost, third behind players who played for rival clubs. Then he is named E.A. Hapgood, 'Eddie' only when safely reimagined behind his desk. The use of the famous 'Eddie Hapgood' is carefully avoided. He is now in some faraway place where, lacking London sophistication, they talk 'northern'. Finally, he jovially confirms his commitment to Blackburn. It's a clever piece of writing that firmly tells the Arsenal fans that the past is past, and calls on their sense of humour but not their emotions.

It seems almost incidental to record that Blackburn beat Arsenal 3-1 that day. It was a worrying result for Arsenal, who had lost 6-1 the previous week away to Wolves, and had now been beaten again by a newly promoted team led by their former player. For Dad there was no pleasure for once in victory, just simple anguish and a first piercing stab of bitterness. The programme, thrust down into his briefcase when the Rovers coach pulled away from Highbury, is a confirmation of Allison's need to keep Dad, his reputation and his known power of influence within strict boundaries.

The story of Dad's rift with Arsenal, of one man's sense of rejection, of grief and bewilderment, is his alone, a purely personal anguish. It runs parallel and irrelevant to Arsenal's story as a thriving business. The board of directors only measured Eddie, as they did all their players, by economic logic. He was an asset. They had invested £1,000 in a raw but promising recruit and it had paid off handsomely. For 12 years or more he was considered a rare asset. From his arrival his particular talents and personality were devoted to the club's ambition to foster success, to foster an identity and a myth.

His price had been pleasingly low, and as years went by the board had to pay more for their assets. Alex James cost £6,000; David Jack became the first player to be bought for £10,000. By 1934, they were paying £20,000 for Jack Crayston and Wilf Copping. The return on their investment in Dad correspondingly increased. And yet in 1944, £750 was not only too much to reward him for his outstanding and distinctive contribution but even, and here lies the economic injustice, as a return on what he had earned for them. The directors would have had no sense of saying 'no' to great players who were part of the Arsenal 'family' and had created its wealth and fame. They had simply made a business decision and said 'no' to three working-class men whose time was over and whose needs were subordinate to executive profits and the future.

When the chairman who was the first to turn down the benefit, is named, the gulf between director and player is cruelly

345

clear. Lord Robin Vane-Tempest-Stewart, the 8th Marquis of Londonderry, educated at Eton and an MP from 1931–45 chaired the board throughout the war years and was unlikely to embrace the idea that the Arsenal family included the many working-class players who came and went through that time. His concerns were to ensure Arsenal's economic viability in a difficult period of transition, to secure the club's future and dividends for the shareholders.

Aristocratic and millionaire directors were the norm at Arsenal until this century, part of an unquestioned set of economic and class relationships in a particular moment of history. Arthur Hopcraft, in his irreverent analysis *The Football Men*, poked fun at such inappropriate loftiness by naming Denis Hill-Wood, chairman from 1961–82, as a 'reminder that it was the Old Etonians, Old Harrovians, Old Carthusians who kicked the game off … a century ago'.

Economic judgements also applied to selling Dad at the peak of his career and not keeping an eye on him when he was injured while class judgements felt it unnecessary to acknowledge his application for assistant manager and to celebrate him in the Arsenal v Blackburn programme. None of these decisions, and many others, were as Dad felt – a devaluation of his achievement, a rejection of who he was. While for him, they belittled the whole of his life's achievements, they are the heart of a story of finance and privilege, a power structure. Dad, resistant to hierarchies, an instinctive leader and a fierce defender of equality, was never able to accept that these qualities were celebrated on the pitch but not, in a working-class man, beyond it.

What the boy from Bristol had earned in money and reputation for his club in the past was always going to be more important than he was. That, I think, was the real message of all the events that Dad experienced as rejection. Although he could never grasp the idea emotionally, through his three managerships he finally began to understand economic imperatives and class divisions could unpick his identity. He could be a myth, he could be a hero, he could even be a 'gentleman', a term frequently bestowed on retired or dead footballers, but he could not be an equal, respected and rewarded in his own right.

In the long term, the investment Arsenal made in him has paid off magnificently. His name became the asset that has been priceless to the present day. When the Emirates Stadium in all its newness was being criticised as just some boring new ground, the project 'Arsenalisation' was launched. Dad's image was chosen to centre the group of players' arms linked across each other's shoulders in an embrace of the new stadium over the entrance in 2009. As an Arsenal 'legend', his story of courage and impeccable conduct is told to fans and officials alike every time there is a stadium tour or when the concourse is filled with waves of supporters trooping past his picture to the turnstiles. His words about team spirit are sculpted above the stairs to the museum where his life-size image still watches the visitors on their tour around Arsenal memories. My younger son on work experience at Arsenal was photographed by another former player, Charlie George, standing next to a life-size cardboard cut-out of his grandfather at Highbury, and his image was chosen to fly over the concourse as a long-term Arsenal supporter at the Emirates Stadium. Loyalty runs deep through the family generations as well.

All this uninterrupted continuity with the power to flow from old stadium to new, from one generation of players and fans to another was what Dad believed in and worked for. It was the legacy he hoped to pass on when he had finished playing, his legacy. It was synonymous with his personal evolution. The divorce of man and name always bewildered him. It wasn't a name that had played brave and exquisite football for Arsenal and consistently led England and Arsenal to victory and yet it is the name alone that defies time and it is the name that belongs to Arsenal. How else could Eddie Hapgood, the great defender, exist in this parallel narrative of man and money? His confidence in his position in the scheme of things and his unequivocal integrity meant he was always blind to the contradictory functions of a football club. For a time, Herbert Chapman had brilliantly reconciled them. That was what he had taught Dad and Dad had learned. Even when Dad began to understand the complexities, he still firmly believed that there was no need for conflict. The success of a club lay in the success of its players and the success of players lay in investment in their talents, their development, their security. He couldn't help seeing Arsenal in this way as a coherent whole, a football family. His parallel recognition that this was not the case, that the relationship was entirely one-sided, was a constant rip of pain for the rest of his life.

Dad was not the only player to wonder if he had seen chinks in Arsenal's white knight armour or to leave Arsenal with a broken heart not quite understanding what had happened. Ted Drake, arriving at Arsenal in 1934, commented on the rifts between players and management. Bernard Joy commented on George Allison's lack of empathy. Both Ted and Jack Crayston suffered career-ending injuries while Arsenal players but received no special support. Ray Bowden, bought in to replace David Jack in 1933, was sold on to Newcastle despite an illustrious career, when an ankle injury temporarily limited his appearances. The lives of these specific cases and many more were constantly threatened by the rebuilding of the team. No matter how brilliant your game or vital your contribution, you would grow older, slower, less resistant to injury. Hungry for novelty, the press inadvertently helped to move players in and out of public consciousness. Horace Cope 'fell out of favour' in 1929. Joey Hulme became 'a bit-part player'. Bob John was 'mainly a reserve player for his final three years', Jackie Lambert was another 'bit-part player' sold on to Fulham in 1933. Tom Parker was 'at the end of his tether'.

Like the flow and ebb of the tide, there were always younger, ambitious players hungry to prove their worth and be blessed by Highbury glory: Bernard Joy for Herbie Roberts, Wilf Copping for Bob John, Jack Crayston for Charlie Jones, Alf Kitchen for Joey Hulme, Ted Drake for Jack Lambert, George Male for Tom Parker, Eddie Hapgood for Horace Cope. Even if you don't know the names, the relentless movement is clear. Tragedy was built in from the first moment a player ran out on to the pitch, each one waiting to be discarded when their own time came. Many years later, in his autobiography, Tommy Lawton reflected on how he had replaced the great Dixie Dean at Everton, concluding, 'Although nobody knew the future, that decision meant that

349

Dixie was finished …. He only played one more game for the first team.' As David Luiz, Chelsea's brilliant and idiosyncratic defender said of the departure of Eden Hazard, whose two goals had just brought Arsenal to their knees in the final of the Europa League in 2019, 'This is the cycle of life: some stories finish and others begin.'

Some players hung around too long and were punished. Jack Crayston is an unhappy example. Transferred in 1934, Crayston played regularly for the Arsenal until the war. After the war, despite being refused the benefit to which he was entitled, he worked for a time with Arsenal's youth teams, became caretaker manager when Tom Whittaker died and then full-time manager. After what might seem a fortunate career to an outsider, he retired, to use his own words, 'broken-hearted'. Arsenal's comment was official and chilly:

'Arsenal Football Club announce their manager Jack Crayston, has tendered his resignation and that it has been accepted by the board of directors.'

Chairman Sir Bracewell Smith dismissed inquiries, commenting, 'I do not think there is much more to say,' and Crayston's 25 years at Arsenal came to an end. He refused to divulge to the press that his frequent impassioned arguments to the board requesting transfer funds to bolster a mediocre team were equally firmly rejected by directors who knew that it would be Crayston himself to pay the penalty. Bruised by Sir Bracewell's whiplash words, he refused, like Dad, to say more than, 'I will not criticise the directors or say a word against the club. It's a great institution and I'm only an individual.' He added in words that Dad would have agreed with, 'Why should I wreck in one minute all that I have enjoyed in the club for the last 24 years?'

Journalists, as always, had their theories, with one article claiming:

'In the taverns and clubs where the soccer class gather they were saying last night that Gentleman Jack had been the scapegoat for Arsenal's prestige-slumping season. They were saying that the men in control – the business minded directors – felt that the quiet and studious Crayston wasn't strong enough to inject the necessary power into the club.'

Crayston was acknowledged a 'gentleman' by those who *were* gentlemen by birth but although he behaved like one, he wasn't treated that way. Dad had also been praised as a 'gentleman' and also behaved like one, but his fault was that he showed a dangerous inclination to claim the rights of his title. Jack was too weak, Eddie too strong; their common denominator was that they were both working class and disposable.

And there were a few players who played until they knew it was over and then stopped. This was true of the sublime Cliff Bastin. His sad story is one of simple neglect. Playing on the left wing from 1927 to 1946, Bastin marked up 350 appearances for Arsenal and held his record of 178 goals for an incredible 50 years. It took Ian Wright to break it in 1997. Cliff was not a cannonball goalscorer but an archetypal winger, an essential part of the unique Arsenal diagonal two-pass goal strike movement, from defender to midfield to winger, perfected by Herbert Chapman.

For Bastin, the shadow began to fall 'on a summer's day in 1938 when the curtain went down on my England career'.

Released from war duties because of a hearing problem, he played on throughout the war, as his former team-mates came and went. 'Gone were Jack Crayston, Ted Drake, Alf Kirchen, Leslie Jones and Eddie Hapgood,' he observed, feeling, just as Dad did, that he was abandoned. Then on Boxing Day 1946, he walked away from Highbury knowing he had played his last game. He never formally resigned, he said, and Arsenal never said anything. 'It was just understood that I would never play again.' Nobody said goodbye. Nobody got around to asking, 'Where's Cliff?' He too was disposable.

This sad 'planned obsolescence' was true of all the big clubs of the time. Read any biography or newspaper interview from that era and you will hear the same puzzled lament. 'It didn't seem to matter who you were or how much service you had given, the manner of departure was unsatisfactory,' said Bill Shankly, released by Preston North End in 1948. 'Football deals badly with mortality. It can be brutal in dealing with those with whom it has finished.'

Whatever the complaints about the growing dominance of television over football, one thing is for sure: retired players today can plan for a long and well-paid continuation of their careers simply by talking about football. Dad was not able to retire into the world of punditry. Instead he passed on Arsenal's heritage and his own legacy through the stories he told. It was a long time before I realised that the joyous energy of those stories we heard as children was powered by more than just family fun. Like the locations and characters, jokes and accidents on the Bayeux tapestry, he could unroll time for himself and for us. He told heroic stories about other Arsenal or England players, about respected opponents over the years and around the country on the big stages of Highbury, Wembley, Hampden Park and the great stadia of Europe, the triumphant and tragic moments, the sublime and ridiculous moments. The borders that ran colourfully around the edge were tales of other clubs, of other players, sad failures, laugh-out-loud anecdotes and always a football bouncing from episode to episode. His tapestry illustrated tackles, clever attacking feints, brilliant defensive clearances, brain-banging headers, flying saves, over-elaborate ball games, idiosyncratic footballing styles all associated with one footballer or another. We knew them all – how to frustrate them, how to beat them, how to celebrate them. His tapestry had entertaining characters too, those who would sometimes forget football and turn into clowns but they had villains too, dangerous characters who might hurt you.

These stories of 'clowns' and 'villains' most clearly reflect Dad's deeply held beliefs about how the game should be played and life should be lived. One player who brought this edge to Dad's mimicry was his own colleague Alex James, the name that graced Arsenal's team sheet for eight seasons from 1929 to 1937, the 'wizard' sometimes compared to Dennis Bergkamp. The Alex James act that caused us all such amusement was the way he sat on the ball as the match was in progress. I always supposed it was a training ground prank or Dad had tipped his own story over into exaggeration as he sank dramatically down on to a convenient footstool, although it is a tale which also crops up in many football histories.

As a child I never questioned its wonderful absurdity although I knew Dad was irritated. Later I realised he was irritated by what he perceived as Alex's lack of professionalism, attention-seeking, playing to his popularity with the crowd. He clearly felt Alex was covering up his lack of fitness. 'Baggy shorts were his hallmark,' he would say sourly, comically demonstrating just how James pulled his shorts high up his waist while the ends still brushed his knees and wide enough to accommodate another player inside them. 'The baggiest of baggy shorts,' Tom Finney, playing against him, would later corroborate. 'And those shorts were heavy. When it was raining he'd get so exhausted he couldn't run. A blow on the referee's whistle for some incident on the field and Alex sat on the ball for a rest!' So it wasn't just Dad exaggerating!

Several invisible barbs were directed at Hughie Gallacher, the brilliant Scottish forward whose incredible tally of 463 goals in 624 professional games sends one back to the record books to check its accuracy. Small, agile, he 'knew where the goal was' as commentators would say today, and he found the goal for Newcastle, Chelsea and Scotland throughout a spectacular career. Dad would imitate Gallacher's savage tackles on the field and his subsequent visits to the Arsenal dressing room after a match, 'He'd be smiling broadly, shaking my hand and saying, "No hard feelings, Eddie. No hard feelings," before vanishing, leaving me limping around and rubbing my shins.' I knew that Dad deplored foul play on the field and there was always an edge to the humorous telling of this story. He felt that a deliberate foul was, like swearing, like lying, like cheating, the last resort of someone who has lost the argument.

'On the field Hughie could be a touch nasty,' his biographer acknowledged.

To us children, Dad conveyed all the wonder and joy of being a footballer and the mystery of how to live life to the full. It was Mum who could best put it into words, borrowed from the RAF's motto 'per ardua ad astra' to express what Dad always believed – through your effort you will reach for the stars (we weren't absolutely sure whether she meant football or Latin). He conveyed it to all those many people who stopped him wherever he went and whatever he was doing, asking, 'Eddie Hapgood?' I think that when he talked, the past became the present and freed his mind of pain. But, if nothing else tells you, this fact will tell you everything. He never took Margot, Mike or me to watch Arsenal play. He took us to watch Aston Villa, Bristol Rovers, Bolton Wanderers, West Ham, Fulham, Wolverhampton Wanderers, Coventry, any team that happened to be nearby. But never Arsenal. We knew about it only as the world we inhabited but didn't own, while we knew it was somehow the origin of why we were who we were.

My mother, more aware of his sadness, once confided to me, 'Your Dad loved football more than he loved me.' That wasn't true. I knew it then and I know it now. She was right, however, that Arsenal had made 'Eddie Hapgood' possible. His heart and his blood forged an unbreakable cord with the club and marked the rhythm of the game and the man. His determination to defend what he thought was right and his love and care for us all came from a spiritual and moral energy engendered on the football pitch, on the grass of Highbury. 'The Arsenal was my heritage,' he wrote in 1961, 'or so I thought.'

16

Weymouth and Elsewhere

Weymouth is 80 miles from Portsmouth, 60 miles from Exeter and 70 miles from Bristol. In 1958, when we moved to Weymouth, it was as nearly a football-free zone as one could find in an English region. In my father's story, it was he who lost the most by our move. His journey from international fame and mesmerising brilliance to ostracism from club and career had taken just over ten years. His attempts to find other work had foundered on that fame. Who knows? Considering what they had endured during the events of the previous few years, perhaps it was a help to Mum and Dad to be physically removed from footballing territory, to be out of the limelight, to be required to create a different world for themselves. Perhaps, but emotionally and psychologically, it was a vague, dislocated existence – a state of unidentified yearning on Dad's part and fathomless anxiety on Mum's. Practically, from day to day, it was safe and straightforward. Temporarily at least that was just what they needed.

We children all shared their loss and our own losses in different ways. Margot had won a place at the Bristol Old Vic Theatre

School. She had dreamed of and worked for this moment since she was a child in Watford and now was her chance to fulfil her dream and to reward all the support and encouragement Dad and Mum had given her. Full of adventure and optimism, she had saved up some money, written her applications, prepared for and performed her auditions. We all knew she would be successful. Sadly her beginnings got tangled up in the family's endings. Not long after her first term in Bristol got under way in September 1957, Dad's case against Arthur Mortimer opened in Bristol Assizes just a short walk from the Old Vic School. As she turned 18, she had to cope with a desperately important, real life drama, anxieties about her parents poised on the edge of disaster and worries about her younger siblings coping without her. She struggled to focus on the competitive world she had chosen. In July 1958, at the end of her first year, she was told kindly but firmly by the school principal that her tutors felt she was not suited to a career in the theatre. Dad collected her from Bristol and brought her to Weymouth, sick with misery and unable to contemplate the purpose of the stream of days stretching out in front of her.

My life at the school I thought I knew was fundamentally, frighteningly changed. The nuns had been saddened when Mum and Dad told them their story and that I would be leaving. They ignored all the bad feeling swirling around Bath at the time and put their faith in us. 'Your father is a good man,' Reverend Mother said to me. 'Don't worry, dear. We will look after you.' The school I had attended as a day girl for seven years was attached to an order of teaching nuns but I had been completely unaware of the life of the convent that now became my home. There were three small dormitories which were used on a need-by-need basis. When I was there, there were 17 of us, the little boarders as I called them to myself, and six older girls. We were refugees rather than boarders, girls who needed help and a home for any number of reasons so we had to live as if we were nuns from when the day girls left to when they returned in the morning.

When I learned later that they had not only offered educational support but the practical help of a free boarding place, I felt ashamed of my resentment and angry ingratitude. My misery prevented me for many, many years from recognising Reverend Mother's generosity. While I was there, all I wanted with a yearning passion, the force of which I could hardly contain, was to escape, to be with my parents. I always felt cold, I remember.

The greatest impact of leaving Bath, however, was probably on Mike because he was the youngest of us and living inside a family crisis he could feel but not understand. He knew we were leaving the house one by one, Margot to Bristol, me to school and Dad to Weymouth to begin preparations for the opening of Egdon Hall, the new hostel. At last he was alone with Mum. When the time came to close the door of 24 Penn Lea Road and post the key through the letter box into an empty house, he didn't want to leave. Of course, he was powerless and uncomprehending. He had to endure a long train journey with Mum to Weymouth, frightened that he had lost forever his father, his two sisters and everything familiar he had ever known.

There had been warning signs. On the last Sunday afternoon we were all together, Mum had brought a table into the sitting room where the fire was lit, and laid it for tea with her Chinese

Rose china. Knowing I was leaving for school the next day, it seemed to be just for me. I remember every taste and every bite but no conversation. It is a moving image without a soundtrack. We had tinned salmon, a luxury in those days, with hard-boiled eggs, radishes, lettuce, tomato sliced with onion and served with thinly sliced buttered bread. Afterwards there were tinned mandarin oranges, lemon junket and a cup of tea poured and distributed by Dad with his usual scrupulous care. Now I realise the meal was for all of us. Perhaps for Mum it was a goodbye to the house and to the life we had known as a family, a celebration of us and a gift to us all.

Some weeks before, we had been told that we were leaving Bath and going to live in Weymouth. How lucky we were to be going to live near the sea, my father said. What lovely bedrooms we would have, my mother said, with pretty quilts and a bedside cabinet each. She had been to see where we would be living and she knew we would enjoy it. It never occurred to us to ask why we wouldn't have our own furniture or what was going to happen to it while we were away. It was a bit further for Margot to visit now she was in Bristol, Mum said, but an easy train journey. It was a very long way for Tony from Burnley to Weymouth but he and Irene and their children Michael and Lori would visit whenever they could. They were very happy with Mike's new school, they said, where he would begin as soon as we had moved. Even earlier than that my mother had asked me whether I wanted to stay at the convent for the rest of my schooling or move to a different school in Weymouth. I wasn't sure what to say, had no evidence to draw on except my life as a day girl. I don't know whether I made a choice. I was never aware of the moving process. Even as I began my life as a boarder, my parents must have been packing up the house, clearing the cupboards and sweeping up the remnants of our life there.

The next home I knew, that we would all know, was Egdon Hall, a new prefabricated YMCA hostel catering for Atomic Energy Authority apprentices on the outskirts of Weymouth, in Chickerell. Despite our parents' conscientious attempts to prepare us, the change when it came seemed sudden. Even on the wilder shores of our imaginations, we could not have conceived of living anywhere other than Bath or being separated from each other. For our parents, hardened by moves from London, Kettering, Blackburn and Watford, the reality was stark. Each of our lives was so fundamentally changed that it seemed almost an act of faith to believe that we were still ourselves, a family. When we were together again, we seemed to act out roles mysteriously allotted. For a time, we were like blindfolded people in one of Dad's games. We moved around, hands stretched out in front of us reaching for a solid surface, for something familiar. Then from time to time, the blindfold would fall and we saw ourselves as we remembered we were, the relieved laughter of a game transformed into moments of joy. The memory of a family, despite being broken apart with each member following a different path and with no home at our centre, was never lost. In this surreal and troubled time, Dad and Mum, who perhaps had no option, were determined to make it work, to make it real. Not surprisingly, Dad was an excellent public face for the hostel, communicating with the press, with local organisations and the administrators and training staff at

Winfrith. The warden's office was immediately opposite the main entrance to the hostel and there are many publicity photographs for the local paper of him sitting authoritatively behind the desk doing various tasks when the hostel was opened. His footballing reputation had alerted the YMCA to his wider potential and Justice Salmon's unequivocal support of that reputation shortly after they had offered him a probationary period confirmed their confidence in him.

During the Weymouth years, Dad's identity as a footballer was virtually extinguished, but that was something he chose. The 12 years he worked at the YMCA was longer than all his managerial career put together but they gave him and Mum some kind of security at last and he carefully insulated himself from the football world. He was happy to give talks locally, to present prizes at fetes and to enjoy local football when his arrival anywhere prompted invitations but he was wary of journalists who came after a story. Often they went away feeling he was brusque and perhaps bitter.

'What football team does he follow?' wrote one. '"One expects the answer 'Arsenal' of course." But the man who thrilled countless thousands in his hey-day says, "I don't follow any team. I haven't watched a match for a long time."'

It was not the answer they wanted. Although some of Dad's wariness was undoubtedly self-protection, he refused to be defined by a past that only existed in a journalist's imagination and determined to rise above old untruths that still surfaced in their questions from time to time. Mum also determined that the past should be left behind where it belonged. If they were to make a success of this new world they had landed in, she too would need to adapt to a new role. Although Dad had had the formal training, she was always much better than him at daily detail so she took the domestic management upon herself. She'd had no experience of working in the public realm since she was 15 years old and never before on the front line. It was a daunting responsibility. She began to read. Books on employment law, national and local food regulations, the economics of mass catering, design of menus, portion control, kitchen timetables and hygiene were borrowed from the local library and their information diligently absorbed. Taking control of a large kitchen, talking to chefs, organising staff, drawing up cleaning schedules, being ready to praise or reprimand were hard-won skills.

Professional football could be consciously assigned to another world but the meaning of football could not be dealt with so easily. Each year there was a different intake of apprentices who did their first year's training at Winfrith before moving on to Harwell in Oxfordshire and a smaller number doing a training year before moving on to university. In the early years, Dad enjoyed getting to know them, settling them in. He organised informal football games, encouraged the keen ones to join local teams in their time off, organised social events for lads away from home for the first time and provided an easy-going and friendly environment.

As soon as he took over his position at Egdon Hall, Eddie hoped to set up a mini under-17 league with the local clubs, something that only happened with patchy success. Schools and youth clubs were already organised – and Egdon Hall had no football pitch. Mike told me how he overcame an intractable obstacle with apparent ease. 'So,' Mike began on another evening of fitting the jigsaw pieces together, 'it was noticed with amusement or bafflement in that post-war era, that Eddie Hapgood, former captain of England, would happily mark out a football pitch himself, as he did once while I was watching, for a nondescript scratch youth team of apprentices. I knew that the degree of precision and seriousness of the marking out of a bumpy pitch, for 22 young lads playing a forgettable game somewhere in England, was driven by the same impulse that brought the captain of England back on to the field of play against Italy in 1934, after having been carried off unconscious with his nose broken by an Italian elbow. No doubt his re-appearance, his white England shirt now red with his blood, played a significant part in England's 3-2 victory, but the significance was not the *footballing* victory, but the *re-appearance* of the man.'

The significance of a football pitch at Egdon Hall laid out on a recent building site barely covered with grass was not its role as a sporting space but its necessary existence and the exactitude of its creation.

Not all such moments Mike shared with me of that Weymouth time were so straightforward. 'There were,' he told me, 'some complicated moments, which while small, almost unnoticeable at the time, are significant. And last. One was a tiny, momentary drama, lasting only seconds, that took place on a late summer's evening very soon after our arrival in 1958 under the floodlights of Weymouth Town Football Club.' My brother can tell a story as vividly as his father did. He continued, 'Almost inevitably, Dad's name drew attention. In those days Weymouth, an old competitor with Bath City, was a decent Southern League team on the threshold of the Football League. The town was packed with holidaymakers and the football club was adding to the summer fun by playing the All Stars, which is to say, a team made up from the entertainers working the summer season at the Pavilion Theatre, the Alexandra Gardens and the Royal Hotel. There were some useful players there too, and a happy occasion was graced by public appearances of well-known, non-playing, faces – I think Johnny Dankworth was there, maybe Matt Munro, "The Man with the Golden Voice" – and by a crowd of maybe 6,000 people.

'At some point in the first or second half, I can't remember which, the referee blew his whistle and signalled a foul throw-in by one of the visiting players. This, then, was the moment – the ref running towards the line, pointing, then miming the correct action for a throw-in, the All-Stars player, who'd committed this minor technical infringement, taken aback, handing the ball over. The manager of Weymouth Town, Arthur Coles, quickly drawing in his breath, saying quietly to himself in that teeth-clenched way, "Eddie, Eddie", shaking his head. I heard and saw all this because I was only ten and invited to sit in the dugout beside Arthur. The referee was Eddie Hapgood. The distance between the Arsenal stadium, Wembley's twin towers, the national stadiums of Italy, Germany, Romania, Hungary, Austria, and the now vanished Recreation Ground in Weymouth was a big one. One might say, unbridgeable. But here, running towards the touchline, signalling a foul throw, was Eddie Hapgood, completely absorbed in a friendly game between players he would never have met on a football pitch in any other circumstances. There was no dispute, it *was* a foul throw. But, in a charitable friendly of this kind? "Eddie.

Eddie." And that was the drama. A drama that an amiable, nice man, and decent non-league footballer, Arthur Coles, didn't understand. The referee was my father, and I did understand.'

Years later, Mike tried to explain to me what exactly it was he had understood. He linked it to the story told by the great C.L.R. James, who learned his cricket in Trinidad and came to England to play in the Lancashire League. James described cricket not only as it was played but as it was *lived*, and told how sport can in some circumstances, maybe in all circumstances, become a metaphor for life. 'Not only for the great players,' Mike emphasised, 'but the Sunday leaguers and the park players, for all of us, it is a kind of moral code. An infringement of it by those who understand it is unthinkable because it is a betrayal of the heart of it … as it was to our father.'

There is another dimension. A player does not just hold the sport within him/herself. The link between sport, player and spectator is part of a trinity as mysterious as any religious doctrine. Sometimes, often, that relationship goes far deeper than witnessing an occasional thrilling triumph, enjoying amusing anecdotes or bouts of temporary fandom. Sometimes the link between a youthful admirer and his hero becomes a living bond as he grows to maturity and a lifelong influence as he sets out on his own adult life. Brian Glanville's journalism was inspired in just this way. As a boy at boarding school he told me, he spent his 'writing home' sessions writing letters to Dad, letters frequently adorned with poems about sporting prowess and 'playing the game'. The teacher who supervised these sessions finally put an end to them. 'No more letters to Eddie Hapgood,' he commanded.

That did not stop him following Dad's career throughout both their lives. So, when Glanville read Bob Wall's book, he knew immediately the tale about Dad's benefit appeal to the FA must be untrue and set about finding the evidence to put the story right. In 1969 he proposed a television programme in the 'One Pair of Eyes' series about changing values in sport and persuaded Dad to participate. It was a difficult, painful experience for him. He had recovered reasonably well from the stroke he had suffered the year before but his long-term health had suffered and he was visibly frail. By the time the programme was screened, he was within a few months of early retirement because of ill health. But even at that late date, Glanville never stopped believing that Dad should have the right of reply. Miles away in Southampton, another former boyhood admirer, Douglas Featherstone, in the days before catch-up TV, 'had rushed back from a meeting in London especially to see you in Brian Glanville's "One Pair of Eyes".' We know because he sat down to write to Dad as soon as the programme finished. 'I have watched football for more than 40 years,' he wrote, 'but have never recaptured the sheer delight of watching you and the Arsenal play from 1930 to 1939. I saw the very first game … I was there when you captained … I gloried in all those home wins … the last time I saw you on a football field … I will never forget Eddie Hapgood because you were as much a part of my young life as all the other significant events of the '30s, and you thereby enriched it. Thank you very much, Eddie Hapgood.'

Sometimes the outside world, overburdened with memories and triggered by some incidental word or event, crashes through time to ask the present, 'Does this really matter? Was it all as important as I thought it was?' And no answer is necessary. Emotional memory can be more powerful than the memory of particular events and is capable of renewing itself long after the details that inspired it have faded. There would have been many other Douglas Featherstones out there, moved and inspired, who never wrote to him but never forgot.

In daily terms, tennis took over from football and it became Dad's chief sporting pleasure. We still all met up in Bude once a year when we could, we still played every evening and Dad still won. Back in Weymouth, he got to know Wilf Dawkins and as congenial opponents they fought to the death for the supremacy of the Greenhill courts on Weymouth front. Mum would go and watch when she could, glad to enjoy his enjoyment. Whenever any of us were home we would join her, half looking at the sea, drowsy with the fragrances from the garden for the blind that surrounded the courts and not taking too seriously her anxiety about his intensity. She would remind him before and after every match that he wasn't playing at Wimbledon but we all knew there wouldn't be any point in his playing if he didn't try to win, and no point in not driving his body towards that victory. He signed up to LTA coaching classes, passed his Amateur Certificate, and planned to help out a tennis club with some coaching in the future. In July, he would always find time to escape from Egdon Hall and drive to Eastbourne to watch the grass court tennis championship preludes to Wimbledon.

By the time the first two intakes of apprentices had come and gone, Mum and Dad had begun to feel more confident of their management abilities and secure in their new life. Mike and I had reconciled ourselves to our different schools. Margot had found an exciting job in London and now shared a flat in Chelsea with a friend. Perhaps outside observers might have said we were happy. Then on 20 October 1960 a letter arrived from Pickford's Removals that sealed off the past with an immutable and shocking finality. It told Mum and Dad with brutal brevity – some five sentences – that the warehouse where all our furniture and possessions had been stored since July 1958 had burned down, 'resulting in the loss of all contents including the effects warehoused in your names'. Nothing had been rescued. Everything had gone.

Our memories were the only inventories. The mahogany table on which my Wembley dress had been sewn. The treasure-trove bookcase, the sideboard where Mike as a little boy had made faces at himself in the mirror. The painting of the old lady crossing the bridge into the forest that I had entered with her so many times. All the grandeur of our front room was extinguished. The pink bedroom, the many-mirrored dressing table reflecting numberless images of Mum, the blue bedroom, the luxurious eiderdowns were heaps of grey ash. The curtains, the carpets, the rugs that Dad had made for Hutton Grove in the early days of their marriage, the cushions that Mum had sewn, the satin lampshades she had so carefully stitched, the footstool I had covered for Dad. The wireless we had all shared in the hours after supper and before bed, the new radiogram and the collection of records. The three-piece suite with its fading art deco loose covers, which Mike and I had ridden and driven with such energy. The story of the family room where we had talked and laughed and listened had vanished. Boxes of baby clothes, our childhood books, toys, Margot's collections of china horses, mementoes, photographs. Glasses, china, plates, pans and bowls – the companions of hours of talking around the now vanished gateleg table with its golden chenille cover. None of us could quite remember everything that was burned because our memories were also burned by two years without our possessions. Perhaps it was kinder that way.

Mike was the only one of us children at Egdon Hall when Mum and Dad turned into the drive on their way back from Bath for the last time. Perhaps that was the day he was 13. He watched them unload two large familiar leather suitcases from the boot. Full of papers, they had been stored separately and were safe. A random selection of images, cuttings, programmes, photographs, one Arsenal shirt with its distinctive white sleeves, one snowy white international shirt with its three lion badge and international caps still wrapped in tissue paper. A few items from Dad's footballing past and some of the props for his many stories had survived. And extraordinary as it might sound, so did they and so did we. With the slate wiped clean, the external world now matched their inner world. They were, in some way, the other side of an invisible line. And there were still fragments. Where there are fragments and a will to survive, survival is always a possibility.

Egdon Hall could never be a home but it turned out to be a secure refuge for which we were grateful as we gathered from school, from university, from first jobs, sometimes, if we were lucky, at the same time – but it was never a home. Oddly, Weymouth, a small seaside town at the central point of the Dorset coast and the southernmost tip of the county of Dorset, became, I suppose you could say, our surrogate home. There was always swimming gear in the boot of the car so we could swim wherever we stopped, a landscape imagined by the novelist Thomas Hardy to roam, the threatening, piratical mystery of the Fleet trapped in the stranded, watery wasteland behind Chesil Beach to explore, the terrifying drama of Chesil Beach itself with its roaring pebbles, its tragic stories, and the bleak grimness of the Isle of Portland as it jutted out into one of the most dangerous tidal waters of Britain. This little promontory, its magnificent stone quarried to build the monumental buildings of our great cities, the Palace of Westminster, St Paul's Cathedral, the British Museum and countless other civic monuments in Leeds, Manchester and Newcastle, was doomed to drown, it was said, from eating itself away. The Dorset hinterland was quite different, gentle, curving swathes of chalky green hiding Iron Age forts and Roman settlements, and bravely erupting pagan signs – the imprint of the fingers of a giant's hand squeezing Eggardon Hill and the brash confidence of the Cerne Giant up for procreation. This is a landscape returned to sheep and emptiness by changes in agricultural practice but so serenely beautiful it is easy to enjoy and hard to grieve for those such as the Tolpuddle Martyrs who fought to protect their way of life way back in the early 1800s.

Whenever Dad and Mum were free we would drive and walk and explore. If they weren't, Mike and I would catch a bus out to the coastal villages, to Lulworth Cove and Durdle Door before the caravans arrived. We hunted for fossils along Kimmeridge Bay and clambered up Maiden Castle Fort where the wind hit us with a spiteful blow as we emerged over the ridge, or we sat sheltered in Maumbury Rings, the small Roman amphitheatre in Dorchester, eating a sandwich and talking. And when the holiday-makers began to go home, there was quaint, dilapidated Weymouth Harbour, the long walk round the Nothe Point to see Portland Bill in the haze, the quixotic tiny horsehoe-shaped bay where the sand-sculptors had abandoned impossible shapes. Perhaps this just seems like a list that could be replicated anywhere in rural, sea-side Britain and perhaps that is true but, for our family, Dorset with Weymouth at its heart, became a shared map where we met up whenever we could and which we coloured in together with our explorations and experiences. When the Winfrith training scheme ended and the hostel closed, Mum was reported in the local paper as saying, 'We are loath to leave Weymouth. We have fallen in love with Dorset.' It probably sounded like a polite gesture but we knew it was true.

In 1970, Dad retired from the YMCA after two years of worsening health and he and Mum moved to Leamington Spa in Warwickshire where my husband Michael and I had lived since we married in 1965. It was a late life gift, all together again, not literally, but with our parents a stable and secure focal point in a home of their own. We all at one time or another converged on Leamington and so the bonds of family were able to be alive and dynamic again. Margot, still mortgage-free, bought a beautiful, 'in need of improvement' Edwardian house in Heath Terrace just round the corner from the attic flat Michael and I had rented. Together and with the help of a student friend who had an eye for design and a need for extra cash, we stripped and wallpapered, cleaned and painted, carpeted and tiled the ground floor ready for their arrival. Margot, driving up every weekend from London, scoured the local auctions for furniture to replace what had been lost in the fire. Mum and Dad organised and made ready for removal the linen and blankets, the cutlery and china and all the bits and pieces they had been gifted by the YMCA when the hostel had closed down in 1968. At last, after a long and difficult, spirit-breaking 25 years they had a home of their own again. This time, it wasn't a borrowed home buoyed up on courage and optimism and generous friendship, however wonderful that was. It was home.

I hope that Mum and Dad gained the most from their move to Leamington Spa. Tony and his family had settled permanently in Burnley. Now 40, he ran a successful sports equipment business. We all exchanged visits when we could. Mike was at university in York, much to Tony's delight as they could meet up at Grassington and explore the Pennines and the Trough of Bowland together. Margot had landed a dream job running the American publisher Time Life's book division in London. She now had a car and the newly constructed M1 very nearly reached Warwick so it was an easy drive. I was teaching in Coventry at the time. I could drop in to see my parents and chat and in the school holidays Mum and I could walk and talk and shop. When I was pregnant in 1971, Mum and I went to horticultural classes at the local further education college together and spent happy hours making hanging baskets. She loved her garden at Heath Terrace and there were few days she wasn't out there planting, weeding, watering or just enjoying. She's the only person I have ever known who can pick up an apparently dead stick on a walk, push it into soil when she gets home and have a sprouting tree by the following spring.

When Dad was studying for his Advanced LTA tennis coaching certificate, I would test him as he walked round the room repeating in response to my questions the size of a court, the height of a net, the weight of a ball and the latest rule changes. He read a lot, particularly biographies, and enjoyed passing on what he learned to me. And there were unforgettable moments. In the days when there was no maternity leave let alone leave for fathers and Michael had to return to work after two days of compassionate leave, it was Mum and Dad who collected me and our new baby from hospital and settled me into our new house in Clarendon Street, a little bit apprehensive as they closed the door behind them and left me and our new baby alone together for the first time.

A year later, at Easter in 1973, Michael and I called round to Heath Terrace to say goodbye on our way to Polruan in Cornwall for a holiday with friends. The back garden gate was slightly open so, carrying baby Sam who was then 15 months old, we walked in. Dad looked round as we smiled hello. He had seemed so much happier and more vigorous since the move. He was standing in front of the high garden wall wearing a flat cap and old clothes covered with dust with a trowel in one hand. 'I'm repointing the wall!' he announced triumphantly, pushing the trowel down into the bucket of mortar on the ground beside him and stretching out his arms towards Sam. 'Oh Dad,' was all I could say as I gave him a kiss and handed Sam to him, watching them both disappear into the house. It had always been a family joke that Dad could do anything with his feet but very little with his hands. Now he was happily intent on reversing that judgement with his new project. Mum and I wandered round the garden chatting. As I hugged her goodbye and turned to go, there was an excited shout from the house and Dad rushed out holding Sam tightly against him. 'Sam's walking! He's walked his first steps. I put my hands out to him and he walked!'

While we were away, Dad was giving a talk at a boys' football weekend that was being held at Honiley Hall, a conference centre not far from Leamington. He had been torn about whether to accept. Of course, he was delighted to have been invited, and looked forward with pleasure to a footballing day with interested lads and to catching up after many years with Stan Cullis, his former international team-mate who was also speaking. On the other hand, he had not been fully well since that frightening day of his stroke in 1968 and the severe angina which had forced his early retirement in 1970. Anticipation made him anxious and bursts of energy left him enervated. If he was honest with himself, he no longer enjoyed public events but he had been persuaded to attend, and characteristically, there was no way he would let them down. So, with another hug, we wished him good luck and goodbye.

As the day began, the hall was full of young lads chatting, jostling into their seats and finally quietening down as the chair of the conference stood up and introduced Dad with the familiar words. 'We are very lucky today to have with us Eddie Hapgood, Arsenal and England defender, the greatest left-back in football history.' Dad knew that if there was a sublime Cliff Bastin, an exquisite Stanley Matthews, a maverick Alex James or a wonderfully imperturbable George Male out there in the audience he would never see him play. He also knew with absolute conviction that at some future date they would be able to say proudly, 'Eddie Hapgood? I heard him talk way back in 1973 when I was a boy.' He did not really want to be there. He wished that Maggie was sitting on the podium behind him.

He was also very glad. He knew he had something worthwhile to say. He always enjoyed being able to honour the continuum of sporting history by talking to the next generation of young footballers. 'And, of course, there's Eddie Hapgood,' the chairman concluded to a storm of clapping. He stepped up to the microphone and smiled at the eager faces in front of him. He spread out his hands to the expectant audience in his instinctively inclusive way as he always did when about to launch into a story, but he never began or finished whatever story he had intended to share. Our father died that day at Honiley Hall on Good Friday 1973.

* * *

It was 2008, 100 years after Dad was born and some 30 years after he died. The signpost at the junction with the A358 said right to the M5, left to Weymouth. I was on my way home to Leamington from visiting friends but on a moment's impulse, I turned left instead of right. The day was hot and brilliant. I wanted to enjoy Weymouth in the sunshine. It was a long time since I had been back. I thought I would drive over to Portland and see the lighthouse against the vivid summer sky.

I parked the car and joining the new spur of the South Coastal Walk, cut up to the plateau before reaching the Bill. At the same moment a car stopped at the locked entrance to what is still Trinity House property. It is one of Dorset's curiosities (or so we used to think) that its three claims to fame are all initialled TH – Thomas Hardy (novelist), Vice-Admiral Thomas Hardy (of 'Kiss me Hardy' fame) and Trinity House. The lighthouse at Portland Bill is the most spectacular of the three famous features. It looks out over the Race, one of the most dangerous convergence of currents around the British Isles, which has ripped up ships and swallowed Romans and Vikings, pirates and smugglers since shipping began. Many of the drowned bodies were eventually cast up on the steep pebbles of the Chesil Beach which links Portland to the mainland, and are buried in their hundreds in mass graves in the huge churchyard of the tiny Wyke Regis Church where I was married. The driver, I now noticed, was very elderly and struggling to get out of the car to unlock the gate. I hurried over to help and among the thanks and exchanges of pleasantries about the extraordinary weather, he asked me whether I was a tourist. Within minutes, he had linked my story to the arrival of Eddie Hapgood as warden of the Egdon Hall Hostel. 'Just wait until I tell the chaps in the pub tonight that I chatted with Eddie Hapgood's daughter today,' he said. 'Who can believe it? Such a long time ago. It was all over the *Echo* when he arrived. Eddie Hapgood. Who can believe it?'

The driver must have been in his 80s and he was remembering with delight an insignificant event that happened some 50 years before. But, for him, this insignificant event was an unforgettable memory. His face lit up as he reached for my hand and held it between his own. 'Well, well. Eddie Hapgood,' he repeated.

Acknowledgements

Many people helped me to research and write *Eddie Hapgood Footballer*. My brother Tony was my witness to events in the 1930s and the careful protector of the family archive until his death in 2011. My younger brother Mike allowed me to steer many conversations about our family history into question and answer sessions and helped me to recognise the often treacherous nature of memory when revisiting childhood events. There are traces of his own writing buried in this book. My two sons, Sam and Jacob, have marked the Arsenal decades with me through the Pat Jennings era, George Graham's triumphs, the arrival of Denis Berkampf, the Invincibles and the new post-Arsène Wenger era. They have vigorously kept modern football issues under review and never allow me to retreat into the past.

A wide range of friends, some of them usefully football neutral, have been valuable readers and critics. Women friends alerted me to the interest of our family story; men to their surprise that so little was known about post-war Eddie Hapgood. Among others, thanks to Alan Wilkinson, Jo Crozier, Imogen and David Graham, David Adams, Heather Purdey, Chris and Lally

Purcell, Jane Beale, Sue Thomas, and Jennifer Lorch, who all read different parts of the drafts at different stages and offered invaluable advice. In particular thanks to Simon Hart, Adam Luck and Ian Grant who advised me on that difficult but crucial next step – being published.

I was able to pursue forgotten details of my father's story via the British Library's extraordinary newspaper archive. I am not sure whether one can thank a database but this book would probably never have been possible without it and the dedicated years of digitalising every newspaper ever printed, however ephemeral or local. My father couldn't escape being unearthed even from the *Sussex Agricultural Press*!

Thanks to Arsenal FC whose stadium concourse, museum and boardrooms are the galleries of my father's career. Researching the past in the Arsenal Museum while watching matches in the present has helped me to understand better the nature of club community and continuity. Before and after lockdown Andy Exley has always been welcoming and helpful. Perhaps my most heartfelt thanks are to all Arsenal supporters, past and present, who have passed my father's name down the generations and contributed so much to keeping his name and reputation alive.

And finally, thanks to the team at Pitch Publishing for their enthusiam and support as they transformed the papers on my desk into this book.

Selected Bibliography

Books:

Bastin, C., *Cliff Bastin Remembers* (Ettrick Press, 1950)

Berry, H., *The Men Who Made Blackburn Rovers F.C. Since 1945* (Tempus, 2006)

Chapman, H., *Herbert Chapman on Football* (Garrick Publishing Co., 1934)

Downing, D., *The Best of Enemies: England v Germany* (Bloomsbury, 2000)

Finney, T., *Tom Finney: My Autobiography* (Headline Publishing, 2003)

Foot, J., *Calcio: A History of Italian Football* (Fourth Estate, 2006)

Football Association, *Victory Was the Goal: The Story of the Football Association in Wartime* (The Football Association, 1946)

Glanville, B., *Football Memories* (Virgin, 1999)

Glanville, B., *The Real Arsenal: From Chapman to Wenger* (JR Books, 2009)

Graham, G., *The Glory and The Grief* (André Deutsch, 1995)

Hapgood, E., *Football Ambassador* (Sporting Handbooks, 1945)

Harding, J., *Alex James: Life of a Football Legend* (Robson Books, 1988)

Henderson, N., *Failure of a Mission: Berlin 1937–38* (Hodder and Stoughton, 1940)

Holden, J., *Stan Cullis, the Iron Manager* (Breedon Books, 2000)

Holmes, O., *Berlin 1936: Sixteen Days in August* (Bodley Head, 2018)

Hopcraft, A., *The Football Man: People and Passion in Soccer* (Collins, 1968)

Hulme, J., *How To Play Soccer* (Eyre and Spottiswoode, 1953)

Imlach, G., *My Father and Other Working-Class Football Heroes* (Yellow Jersey Press, 2006)

Jackman, M., *Blackburn Rovers: The Complete Record* (Breedon Books, 2009)

James, C.L.R., *Beyond a Boundary* (Hutchinson, 1963)

Jennings, H., *Sixty Years of Change 1911–1971* (University Settlement Bristol, 1961)

Joannou, P., *The Hughie Gallacher Story* (Breedon Books, 1985)

Joy, B., *Forward Arsenal* (Phoenix House, 1952)

Kuper, S., *Ajax, the Dutch, the War: Football in Europe During the Second World War* (Orion Books, 2003)

Lawrence, A., *Proud To Say That Name: The Marble Hall of Fame* (Mainstream Publishing, 1997)

Lawton, T., *Football is My Business* (Sporting Handbooks, 1947)

Lawton, T., *My Twenty Years of Soccer* (Heirloom Modern World Library, 1955)

Lee, L., *As I Walked Out One Midsummer Morning* (André Deutsch, 1969)

Lyes, J., *Bristol 1920–1926* (Historical Association, 2003)

Malam, C., *Clown Prince of Soccer? The Len Shackleton Story* (Highdown Press, 2004)

Martin, S., *Football and Fascism: The National Game under Mussolini* (Berg, 2004)

Matthews, S., *The Way It Was: My Autobiography* (Headline, 2000)

Mercer, J., *The Great Ones* (Oldbourne, 1964)

Mortensen, S., *Football is My Game* (Sampson, Low, Marston and Co., 1949)

Richardson, M., *Trade Unionism and Industrial Conflict in Bristol* (Bristol Business School Research Unit, 2000)

Rous, S., *Football Worlds: A Lifetime in Sport* (Faber, 1978)

Spurling, J., *Highbury: The Story of Arsenal in N.5* (Orion Books, 2000)

Studd, S., *Herbert Chapman Football Emperor: A Study of the Origins of Modern Soccer* (Peter Owen, 1981)

Taw, T., *Football's War and Peace: The Tumultuous Season of 1946–47* (Desert Island Books, 2003)

Wall, B., *Arsenal From the Heart* (Souvenir Press, 1969)

Whittaker, T., *Tom Whittaker's Arsenal Story* (Sporting Handbooks, 1957)

Widdows, R. ed., *Sixty Memorable Matches* (Marshall Cavendish, 1974)

Newspapers:

Bath Chronicle and Herald

Bristol Evening Post

Birmingham Post and Gazette

Coventry Evening Telegraph

Daily Express

Daily Herald

Daily Mail

Daily Mirror

Daily Record

Daily Telegraph

Derby Daily Record

Dorset Evening Echo

Edinburgh Evening News

Manchester Guardian

Gloucester Citizen

Gloucestershire Echo

SELECTED BIBLIOGRAPHY

Kettering Evening Telegraph
Lancashire Evening Post
Leicester Mercury
Lincolnshire Echo
Liverpool Echo
London Evening Post
Morning News
Newcastle Evening Chronicle
Northern Daily Mail
Observer
Portsmouth Evening News
Reynolds News
Sussex Agricultural Press
Sunday Chronicle
Sunderland Daily Echo
The Sun
The Times
Weekly Illustrated
Western Morning News

Unpublished archives:
Arsenal Football Club archives – J.H. Catton Collection; Harry F. Homer
   (The Marksman)
Bastin family archive, currently on loan to Arsenal FC
Hapgood, Eddie. *Unpublished Memoir*
Hapgood family archive

Film:
The Lucky Number (1933)
The Arsenal Stadium Mystery (1939)
89 (2017)

Selected websites (excluding statistics and records):
https://blog.woolwicharsenal.co.uk/archives/378
https://aculturedleftfoot.wordpress.com/2010/01/16/review-football-
   ambassador-by-eddie-hapgood/
https://www.rovers.co.uk/club/history/club-history
https//www.watfordobserver.co.uk
http://www.com/arsenal-history/arsenal-player-database/eddie hapgood

Index